DATE DUE

DEMCO 38-297

Tennessee Studies In Literature

Editor
Richard M. Kelly

Associate Editor
Allison R. Ensor

VOLUME XVIII

THE UNIVERSITY OF TENNESSEE PRESS · KNOXVILLE · 1973

Tennessee Studies in Literature

Persons interested in submitting manuscripts should address the Editor, *Tennessee Studies in Literature*, McClung Tower 306, University of Tennessee, Knoxville, Tennessee, 37916. Contributions from any qualified scholar, especially from this state and region, will be considered. Return postage should accompany manuscripts. Papers (ribbon copies on non-erasable bond paper) should be no longer than five thousand words. Contributors will receive fifty offprints. Other inquiries concerning this series should be addressed to the University of Tennessee Press, Communications Building, University Station, Knoxville, Tennessee, 37916.

CONTENTS

Abstract. Since Gower treated the theme of "a knight in love" extensively in *Vox Clamantis* and since Chaucer dedicated *Troilus and Criseyde* to Gower, we have in this poem a clear frame of reference for understanding Chaucer's treatment of the same theme. In Gower the behavior of a knight in love is not regarded as independent of our moral code; nor is there any mention of love's ennobling effects; indeed love is consistently viewed as a debilitating force. Essentially the same attitude is to be found in *Troilus and Criseyde.* Unfortunately too much attention has been given in the past to the pathetic aspects of Troilus' love and too little attention to the satiric undercurrent in all the key sections. Moreover the matter has been obscured by the narrative voice, which ought to be regarded with considerable caution, as in all of Chaucer's poems. Ultimately we must distinguish between the narrator's sympathy and the poet's intellectual awareness, occasioned by a tension within the poet himself, for in this dichotomy lies most of the irony of the poem, the humor, and the sense of inevitability. (FHW)

Abstract. Although "Sumer Is Icumen In" has always been taken as a welcome to spring and the cuckoo, it is noteworthy that the cuckoo as parasite is out of place in a poem which otherwise rejoices in the solicitude of beasts for their young. The poem has two voices: a description of spring's rebirth which moves from plant to animal, but ignores man; and the invocation to the cuckoo never to stop singing. The invocation attempts to remedy the individual man's exclusion from nature's regeneration by perpetuating this particular spring in the perpetuation of the cuckoo's song. As long as the bird sings, summer lasts—a theoretical possibility since, as a round, the lyric is conceivably endless. The irony, first noted in the choice of the parasitic cuckoo to carry out this task, is compounded by the fact that the cuckoo, although a harbinger of spring, never sings in the summer. (JAH)

Abstract. John Skelton's *Garlande of Laurell* has been considered the poet's rejection of his satiric muse, as well as his capitulation to his former satiric butt, Thomas Cardinal Wolsey. But evidence in the poem suggests that Skelton was indeed serious in defending his satiric artistry and was only ironically concerned with flattering Wolsey. Skelton's careful reference to dream lore and astrological signs signals his readers that the poem may have hidden satiric meaning. And startling echoes of earlier anti-Wolsey satires warn that the poem is no simple gesture of reconcilation. The poem is an affirmation of Skelton's satiric writing style as well as his preoccupation with the folly and vice of courtly figures.   (JSC)

Abstract. Chapman's *Blind Beggar of Alexandria*, enormously well received in its own day, has offended modern tastes. This attempt at re-evaluation is based on a study of the folk tales and legends combined in the curiously "primitive" work. For example, the relationship between Cleanthes and Aegiale represents one version of the story of "Potiphar's Wife." Cleanthes is also linked with the "protean beggar" who assumes a variety of disguises to cheat his victims, and his marriages and self-cuckolding recall popular accounts of sexual misadventures. These parallels suggest the following conclusions: the original work (which is not fairly represented by the extant text) featured more prominently the "Potiphar's Wife" theme. Elizabethan audiences probably responded enthusiastically to the familiar folk matter in the play. The similarities between Cleanthes and several folk "heroes" indicate that he is not simply a low-comedy rogue but a dramatic spokesman expressing a significant view of life not normally allowed the author.   (JER)

Abstract. An examination of *Hamlet* against the background of the various archetypal readings of the tragedy indicates that myth does indeed play an important part in defining Hamlet's predicament. However, these archetypal readings generally fall short in failing to account for the ironic distortions of myth in the play. What we are to see in Hamlet is a hero striving for mythic dimensions of heroism, but inhibited by history: the dual time-frame of the tragedy places him in a historical context which makes mythic heroism inaccessible to him. Thus Hamlet tests several versions of heroism, including the mythic roles of winter-king, scapegoat, and fool-prophet; but the fundamental principle of structure in this tragedy is that all patterns seem to be abortive. Thus the tragedy of Hamlet consists in the fact that he fails, on both levels of his quest—word and deed—to find self-definition as a hero. On the level of the deed, his endeavors simply lead to a meaningless death with the succession of Fortinbras providing little hope of renewal for the "drowsy age"; on the level of the word, the "prophetic tongue" of Hamlet gives issue to what must finally be recognized as a hollow rhetoric that yields no saving truth.   (REF)

Abstract. The often-noted self-deceptions of the characters of *Twelfth Night* stem ultimately from their self-centeredness. Orsino loves in the grand style because he wants to display the exquisiteness of his own emotions, just as Sir Andrew struggles in a cruder way to be an admired courtier. Narcissistic Olivia falls in love with Cesario because this disdainful critic presents an ideal image of her own Petrarchan haughtiness to Orsino, just as her steward Malvolio, self-loving in a cruder way, worships himself as the chosen of the gods. In contrast to these characters who are imprisoned in their self-gratifying, artificial fantasies, Sir Toby lives by natural and unpretentious appetite. But his vision of the world is too selfish and too materialistic to do justice to the kinds of faith and love exemplified by the noblest characters of the play, Viola and Sebastian, whose response to the world is neither artificial nor natural, but essentially religious.   (CD)

Abstract. In three of his best-known verse satires, "The Last Instructions to a Painter," "The Loyall Scot," and "A Dialogue Between the Two Horses," Andrew Marvell uses dramatic frame devices. These free him to an extent from the demands of internal consistency and permit him to use multiple voices and multiple modes of discourse, though these freedoms have caused critics to declare the poems artless and obscure. When proper attention is devoted to the functions and effects of the frame devices, however, it becomes apparent that the advice-to-a-painter frame of "Last Instructions" *allows* the poet the luxury of some rhetorical flaws, that "The Loyall Scot" derives virtually its entire satiric thrust from the frame, that the unordered discourse of the statue personae in "A Dialogue" becomes ordered and meaningful when recognized to be controlled by the speech motif advanced in the frame. Thus, the poems are considerably more skillfully constructed than is commonly supposed.   (JQ)

Abstract. The bee and the spider episode in *The Battel of the Books* is the key to any understanding of Swift's aesthetic outlook. As antithetical metaphors, they represent aesthetic theories which are, respectively, object-centered and artist-centered. Within the framework of object-centered art (mimesis), Swift defines the function of the imagination and genius, demands originality, and accepts traditional literary values without the sterile prescriptivism which mars much of eighteenth-century literary criticism. Also, "Sweetness and Light," the results of the bee's (or artist's) flights, have their counterparts in the critic's response: taste and candor. Finally, the fruits of the bee's labors shed light on both Lemuel Gulliver and the Grub street narrator of *A Tale of a Tub*. Both "authors" deviate from a classical aesthetic norm; Gulliver wishes to instruct man without entertaining him, and the Modern writer concludes that entertainment is the only good he can hope for. (CS)

Abstract. Jonathan Swift's *Verses on the Death of Dr. Swift* carries much more self-praise than has ever been deprecated or even discerned, and is the better for it. The poem eulogizes Swift not only in the testimonial close but also in the wry presumption and mock self-disparagement of the opening, in the attentions and honors of the middle, and in several strands of self-aggrandizement that span the poem. The extensiveness of the self-praise is made hard to detect and to dislike, partly by shifts in methods and concerns within the between sections, partly by comic uses of dramatic, rhetorical, and logical forms. Eulogy managed with such profusion, diversity, and deviousness is a feat. Its by-products include a curious elegy for oneself and a remarkable tribute to mankind. (HMR)

Abstract. Until recently, interpretations of *The Eve of St. Agnes* have tended to diverge radically from their predecessors. The latest study, though, offers a kind of compromise to "metaphysical" and "realistic" readings. Though that essay is right to argue the poem has both realism and romance, as well as affirmation and scepticism, its specific arguments seem unsatisfactory. Re-examination shows that, instead of a validation (Wasserman) or repudiation (Stillinger) of visionary imagination, or, now, a self-conscious romance of wish-fulfillment (Sperry), *St. Agnes* focuses on a sharply defined approach to experience. This approach is spotlighted within the Madeline-Porphyro plot by contrast with the "ways" of both the Beadsman and the revelers; through the close parallel between the Beadsman's religious ritual and both Madeline's superstitious ceremonies and Porphyro's worship of her; and by means of the union of sensuous-sensual and religious imagery. The poem emerges as a crystalization of an experience that acquires religious meaning for Porphyro. For him, as well as for Keats, religious significance lay, not in conventional modes, but in the experience of intense, exalted moments. Worldly and realistic, the poem insists on the impermanence of such moments. More than a thesis-poem affirming the limited possibilities for fulfillment in a brutish world, *St. Agnes* is one of the consolations it describes and advocates. (GDA)

Abstract. Both the form and the style of William Bartram's *Travels* reflect its author's deeply rooted ambivalence toward the wilderness. Perhaps accidentally, but nonetheless significantly, the narrative features the classic pastoral pattern of withdrawal, contact with nature, and return to civilization, a pattern that takes on special meaning for the book in light of Bartram's later refusal to accompany Jefferson's Lewis and Clark expedition. The style dramatizes a tension in his mind between cultivated and untrammeled nature, useful and merely picturesque landscapes, which gives added point to the tripartite pastoral design that controls the structure of the book. (RDA)

Abstract. The poetry of George McClellan (1860–1934), which has never previously been studied, sensitively records the black artist's struggle to be both a Negro and an American. The poet, an exceptionally gifted and learned man, earned three college degrees, served as a minister and teacher in the deep South, and published four volumes of poetry and fiction from 1895 to 1916. His stories denounce white hypocrisy and racial injustice, which he suffered, and his sixty-seven poems are spiritual autobiographies of a frustrated, race-proud black man. Although superficially traditional in subject and versification, the poems, through complex image clusters and unresolved appositions of neo-classical and romantic elements, reveal McClellan's "double consciousness," his anguished sense of being alienated from both black and white worlds, his futile striving to express Negro soul-beauty and to recapture the Negro self while simultaneously longing to please white audiences. McClellan's graceful, precise poetry of Southern landscapes and youthful loves and dreams significantly illumines both racial history and American literature of the turn of the century. (JRS)

FRANK H. WHITMAN

TROILUS AND CRISEYDE
AND CHAUCER'S DEDICATION TO GOWER

The second last stanza of *Troilus and Criseyde* contains Chaucer's dedication to Gower and Strode:

> O moral Gower, this book I directe
> To the and to the, philosophical Strode,
> To vouchen sauf, ther nede is, to correcte,
> Of youre benignites and zeles goode.
>
> v, 1856–59

Of "philosophical Strode" we unfortunately know too little, and what we do know seems to bear small relation to the matter of Chaucer's poem. Of "moral Gower" we know a good deal more, of course, and that particularly on the theme of "a knight in love" he had much to say. Yet, as far as I know, this has been almost totally overlooked as a means of understanding *Troilus*, since for the most part critics have rarely thought that the dedication was relevant to the meaning of the poem as a whole. The outstanding exception is Fisher,[1] who finds significant points of contact between *Troilus* and the works of Gower generally. The philosophy of Chaucer's poem, he argues, is but a development of the first thirty-six lines of Gower's *Mirour*, as summarized in the following lines:

Car s'un soul homme avoir porroit	For if a man could have
Quanq'en son coer souhaideroit	whatever his heart desired
Du siecle, pour soy deliter,	of the world, to delight him,
Trestout come songe passeroit	it would all pass away like a dream
En nient, et quant l'en meinz quidoit,	into nothing, just as he thought it in his hands—
Par grant dolour doit terminer:	it would end in great sorrow.
Et puisque l'amour seculer	And thus secular love
En nient au fin doit retorner,	must in the end return to nothingness.

1

But, says Fisher, there is a fundamental difference in the technique of both works, a difference which is evident from the beginning: Gower denounces temporal love as a degrading force, whereas Chaucer refines it and makes a tragedy of its eventual insufficiency. "The subtlety and human interest of Chaucer's poem," he goes on, "derives from its use of this spiritualized conception of courtly love as a vehicle for its moralization"; Gower's poem, on the other hand, shows "no awareness of the literary possibilities of spiritualizing the romantic conventions."[2]

With this I agree in the main, but I think the claim consistently made by critics that Chaucer "refined" ("elevated," "spiritualized") temporal love can be very misleading. It is true that Troilus' love is almost totally purged of sexuality and that it is sometimes viewed cosmically as a life force. It is also true that the whole drama is clothed in a language with a distinct "ecclesiastical" ring. But, unless we choose to disregard the obvious, we must remember that the action is filtered through a narrator whose understanding of Boethius, and his underlying Platonism, is poor and whose judgments constantly require scrutiny. In spite of the appearance, Troilus' love is in no way Platonic, at least not in the sense of reflecting the soul's escape from carnality, with love beginning in natural desire but rising beyond carnality to something higher and better; for it is one thing to worship the divine as human, quite another to worship the human as divine—a fundamental distinction, of course, but one that the narrator fails to make. He also fails to evaluate soberly Troilus' reaction to love's force. According to him the effects on Troilus are ennobling, but for this, there is little evidence; indeed such a view is contradicted by each of the poem's major movements. In my opinion, too much has been made of Troilus as a tragic figure and insufficient of his foolishness. Admittedly, critics have always been aware of the comedy inherent in the drama, but it has been underplayed; if it is given its due weight, then I believe it will be seen that Chaucer is even closer to Gower in sentiment than Fisher credits.

In *Vox Clamantis* Gower devotes more than six chapters to the theme of "a knight in love."[3] Knighthood, he begins, was established for three reasons: to protect the rights of the Church, to promote the common good, and to help those in need. For these reasons, he says, a knight in arms should be ready to go into battle, and if he does he ought to be praised; but if he wages war for other reasons, such as fame or the praise of a woman, he deserves none. What honor will a victorious knight have, Gower asks, if a woman's love in turn conquers him? He will certainly receive no praise from Christ; indeed, if he is led into battle by Venus, he is simply a fool. A woman rarely releases a knight whom she has ensnared, and any knight who was once free but has voluntarily subjugated himself is stupid. If he understood the real nature of love, its changeability, he would avoid it; for among other things it causes the very natures of things to deteriorate. The knight in love thinks his lady's beauty transcends human kind; he thinks of her as a goddess. Scarcely does he look at her but that he wants to kneel before her and offer his devotion. His mind's eye grows dull, blind from the darkness of lust, and he sinks down to his own destruction. He burns, he freezes. His imagination is constantly at work; now he is elated, now depressed. Thus blind love leads foolish lovers so that they do not see what is good for them, and their honor dies. Snared by carnal love, the reason becomes irrational; and in the end the fool will say, "Alas, how wretched Fortune is! For after such a long time my efforts have turned out to be nought." This is a foolish lament because the suffering has been self-inflicted. Why, then, does a knight wish for things which are senseless? His praises will be sung in vain unless God is their author, and honor which does not come from God is really a disgrace.

What is interesting about all this, and much else that I have had to omit, is not that we find many of the same motives in *Troilus*, for these are a commonplace in the literature of the period, but that they are ordered by a singular vision. The behavior of the knight in love is not held to be independent of our code of morality, nor, alternatively, is there any talk about love's ennobling effects; indeed, love is consistently viewed as a debilitating force and the knight who falls under its power as a poor wretch whose destruction is inevitable.

Now it has always seemed to me that the effect of love on Troilus is precisely this—debilitating. It is true that it is not degrading—the romance conventions preclude any such quality—but it is nevertheless debilitating and utimately destructive. If there is a difference between Gower and Chaucer, it arises only from their manipulation of the same conventions: one is dramatic, the other not. Moreover in Gower the real world intrudes, or, if you like, conventions which are essentially romantic (that is, which take their life from the heightened world of imaginative literature) are applied to the real world of knighthood in the fourteenth century with the result that they seem silly and in the final analysis degrading; in Chaucer the real world never intrudes—the nearest it comes is in the person of Pandarus, who brings a certain mocking practicality to bear on the problems at hand—so that degradation has no place. These are clear differences, but in spite of them the moral drift of each work seems quite the same: as Fisher himself observes, the discussion of knighthood in *Vox Clamantis* is "replete with the sort of moral judgments that Chaucer was to make dramatically."[4]

If there is doubt about this, it ought to be dispelled by focusing upon Troilus in any key passage, where for the most part he will be seen to be a ludicrous figure whose absurdity gives the work much of its moral force. This is particularly evident in Book III, the consummation, which in every way is the center of the poem. The essential tone of this section is satiric and arises in three principal ways, from the inherent comedy of the situations, from an intensification of this comedy by means of satiric comment on the action, and, at a deeper level, from an ironic counterpoint which allows the reader no alternative but to focus upon the transience of all temporal joy even at those moments when the lovers are at the very height of bliss. Consider the situations in which we find Troilus: at the opening, in bed, feigning sickness, groaning, blushing, lamenting, professing his love, while Pandarus wept "as he to water wolde" and "poked evere his nece new and newe"; in the next scene, waiting in the "stewe," forlornly looking through "a litel window" at the women gathered around; then, when it is time to go, dallying, calling upon the gods for strength with extensive prayer-making; at last, dragged into Criseyde's bedroom "by the lappe," falling on his knees—Criseyde in bed, Pandarus to the side, reading a romance; shortly after, swooning, then being thrown on the bed and eventually brought back to life. The comedy inherent in all this is further enhanced by a satiric commentary, arising out of the reactions of Pandarus and Criseyde to Troilus' unlikely behavior. Thus Pandarus on Troilus' prayers (themselves satiric in their rhetorical bombast), which delay entrance into Criseyde's chamber:

> . . . "Thow wrecched mouses herte,
> Artow agast so that she wol the bite?"
> III, 736–37

Again Pandarus, pointing to Troilus as he kneels, before running for a cushion:

> . . . "Nece, se how this lord kan knele!
> Now, for youre trouthe, se this gentil man!"
> III, 962–63

Pandarus, attempting to salvage the situation when Troilus faints:

> "O nece, pes, or we be lost!" quod he,
> "Beth naught agast!" but certeyn, at the laste,
> For this or that, he into bed hym caste,
> And seyde, "O thef, is this a mannes herte?"
> III, 1095–98

Criseyde, so taken aback by the course of events:

> ... "Is this a mannes game?
> What, Troilus, wol ye do thus for shame?"
>   III, 1126–27

And finally Pandarus, at rest content that the consummation must take place:

> ... "If ye be wise,
> Swouneth nought now, lest more folk arise!"
>   III, 1189–90

If the situations and the commentary do not in themselves point up the absurdity of Troilus' behavior, the irony certainly does, particularly in the latter part of this book, by juxtaposing the lovers' happiness, their talk of true felicity (1691–94) and heaven (1597–1600), with a keen sense of its ephemerality, by means of Criseyde's vows of fidelity (1493–98), soon to be broken, by the symbolic exchange of rings, and above all by a strong suggestion of time's passage, symbolized by the inevitability of the approaching day, which dominates the thoughts of the two lovers.

If we look at the tenderest scenes, we find that they are immediately followed by others in which Troilus' absurdity is paramount, so that in large measure the pathos is destroyed. I point to only two. The first is in Book IV when Troilus and Criseyde are together for the first time after hearing that they must be separated. In perhaps the tenderest moment in the whole work Criseyde lays her face upon Troilus' breast, speaks briefly with broken voice, and then faints away. What follows— Troilus' assumption that she has died, his readying her for the bier, his own preparation for suicide, his long rhetorical dallying, her awakening and seeing the sword—all this has a devastating effect on the pathos which for a moment has dominated the mood. The other scene that I have in mind is in Book V, the departure of Criseyde and its aftermath. The pathos here is very strong, particularly when Troilus has to make much of Antenor, the real cause of the exchange; and it is intensified by Diomede's forthright wooing of Criseyde. But immediately afterwards we find Troilus in another of his absurd postures, this time directing Pandarus in the details of his own funeral and the disposition of his weapons. The reaction of Pandarus, it is interesting to note, is typically satiric:

> "... fro many a worthi knyght
> Hath his lady gon a fourtenyght,
> And he nat yet made halvendel the fare.
> What nede is the to maken al this care?"
>   V, 333–36

The effect of love on Troilus, rather than producing an ennobling transformation, as we are usually told by critics, is ironically enough one of emasculation, leading to a loss of identity, and producing something akin to role switching. Put bluntly, Troilus, the great man of Troy, a spirited and energetic soul, becomes impotent, and Criseyde, the "fearfulest of wights," his master. It is precisely the kind of role switching that Gower laments in Book VII of *Vox Clamantis*: "the female has now become the lord and master of the male, and the gentle, submissive, and compliant handmaiden has become the man"; "weak folly assails and conquers the man of strength, and the man who should be wise falls, being made of clay."[5] Significantly, Troilus consistently plays the passive role: he can neither initiate the affair nor promote it; instead he faints away like a woman and has to be patted back to life, so that eventually it is Criseyde, not he, who does the seducing, if this is the right word for it. His inactivity and debilitation are symbolized by his bed, which he instinctively turns to whenever he faces an emotional crisis; he is ever prostrate—this fact impresses itself most upon us. Surely we find ourselves in sympathy with Pandarus, if not with his specific plan, when, trying to rouse Troilus out of his characteristic lethargy on hearing of the planned exchange of Criseyde for Antenor, he says:

> "Ris up anon, and lat this wepyng be,
> And kith thow art a man . . . ."
> IV, 537–38

And again later, when addressing Troilus rather like an adult to a child:

> "Forthi ris up, as naught ne were, anon,
> And wassh thi face, and to the kyng thow wende,
> Or he may wondren whider thow art goon."
> IV, 645–47

This impotence and loss of identity are but a dramatic representation at a temporal level of the Boethian discussion in Book IV of *De Consolatione* which turns upon what happens to a man who has had his natural tendency toward good dulled, except that "good" in Chaucer's poem is given the narrower and more manageable meaning of "the need for the soul to be ruled by love, just as everything is." Speaking of the "good," Boethius notes that man is instinctively governed by it—both good and bad men alike—but, he adds, only the former attain it because their approach is through virtue; bad men fail because they try to achieve it through concupiscence. The quality of good men, he concludes, is strength; that of wicked men, impotence. Not only are the latter deprived of strength, he goes on; they are also deprived of their real being, for they fail to do what is their nature and thus lose their very character. Their appearance shows that they were once men, but they have ceased to be what they were. Just as virtue can raise a person above human nature, so vice lowers those whom it has seduced from the condition of men; for this reason, anyone found transformed cannot be counted a man.

In *Troilus* "good" and "love" are nearly synonymous; at least "love" is the sine qua non of everything. As the Chaucerian narrator says, "in this world no lyves creature / Withouten love is worth, or may endure." But, as he goes on to point out, there are those who "stryve" with it; and it is precisely this fact that produces the Boethian lament, "O how happy the human race would be, if that love which rules the heavens also ruled your souls." But that Troilus and Boethius have different understandings of the meaning of love is at once apparent: Troilus associates it with Venus, Boethius with divine essence. And herein is the explanation for Troilus' debilitation and impotence: in Boethian terms, he is the man who has sought the highest good through unnatural means—in this instance, idolatrous love.

What is idolatrous about Troilus' love is not that it is human but that it never develops beyond this. In so doing, it differs totally from Platonic notions popularized at Chartres or the speculative mysticism of Clairvaux, both of which sang the praises of human love but viewed it in relation to higher forms. To the Platonists the most striking feature of beauty (the object of love) was its universality, so that the proper business of a lover was its recognition in all phases. Beauty, Plato had argued, is not a particular thing: a man should love beauty in a particular body, but then he should note that this beauty is cognate to the beauty found in all other forms; ultimately he should set an even higher value on the beauty of souls; and finally he ought to love the very essence of beauty.[6] In Bernard of Clairvaux we find the same progression. Bernard did not disparage human love either; on the contrary, he regarded it as a normal introduction to divine love: because we are born from the flesh, he argued, love must have its beginning in the flesh, but when guided by the grace of God it will be consummated in the spirit. The first step in love is thus the flesh, which appreciates nothing beyond itself; but man soon perceives that he cannot exist by himself and so will begin to seek God—for his own selfish ends; then, through worship, he will gradually come to understand and to love God, not for selfish reasons this time but solely as God; and finally it may be possible for him to reach perfection, by loving himself solely for God's sake.[7]

Of these various stages in love's development only the first finds expression in Chaucer's poem. Here the love is firmly rooted in the physical world: its object is Criseyde and has no meaning without her; it is an end in itself, without progression to a "purer" ("higher") form. What seems to be lacking is the exercise of the reason. Reason has the greater sobriety, Bernard observed, love blessedness, and unless they function together little is achieved; but when reason teaches love and love illuminates reason (similarly when reason yields to the affection of love and love is agreeable to the restraints of reason) much is accomplished.[8] Troilus' love is sudden and never tempered by reason and as such conflicts with characteristic neoplatonic notions of fulfilled love. "I indeed marvel profoundly at all those who pretend to fall in love at first sight," observes Ibn Hazm; "I cannot easily prevail upon myself to believe their claim, and prefer to consider such love as merely a kind of lust, [and] as for thinking that that sort of attachment can really possess the inmost heart, and penetrate the veil of the soul's recess, that I cannot under any circumstance credit."[9] "The soul must first be made aware of its points of resemblance and concord with its fellow-soul," he writes in another place; "it must confront its own hidden temperaments with the corresponding temperaments of the beloved; then and then only will veritable union be consummated, and that without further let or hindrance."[10] We find nothing like this in *Troilus*; this love is of an entirely different character—blind, idolatrous and destructive. Gower, better than anyone, summarizes its effects:

When a man sees her womanly beauty—so sweet, elegant and fine, but more like an angel's—he thinks her a goddess, and puts his fate of life and death in her hands. As he turns such marvellous beauty over in his mind, having been turned by it, he withdraws without turning around. Outwardly, he does not show what the sight of her means to him; inwardly, the sting of love pierces his heart. He stands as motionless as a stone and does not move from her sight, as if he were in a trance. His mind's eye grows dull, blind from the darkness of lust, and he sinks down to his own destruction.[11]

This distinction, between human and divine love, is in part obscured by the narrative voice. The narrator's conception of love is certainly colored by Platonic notions ("As man, brid, best, fissh, herbs, and grene tree / Thee fele in tymes with vapour sterne"), but, like Troilus, his main concern is with Venus:

> Now, lady bryght, for thi benignite,
> At reverence of hem that serven the,
> Whos clerc I am, so techeth me devyse
> Som joye of that is felt in thi servyse.
> III, 39–42

It follows, then, that we have to regard the narrative voice with considerable care. What I think we must clearly come to accept is that there is a fundamental difference between the narrator's pronouncements throughout and Chaucer's own position—in short, what has become virtually a cliché of Chaucerian criticism, that the narrator is simply another character. Like all Chaucer's narrators, particularly those in the *General Prologue, The House of Fame,* and *The Parliament of Fowls,* he is the butt of considerable humor: he is naive and frequently misguided. He is just as misguided in his veneration of Venus and praise of Troilus as the narrator in the *General Prologue* is in his evaluation of the pilgrims. He grasps part of the truth, but only part; and in this he is unquestionably the most important instrument of irony in a work which is ironic at its very core.

This manipulation of the narrator arises, I suspect, from a tension within the poet himself, a tension between his intellectual awareness of the instability and impermanence of everything earthly on the one hand and his reluctance to abandon such ephemeral joys on the other. As is usually the case in Chaucer, this conflict crystalizes in love, in an analysis of its duality, both its power of attraction and its concomitant sorrows. In *Troilus* this dichotomy finds expression in a narrator who at the beginning sympathizes with his hero and ardently defends the religion of love and the poet who in the end is philosopher and must reject all as earthly vanity. Here, in this conflict between awareness and desire, is where the emotional energy of the poem is generated. In Troilus, the poet, through his narrator, finds a man whom he can identify with at an emotional level, a man who is not emotionally equipped to adapt to changing situations (love's torment, love's bliss, love's loss), and who will rail at Fortune in times of adversity; yet, as poet, he realizes that Fortune is nothing more than a reflection of the earthly situation, a mirroring of the constant flux between periods of prosperity and adversity, and that all is to be viewed within a larger framework. The difference between the narrator's sympathy and the poet's awareness is what accounts for most of the irony, the humor, and the sense of inevitability.

Unless we make this basic distinction we are likely to read the poem like Kirby, who sums up his study in the following way: "he [Chaucer] found a poem of courtly love, saw fit greatly to enhance that element, and succeeded in making the finest courtly love poem ever written." "Then," he goes on to say, "his work done, he stopped, looked back, saw the artificiality not only of courtly love but of all earthly endeavor and consequently urged his readers to devote their efforts to the things of eternity."[12] Such a view as this—which, by the way, strikes me as naive and, though unintentioned of course, a slight of the worst kind in that it implies Chaucer approached his material uncritically—makes this elementary error and leads, I think, to a view of Troilus that is sentimental. I use the word "sentimental" advisedly because this surely is the danger, given, as we are, a frame of reference in the epilogue within which the whole action may be viewed, and more significantly perhaps a comic tone, deriving primarily from Troilus' behavior, which permeates the very fabric of the poem. What is usually overlooked is that the apparent dichotomy between the direction of the poem proper and the epilogue is paralleled by a similar dichotomy between the narrator and the poet throughout. In the end, therefore, when Troilus rises up and is able to view his actions from a new perspective, there is no sense of incongruity. Troilus sees for the first time how ludicrous he has been, what a ridiculous figure he must have cut to other eyes, obsessed as he was, blind, prostrate, hardly a man at all, the main figure in an affair which at its climax teeters on the brink of farce: all this is a revelation to him and he laughs. But to us it is no surprise, for we have been prepared for this renunciation from the beginning by the poet's awareness, which plays over the material undercutting the pathetic and creating a sense of irony at every turn. The poem is in no way a tragedy then, at least in the classical sense. John of Salisbury is closer to the spirit when he says, "almost everything that takes place in the seething mob of the irreligious is more like a comedy than real life . . . where each forgetting his own plays another's role."[13] But of course it is no comedy either; that there is considerable pathos is obvious, because, however well we may understand the drama at a philosophical level, like the narrator, we find ourselves responding emotionally to the situations.

According to Lewis, *Troilus* is "a great poem in praise of love."[14] If this were true, we would have to see Gower and Chaucer standing at polar extremes in their treatment of "a knight in love." But I think we have to ask ourselves what there is in Troilus' love that is praiseworthy. Very little, I suspect! It is true that the narrator talks of the admirable transformation in Troilus:

> . . . he bicom the friendlieste wight,
> The gentilest, and ek the mooste fre,
> The thriftiest and oon the beste knyght
> That in his tyme was or myghte be.
> Dede were his japes and his cruelte,
> His heighe port and his manere estraunge,
> And ecch of the gan for a vertu chaunge.[15]

But this is the narrator's estimation, and he is a self-proclaimed servant of love, whose identification with Troilus is so strong that at one point he seems willing to sell his soul for a night of similar bliss:

> Why nad I swich oon with my soule ybought,
> Ye, or the leeste joie that was theere?
>
> III, 1319–20

Dramatically, and this is more important, we simply do not feel that the transformation is for Troilus' good. Quite the contrary, we are more apt to agree with Andreas, that "any man who devotes his efforts to love loses all his usefulness."[16] Certainly this is Gower's view, and, I suggest, Chaucer's.

NOTES

[1] John Fisher, *John Gower* (New York: New York Univ. Press, 1964), 204–302.

[2] Ibid., 227–35.

[3] A convenient translation may be found in Eric W. Stockton, *The Major Works of John Gower* (Seattle: Univ. of Washington Press, 1962), 47–288. For the theme of "a knight in love" see particularly 196–206 (v, 1–7).

[4] Fisher, 228.

[5] Stockton, 257–58 (VII, 3).

[6] *Symposium*, trans. W. R. M. Lamb, *Plato* (London: Heinemann, 1946), 203–207.

[7] *De Diligendo Deo*, xv (*PL*, 182, 998–1000).

[8] *De Natura et Dignitate Amoris*, VIII (*PL*, 184, 393).

[9] *The Ring of the Dove*, trans. A. J. Arberry (London: Luzac, 1953), 56.

[10] Ibid., 57.

[11] Stockton, 199 (v, 3).

[12] Thomas A. Kirby, *Chaucer's Troilus* (Baton Rouge: Louisiana State Univ. Press, 1940), 284.

[13] *Policraticus*, III, 8.

[14] C. S. Lewis, *The Allegory of Love* (New York: Oxford Univ. Press, 1958), 197.

[15] Moreover Troilus' actions are of questionable virtue because it is not clear whether they are inspired by the hope of making a good impression on Criseyde or by "the good, the right, and the reason." See Jehan le Bel, *Ars d'amour*, summarized by D. W. Robertson, Jr., *A Preface to Chaucer* (Princeton: Princeton Univ. Press, 1962), 454.

[16] *De Arte Honeste Amandi*, III.

University of British Columbia

JEFFREY A. HELTERMAN

THE ANTAGONISTIC VOICES OF
"SUMER IS ICUMEN IN"

Svmer is icumen in,
Lhude sing cuccu!
Groweþ sed and bloweþ med
and springþ þe wde nu.
Sing cuccu!

Awe bleteþ after lomb,
lhouþ after calue cu,
Bulluc sterteþ, bucke uerteþ.
Murie sing cuccu!
Cuccu, cuccu,
Wel singes þu cuccu.
ne swik þu nauer nu!

Pes {
Sing cuccu nu, Sing cuccu!

Sing cuccu, Sing cuccu nu!
}

Hoc repetit unus
quociens opus est.
faciens pausacionem in
fine
Hoc dicit alius pausans
in medio & non in fine.
Set immediate repetens
principium.[1]

The popular round "Sumer Is Icumen In" has always been taken to be a joyous welcome to spring and its harbinger, the cuckoo. The imagery of rebirth—the growing seed, the lamb, the calf—salutes Nature's regeneration as the poet's eye moves up the order of created being from plant to animal. The chain does not extend to man as does the *reverdie* at the beginning of *The Canterbury Tales*. This in itself is not significant until we remember that the cuckoo's song in a similar context of *reverdie* in "The Sea-Farer" brings not joy, but bitter sorrow:

Bearwas blostmum nimað, byrig faegriað
wongas wlitigað, woruld onetteð;

13

ealle þa gemoniað modes fusne
sefan to siþe þam þe swa þenceð
on flodwegas feor gewitan.
Swylce geac monað geomran reorde;
singeð sumeres weard, sorge beodeð
bitter in breosthord.[2]

(ll. 48–55)

The Anglo-Saxon poem does not explicitly state the reason for this sorrow, but the bird's song calls to mind the speaker's separation from the rest of Nature, with the moral implication that it is not enough for man simply to grow; he must take to the sea and strive in pain for self-definition. With this tradition of the sorrowful song of the cuckoo in mind, we may find that the purposes of the Middle English poet are less joyful than has previously been acknowledged.

Although the cuckoo is a traditional harbinger of spring, the parasitic habits of the bird, well known from the time of Pliny on,[3] are somewhat out of place in a poem which rejoices in the solicitude of other beasts for their young. If the poet has in mind the very widespread tradition that allows the Fool in *Lear* to compare Goneril to the cuckoo,

The hedge-sparrow fed the cuckoo so long,
That it had it head bit off by it young,
(I.iv.235–36)

then there is an implied tension between the song of the bird and the presence of the ewe that bleats after its lamb and the cow that lows after its calf. The medieval reader was well aware of this unattractive side of the cuckoo. Chaucer makes a passing allusion to the cuckoo's habits in *The Parlement of Foules* where he refers to the "cukkow ever unkinde" and Brunetto Latini fully describes the cuckoo's failure to care for its young:

It is so lazy and negligent that it does not wish to brood over its eggs. And when the time comes to lay its eggs, it goes to the nest of a small bird called the scerpafolea which fears larger birds, and picks up one of its eggs, and put one of its own in its place. In this manner, the cuckoo disposes of its eggs, and thus is not troubled with its offspring.[4]

If we look carefully at the strategy of "Sumer Is Icumen In," we will discover that it is divided into two parts: the description of spring, which uses indicative verbs, and the invocation to the cuckoo, which uses the imperative mood. The whole poem has been taken as a celebration of spring because of the joy and energy delineated in the description, but the celebration is limited *only* to the descriptive part, while the invocation simply asks the cuckoo to sing *without stopping*.

The invocation is motivated by the speaker's realization that as an individual he is isolated from what he celebrates—Nature's regeneration. Since he is not renewed every year like the rest of Nature, the speaker's only hope is to keep this particular spring from fading. He tries to do this by perpetuating the cuckoo's song: all of the "sing cuccu's" reinforce the plea "ne swik þu nauer nu!" in an attempt to stave off the coming of winter and metaphorically, Death.[5] As long as the bird sings, summer lasts. A contemporary lyric equates the duration of summer and bird's song:

> Mirie it is while sumer ilast
> Wiδ fugheles song,
> oc nu necheδ windes blast
> and weder strong,[6]

but it views their identity from the bleak time of winter, thereby acknowledging that the bird's song and the summer of man's life must end.

The adverb "murie" in line 9 ("murie sing cuccu") marks the near desperation in the poet's desire to retain the "mirie sumer" of the lyric, but the speaker's use of the adverb in juxtaposition with the plea for the permanence of the song ignores momentarily the ironic fragility of both the joy and the bird's voice. The limited duration of the cuckoo's merry song is set forth in *Summer's Last Will and Testament*, where Spring arrives with the cuckoo's song,

> And we heare aye birds tune this merry lay,
> Cuckow, iugge, iugge, þu we, to witta woo,[7]

but then reveals his own inability to stay beyond a moment of pleasure:

nam quae habui, perdidi; what I had, I haue spent on good fellowes: in these sports you haue seene, which are proper to the Spring, and others of like sort . . . haue I bestowde all my flowry treasure.[8]

By choosing the cuckoo's song to perpetuate his summer, the poet of "Sumer Is Icumen In" has undertaken a seemingly impossible task.

The effort, nevertheless, is supported by a second strategy at work in the poem—the choice of the round as the vehicle for the invocation. Theoretically, a round can be sung endlessly so that the poem's form represents iconographically the attempt to make summer last forever. As long as the bird will respond to the continued repetition of "sing cuccu!" the bitter season will not come. This follows a tradition, dating back at least to Alcuin, that he and winter are fierce antagonists (*"veniat cuculus cum germine laeto. / Frigora depellat"*).[9] The poet, however, is no sentimentalist and the theoretical hope for endless repetition is set against his knowledge that the round must at last end.

The tension between the attempt to perpetuate the summer of man's life and the certainty of its failure is focused in the choice of the cuckoo as the object of the invocation. Not only is the cuckoo unfit company for the cow and the ewe, but also its song has a second pejorative meaning for the Middle Ages as Phoebus learns in "The Manciple's Tale" when the crow "contrefetes" the cuckoo's song to tell of his wife's deceit. It is a song of mockery, the French "cocù" that warns man that he has been betrayed by what he loves. Although it is not certain that the poet has this secondary meaning in mind, "sing cuccu" as a warning of cuckoldry was commonplace enough in the thirteenth century and by Shakespeare's time the invocation to spring included the mockery:

> When daisies pied, and violets blue,
> And lady-smocks all silver-white,
> And cuckoo-buds of yellow hue,
> Do paint the meadows with delight,
> The cuckoo then on every tree
> Mocks married men, for thus sings he,
> Cuckoo.
> Cuckoo, cuckoo, O word of fear,
> Unpleasing to a married ear.
> (L.L.L.v.ii.905–12)

Furthermore, if the poet knew Pliny, he might have noted that the cuckoo is called the cuckolder of the foster parent's nest: "*educat ergo subditum adulterato feta nido.*"[10]

In any case, the cuckoo's song is a song of mockery in "Sumer Is Icumen In." Not only must the summer end, just as the singers must tire of the round, but also the cuckoo is the last bird that one should invoke to correct this situation. Despite the title of the poem, we must not forget that this is a spring song. The cuckoo, traditionally, does dispel winter, but it does not sing in the summer! Pliny notes its disappearance after a brief visit at the beginning of the warm season: "*Ipse quoque modico tempore aestatis visus non cernitur postea.*"[11] Brunetto is even more emphatic about the cuckoo's not singing in the summer and gives an elaborate, if fanciful, explanation for its silence:

And you should know that the cuckoo does not sing in the summer when the cicadas, who detest it, begin their song. For when the cicadas hear the cuckoo sing, they go immediately to where it is, and climb upon its wings. The cuckoo cannot push them off its back, and they cause it so much pain, biting its flesh, that it cannot stay in one place, but goes flying from tree to tree, no longer pecks, and lets itself die.[12]

The speaker's fallacious dependence upon the song of the cuckoo to ward off the coming winter is similar to that of a sorceress in a medieval tale who depended upon the voice of the cuckoo to guarantee her life against a grievous illness. When the sorceress fell sick she refused any sacrament because she was certain that it was not yet time for her death:

[her friends] axkid hur how sho knew þat, and sho ansswerd agayn & said þat on þe furste day of Maij þe goke ansswerd hur & sayd V tymys, "cukkow!" And be þat sho sayd sho wiste wele liff V yere. And þus onone after in þis belefe, wiþ-owten any sacrament, sho dyed.13

The urgency of the round as invocation, then, pulls against the irony of addressing it to the cuckoo. The lyric intensity of the song is derived from the tension between the desire to perpetuate the spring it describes and the certainty that this wish cannot be fulfilled—the tension, in fact, of the human condition viewed from its purely secular aspect.

NOTES

[1] Carleton Brown, *English Lyrics of the XIIIth Century* (Oxford: Clarendon Press, 1932), 13.

[2] I. L. Gordon, *The Sea-Farer* (1960; rpt. New York: Appleton-Century-Crofts, 1966), 39.

"The groves begin to blow, cities grow fair, the fields are lovely, the world revives; all these urge the heart of the eager-minded man to a journey, him who determines to go far on the flood-ways. Likewise the cuckoo admonishes with a sad voice, the warden of summer sings, bodes bitter sorrow to the breasthoard." The sad voice of the cuckoo is also heard in the Anglo-Saxon "The Husband's Message."

[3] Pliny, *Natural History*, ed. H. Rackham (Cambridge, Mass.: Harvard Univ. Press, 1940), III, 308 (Bk. x, ch. xi).

[4] Brunetto Latini, *Il Tesoro*, ed. P. Chabaille, volgarizzato da Bono Giamboni (Bologna: Presso Gaetano Romagnoli, 1877), II, 202, my trans.

[5] Since the poem is from the West Midlands, the poet may have absorbed from neighboring Wales the association of the cuckoo with mortality. There, the cuckoo's cry is identified with the interrogative "cw?" (pronounced "coo"), the "where" (Lat. "quo") of the "ubi sunt?" theme; Ifor Williams, *Lectures on Early Welsh Poetry* (Dublin: Dublin Institute for Advanced Studies, 1944), 11.

[6] Brown, 14.

[7] Ronald B. McKerrow, ed., *The Works of Thomas Nashe* (1904; rpt. Oxford: Basil Blackwell, 1958), III, 238.

[8] Ibid., 240–41.

[9] Alcuin, "*Conflictus veris et hiemis*," in K. P. Harrington, ed., *Medieval Latin* (1925; rpt. Chicago: Univ. of Chicago Press, 1963), 130.

[10] Pliny, III, 308.

[11] Ibid.

[12] Brunetto, II, 202, my trans.

[13] Mary Macleod Banks, ed., *An Alphabet of Tales*, EETS, O.S., No. 126 (London: Kegan Paul, Trench, Trübner & Co., 1904), 487.

University of South Carolina

JOHN SCOTT COLLEY

JOHN SKELTON'S IRONIC *APOLOGIA*:
THE MEDIEVAL SCIENCES,
WOLSEY, AND THE *GARLANDE OF LAURELL*

John Skelton's *Garlande of Laurell*, an unparalleled 1600-line chronicle of ironic self-praise, has remained enigmatic despite frequent critical attention. In recent years two interesting points have been made about the poem. It is said that the *Garlande* demonstrates that Skelton was not seeking fame in terms of his role as a satirist but because of his purely poetic talent for pleasing ladies and gentlemen.[1] Moreover, the *Garlande* constitutes the poet's capitulation to his former satiric butt, Thomas Cardinal Wolsey,[2] but evidence in the poem suggests that Skelton was indeed serious in defending his satiric artistry and was not sincere in his flattery of the Cardinal at the end of the dream vision. Skelton's careful reference to certain "scientific" data (astrological signs as well as dream lore) signals his readers that the poem may have a hidden meaning. And his startling echoes of earlier anti-Wolsey satires warn that the poem is not simple gesture of reconciliation. Skelton does display an ability to write in the high style in the *Garlande*, and the poet does address a complimentary "envoy" to the Cardinal. But the degree to which Skelton carries his ironic quest for fame mitigates against the seriousness of his elaborate postures of poetic and political respectability. With energy and daring, Skelton reveals that he has no intention of rejecting his verse style or his obsession with satire.

In his dream vision the poet perceives a debate between the Queen of Fame and Dame Pallas about the merits of Skelton's literary reputation. The Queen notes that Skelton will not write sugared words in

19

praise of ladies and for that reason is no poet. Pallas argues in reply that Skelton is no mere flatterer and must write plainly and satirically: "who wryteth wysely hath a grete treasure."[3] Soon many of the great poets of antiquity, including Gower, Chaucer, and Lydgate, come out to greet Skelton and to support his bid for fame. Later, Skelton composes a series of love lyrics for the Countess of Surrey and her ladies and thereby earns a "garlande of laurel." Having proved that he can write in the accepted poetic manner, he returns to the court of Fame where an interminable catalogue of his works is read. As the crowd shouts in his favor, the poet awakens and offers envoys to the King and Cardinal. Skelton thus has demonstrated his claim to fame by writing in the aureate style, and perhaps has protected his future by bowing deeply and reverently before Wolsey. But the poet's exaggerated and hyperbolic use of accepted literary conventions tends to weaken the force of his conversion to the poetic high style.[4] And indeed, his love lyrics, while superficially quite lovely, are replete with images of incest, perversion, and sadism from mythology.[5] One wonders if such an ironic bid for poetic respectability could ever be considered a peace overture to Cardinal Wolsey.

A clue to the underlying mood of the *Garlande* may be found in the first stanza:

> Arectyng my syght towarde the zodyake,
> The signes xii for to beholde a farre,
> When Mars retrograndant reuersyd his bak,
> Lord of the yere in his orbicular,
> Put vp his sworde, for he cowde make no warre,
> And whan Lucina plenarly did shyne,
> Scorpione ascendyng degrees twyce nyne . . . .
> (1–7)

Consistently these lines have been read only as Skelton's attempt to "date" the poem.[6] Yet the poet has more in mind than establishing the time of composition. Skelton seems primarily concerned with a revelation of the "complexion" of the events related in the poem. From the start he wishes the reader to understand his poetic intentions in terms of some astrological clues. Astrologists would see significance in the peculiar conjunction of Mars and the Moon in the Ascending Scorpio:

If Mars is in an evil position [Scorpio] or if he is evilly affected by being retrograde or by being cadent from an angle it signifies that he is powerful in planning and producing that which is in accordance with his nature, namely, fears, terrors, anxieties, perturbations of mind, evil thinking, wicked deliberations, and that which follows the execution of such.[7]

Moreover, "if Luna is joined with Mars, you may expect false rumors, lying reports and the effusion of blood."[8] In a poem which discusses in part the insubstantial nature of fame and fortune, it is significant that Skelton provides astrological clues to the ambiguous and tentative nature of his dream vision:

> The location of Luna in all parts of Scorpio is the cause of much anxiety and sorrow, and because of such inadvertance she precipitates great evil upon herself. Great impediments and hindrances shall be set up for her because of wicked reports and rumors.[9]

With these signs present, one should expect to find anxieties, perturbations, lies, and false rumors in Skelton's poem. He may be suggesting that the poem has been written to quell false rumors, or more likely, he may be daring the reader to find more rumors and false reports within the body of the poem. Certainly the astrological information serves to prepare for the ironic undercutting that is present throughout the sixteen hundred lines of self-glorification.

Skelton does not stop with the complexion of the planets. He adds to the exposition more signs of ambiguity, mystery, and doubt:

> Whylis I strode musynge in this medytatyon,
>   In slumberynge I fell and halfe in a slepe;
> And whether it were of ymagynacyon,
>   Or of humours superflue, that often wyll crepe
>   Into the brayne by drynkyng ouer depe,
> Or it procedyd of fatall persuasyon,
> I cannot wele tell you what was the occacyon.
> (29–35)

Macrobius' *Commentary on the Dream of Scipio* (c. 410) supplies some suggestions that may clarify the "meaning" of Skelton's dream. There are five classes of dreams, writes Macrobius. Of these, three (*visio*, *oraculum*, and *somnium*) are valuable as sources of information and must be interpreted carefully, for they signify great truths for mankind. But there are two other types of dreams that are misleading and are not to be trusted. One (*phantasma*) is really a hallucination, and the other (*insomnium*) is equally untrustworthy. Macrobius' description of the *insomnium* is remarkably similar to Skelton's dream.

> [The *insomnium*] may be caused by mental or physical distress, or anxiety about the future: the patient experiences in dreams vexations similar to those that disturb him during the day. As examples of the mental variety, we might mention ... the man who fears the plots or might of an enemy and is confronted with him in his dream or seems to be fleeing from him. The physical variety might be illustrated by one who has indulged in eating or drinking.... Anxiety about the future would cause a man to dream that he is gaining a prominent position or office as he hoped or that he is being deprived of it as he feared.
>
> Since these dreams and others like them arise from some condition or circumstance that irritates a man during the day and consequently disturbs him when he falls asleep, they flee when he awakes and vanish into thin air.... [T]hey are noteworthy only during their course and afterwards have no importance or meaning.[10]

Later medieval experts also describe such dreams as Skelton relates. Petrus de Abano and Vincent de Beauvais argue that there are three types of dreams: *somnium coeleste,* caused by celestial beings and completely reliable; *somnium naturale,* caused by bodily humours and not to be trusted; and *somnium animale,* caused by anxieties or "perturbations" of the mind, and like the *naturale,* untrustworthy.[11]

Skelton's dream vision is either Macrobius' *insomnium,* or perhaps, in the medieval sense, a *naturale* or *animale.* At any rate, it is clearly a pipe-dream, stemming from hopes, fears, anxieties, or heavy drinking, and certainly not of the variety to be believed. It may be no accident that so many of the conditions that Skelton mentions are those enumerated by dream experts.

Skelton, indeed, goes to some lengths to characterize his dream as the misleading variety. He tells of his despair as he mused about "How all thynge passeth as doth the somer flower" (9).

> So depely drownyd I was in this dumpe,
> Encraumpyshed so sore was my conceyte,
> That, me to rest, I lent me to a stumpe . . . .
>
> Thus stode I in the frythy forest of Galtres,
> Ensowkid with sylt of the myry wose.
>   (15–17; 22–23)

Deeply troubled, sitting in the miry ooze of the forest, he falls into a light sleep. Macrobius warns that dreams that come in the moment between wakefulness and slumber are especially fantastic and misleading.[12] The poet has been worrying about the future, and he may have been drinking heavily. The picture of the possibly drunken Skelton, sitting deep in mire and dreaming of fame, certainly contributes to the developing mirth of the poem. No expert would have trouble classifying the dream as either *somnium naturale* or *animale,* or perhaps Macrobius' *insomnium:* it is clear that the dream has no significance except as an indication of the poet's state of mind. Skelton emphasizes that his vision is ambiguous, or even meaningless. With the position of the planets complicating the situation, Skelton's dream must be of a dubious and perhaps dangerously misleading nature. Not only false, terrifying, and ambiguous, Skelton's defense of his art is also presented as a fleeting and insubstantial fantasy. But the poet means the opposite of what he seems to be saying.

The poet has previously used astrological and dream lore to contribute to the ironic tone of a poem. In the prologue to *The Bowge of Courte* (1498), Skelton similarly presents the circumstances of the

blasts of gold and scuts (coins). In *Why come ye nat to courte?* the
French had shot at Wolsey's cap, the symbol of his position in the
church, and were able to influence him with the blasts of gold. In the
Garlande the blast is also aimed at the cap, and Skelton takes pains to
comment upon it. Indeed, Skelton seems to have had a preoccupation
with hats, particularly the Cardinal's hat, and often directs his satiric
attacks upon the symbol of office rather than the man. Throughout
Why come ye nat to courte? Skelton speaks of the Cardinal's cap, constantly juxtaposing images of Wolsey's baseness with the vision of his
red cap of ecclesiastical office (ll. 172, 235, 278, 380, 740, and 1105).
Predictably, he once calls the red cap a "cockes come" (1232). In
Colyn Cloute the poet also speaks of religious figures who share his
interest in hats:

> They gaspe and they gape
> All to haue promocyon,
> There is theyr hole deuocyon,
> With money, if it wyll hap,
> To catch the forked cap.
> (85–89)

In *Colyn Cloute* the "forked cap" is the miter, the coveted symbol of
authority in the church. Could the strange figure in the *Garlande*, with
his jagged cap, bring to mind one who wears a forked cap? A jagged
cap is not necessarily forked, but considering the parallel instances of
an unusual retreat before cannon fire in both the *Garlande* and *Why
come ye nat to courte?* it may be possible that Skelton is alluding to
Wolsey as he stands with Occupation looking over the battlements of
Fame's stronghold.

The most striking echo of anti-Wolsey satire is also found in the
Garlande passage in question. Skelton notes that the cannon fire directed against the unruly mob killed some and lamed others: "Sum
were made peuysshe, porisshly pynke iyd, / That euer more after it
they were aspyid" (626–27). In *Why come ye nat to courte?* Skelton
makes great fun of an eye infection that was causing Wolsey some
trouble. The poet mentions syphilis as the cause, but does hint that
the malady could be part of God's retribution:

> This Naman Sirus
> So fell and so irous,
> So full of malencoly,
> With a flap afore his eye,
> Men wene that he is pocky,
> Or els his surgions they lye,
> For, as far as they can spy

> By the craft of surgery,
> It is *manus Domini.*
> . . . .
> Balthasor, that helyp Domingos nose
> From the puskylde pocky pose,
> Now with his gummys of Araby
> Hath promised to hele our cardinals eye;
> Yet sum surgions put a dout,
> Lest he wyll put it clene out,
> And make him lame of his neder limmes:
> God send him sorrow for his sinnes!
>   (1163–71; 1191–98)

Wolsey's eye infection was evidently well known and was mentioned in several diplomatic dispatches during late 1522.[16] It is remarkable that Skelton would repeat the reference to Wolsey's pink eye in the *Garlande*, especially after stating that his satiric "ship" had been prepared for more "heavy weather" and that he was intending to protect himself against political censure. The reference to Wolsey's eye, indeed the combination of references to Wolsey, may not have been obvious enough to bring new difficulties to the poet. But after the *Garlande* was first published, Skelton saw fit to add the envoy to the Cardinal in order to becloud any satiric relevance of the poem. The conciliatory "Lautre Enuoy" did not appear until Marsh's edition of 1568, years after the initial publication of the poem. Skelton may have regretted the exuberance of the *Garlande*, and, heeding Occupation's warnings, added the final note of "respect" for Wolsey.

Occupation's reading of Skelton's "bibliography" at the end of the *Garlande* has long been recognized as another of Skelton's ironic gestures. The exaggerated length of his list of publications and the hyperbolic mode of Occupation's commentary are probably contrived to make a point. Several critics have felt that the emphasis placed upon some works, and not upon others, constitutes a further dig at the Cardinal.[17] By omitting the title of the recent *Why come ye nat to courte?*, the poet's most outspoken attack against the prelate, by calling *Speke Parrot* a poem in commendation of women, and by purposely misinterpreting *Colyn Cloute* as a "trifle," and a piece of "honest mirth," Occupation may in fact be drawing attention to these poems and their contents. Perhaps it is with a spirit of subterfuge that Skelton included the short echoes of earlier poems in the *Garlande* in order to launch one last satiric attack upon the Cardinal. It must have pleased the poet to have been welcomed to the palace of Fame by the great English poets and to have been "sponsered" by Dame Pallas. He must have especially enjoyed watching as "Wolsey" was driven off with the other scum that was clamoring for admission to the annals of Fame.

Dreams must end, and Skelton relates that the noise raised in his honor caused him to awaken:

> A thowsande thowsande, I trow, to my dome,
>   *Triumpha, triumpha!* they cryid all aboute;
> Of trumpettis and clariouns the noyse went to Rome;
>   The starry heuyn, me thought, shoke with the showte;
>   The grownde gronid and tremblid, the noyse was so stowte:
> The Queen of Fame commaundid shett fast the boke;
> And therwith sodenly out of my dreme I woke.
>
>   (1505–11)

With the culmination of his vision, and with the appended envoys, Skelton ends the *Garlande* on contrasting notes of bravado and "humility." In some Latin verses, the poet says he is Britain's Catullus, or Adonis, or Homer. His English poetry now runs an equal race with Latin verse, he claims, and is no longer to be considered uncouth (1522–32). And with the final bow, "Twene hope and drede" (1594), in the direction of Wolsey, the poem is resolved, remaining partially serious, partially mirthful, and completely ambiguous as to its exact satiric applicability.

If the echoes from *Why come ye nat to courte?* were intended to tease the reader of the *Garlande* into identifying Cardinal Wolsey, certainly Skelton's other references in the poem have the reverse effect. He makes a number of veiled comments about people he does not like, including more characters who clamor about the gateway to fame. But his satiric focus is so blurred that, rather than being enlightening, his attacks confuse and confound the reader. He speaks of one "blunderar" who "fyndith fals mesuris out of his fonde fiddill" (741), and includes an interpolated Latin satire that appears to be nothing more than a kind of Juvenalian double-talk (741–51). Indeed, he adds a numerological puzzle that, even when decoded, adds little clarification of his satiric intentions.[18] Many of the jumbled portraits and sly references have been nothing more than conscious attempts to render the poem meaningless as a consistent satire of recognizable persons. Once he has teased the reader into identifying a satiric butt, Skelton may have deliberately retreated into murkiness and incomprehension. Parts of the *Garlande* seem almost a parody of the circumspect, indirect method of *The Bowge of Courte*.

But even as the *Garlande* confounds, it astounds. Throughout the poem Skelton encourages the reader to seek rumors, dangerous reports, double meanings. The astrological and dream lore suggests that the dreamer has good reason to fear the evil plots of a powerful enemy, or that the dreamer's vision may portend "false rumors, lying reports,

and the effusion of blood." Or the "scientific" data may suggest only
that the dream is no more than a neurotic wish-fulfillment fantasy,
prompted by the poet's despair and drunkenness as he lay in the ooze
and slime of the forest of Galtress. But the poet's adoption of a conventional aureate style is certainly not ambiguous. The lyrics, the rime
royal, the conventional dream vision, are all exaggerated, twisted, and
turned against any detractors of the mighty Skeltonic.

Not so clear are Skelton's attitudes as he "forsakes" satire and
"makes peace" with his old political enemy. If the ironic tone of the
Garlande serves to bolster the poet's literary arguments, one wonders
what political value Skelton could see in his long *apologia.* It seems
clear that the poet was still musing over his recent difficulties with
Wolsey. *Why come ye nat to courte?* had been circulating hardly a
year before the *Garlande* appeared and Skelton was certainly aware
of the possible consequences of the Cardinal's anger. Indeed, the poet
may have found himself in deep trouble because of his last two or three
satiric poems. There is no definite evidence that Skelton suffered for
his satires against the Cardinal, but it is evident that after 1522 he
radically changed his approach to poetry: there is no unmistakable
criticism of Wolsey in Skelton's verse from the time of the *Garlande*
to the poet's death in 1528.

A clue to the poet's mood in the *Garlande* may be found in some
lines from *Why come ye nat to courte?*:

> Some men myght aske a question,
> By whose suggestyon
> I toke on hand this warke,
> Thus boldly for to barke?
> And men lyste to harke,
> And my words marke,
> I wyll answer lyke a clerke;
> For treuly and vnfayned,
> I am forcebly constrayned,
> At Iuuynals request,
> To write of this glorious gest,
> Of this vayne gloryous best,
> His fame to be encrest
> At euery solempne feest;
> *Quia difficules est*
> *Satiram non scribere.*
> (1199–1214)

Even in a "peace" gesture, Skelton was not able to restrain his satiric
imagination. In the *Garlande* the poet refuses to retract his poetic techniques, his preoccupation with satire, as well as the statements he had
made earlier about certain notable figures. He insists that his methods,

his subject matter, and his poetic "truths" are worth defending. But he realizes that words can cause trouble, and he carefully presents his defense of his art in a manner that will exempt him from more tempests, and more batterings. Early in the *Garlande*, Occupation says, "Beware for wrytyng remayneth of recorde" (89). The poet's written words live on and on, and he must use them with care. Yet Occupation adds that a poet must not "Displease . . . an hundreth for one mannes pleasure" (90). Skelton must exercise discretion, but he cannot be expected to deny his muse for "one mannes pleasure." Sometimes it must be the poet's "fortune to wryte true and plaine, / As . . . he must vyces remorde" (84–85). The trueness, and the plainness, represent Skelton's claim to fame. He must be careful, but he must honor his "Occupation," his peculiar role as a satirist.

Several points about the *Garlande* would become clearer if Skelton indeed had Wolsey in mind as he wrote of the strange mob below the walls of Fame's castle. Such references would explain why Skelton added the complimentary envoy to Wolsey after the poem was first published: the poet may have felt compelled to negate any possible jibes in order to stay out of trouble. Moreover, the presence of hidden mockery of the Cardinal would strengthen the poet's most important arguments of the *Garlande*: his satiric art is indeed defensible and he merits fame for speaking out truly and plainly in reproof of vice.

Hence the *Garlande* is not necessarily the capitulation that many have thought. Or if it is to be considered a "capitulation," it is a grudging one. Skelton refrained from writing in the style of *Why come ye nat to courte?*, but he did not refrain from writing "wysely" and satirically. He altered his approach, but not his conception of poetry.

Therefore one should reconsider the hypothesis that Skelton framed the *Garlande* to represent his rejection of any claim to poetic fame, or that he was seeking fame not in terms of his role as a satirist, but because of his purely poetic talent for pleasing ladies and gentlemen. It may be more likely that the poet claims fame because of his satiric talents, and because of his ability to ridicule the foibles of ladies, gentlemen, and cardinals.

NOTES

[1] A. R. Heiserman, *Skelton and Satire* (Chicago: Univ. of Chicago Press, 1961), 311. Stanley Eugene Fish, *John Skelton's Poetry* (New Haven: Yale Univ. Press, 1965), 234, feels that Skelton was in fact rejecting *any* claim to fame in the *Garlande*.

[2] The most recent statement of Skelton's "capitulation" is by Owen Gingerich and Melvin J. Tucker, "The Astronomical Dating of Skelton's *Garland of*

Laurel," *HLQ* 32 (1969), 207–20. Similar statements have been made by Leslie John Lloyd, *John Skelton: A Sketch of his Life and Writings* (Oxford: Blackwell, 1938), 123; and H. L. R. Edwards, *Skelton: The Life and Times of an Early Tudor Poet* (London: Cape, 1949), 228.

[3] All quotations from Skelton's poetry are from Rev. Alexander Dyce's edition, 2 vols. (London: T. Rodd, 1843; rpt. New York, 1965).

[4] For an intelligent and convincing analysis of Skelton's ironic manner, see Fish, 225–39.

[5] See Edwards, 234–36; and Fish, 238–40.

[6] Helen Sterns, "The Date of the *Garland of Laurel*," *MLN* 43 (1928), 313–16; William Nelson, *John Skelton Laureate* (New York: Columbia Univ. Press, 1939), 190–92; and Gingerich and Tucker, *passim*.

[7] Albohazen Haly, *Libri de ivdiciis astrorum* (Basle, 1551), cited by W. C. Curry, *Chaucer and the Medieval Sciences* (New York: Barnes & Noble, 1960), 180.

[8] Haly, cited by Curry, 181.

[9] Haly, cited by Curry, 179. Supporting Haly's warnings is Johannes Regiomontanus, *Ephemerides 1475–1506* (Venice, 1484), fol. 6^r (cited by Gingerich and Tucker, 216), who advises men to flee from quarrels and to avoid strong men and soldiers during the conjunction of Luna and Mars.

[10] Macrobius, *Commentary on the Dream of Scipio*, trans. William Harris Stahl (New York: Columbia Univ. Press, 1952), 88–89.

[11] Cited by Curry, 207–208.

[12] Macrobius, 88–89. John of Salisbury would add that a dream in a swampy place is especially productive of fantasies (*The Frivolities of Courtiers and Footprints of Philosophers*, trans. Joseph B. Pike [Minneapolis: Univ. of Minnesota Press, 1938], 78).

[13] Heiserman, 32–34. It was Heiserman's discussion of *The Bowge of Courte* that prompted my investigation of the *Garlande*.

[14] Skelton also appends a straightforward defense of satire at the end of *Why come ye nat to courte?* (1199–1248) and at the end of the *Replycacion agaynst certayne scholers* (300–408).

[15] For Skelton's problems with Wolsey, see Edwards, 221–25; Nelson, 185–211.

[16] Nelson, 162.

[17] Notably Fish, 237–38.

[18] See Edwards for the "solution," 236–38.

Vanderbilt University

JACK E. REESE

"POTIPHAR'S WIFE" AND OTHER FOLK TALES
IN CHAPMAN'S *BLIND BEGGAR OF ALEXANDRIA*

Devoting an entire essay to George Chapman's *The Blind Beggar of Alexandria* might be viewed as an almost perverse celebration of mediocrity. Chapman's comedies have long been overshadowed by his Homer, his non-dramatic poetry, and his tragedies; and *The Blind Beggar* is customarily regarded as the weakest of the comedies. Millar MacLure, for example, warns that the modern reader can only be "baffled and irritated" by the piece; the play's original popularity, he says, gives one "cause to reflect grimly . . . on the curious tastes of our ancestors—or, if he stops to think further, he may notice in these ridiculous antics a strong resemblance to the quality and in some cases the substances of the fare produced on commercial television."[1]
There is no denying, however, that the work was extraordinarily well received in its own day. Henslowe's *Diary* records that it was performed twenty-two times by the Lord Admiral's Men during the 1595–1596 season, and it continued to attract audiences after its revival in 1601. Only a few perennial favorites such as Marlowe's *Doctor Faustus* and Kyd's *Spanish Tragedy* were as insistently popular.[2] Such lasting appeal indicates that *The Blind Beggar* merits re-evaluation rather than condemnation as a glaring example of the puerility of Renaissance tastes. Moreover, the fact that the surviving text is obviously debased calls for a reassessment that attempts to deal with the probable shape of the original play. As Thomas Marc Parrott points out, the 1599 edition prepared by William Jones (the only source for modern editors) represents a severely truncated version of Chapman's original manuscript, "for the printed play contains only about 1,600 lines, and

33

the omissions are such as to render the serious part of the play almost unintelligible . . . . As a consequence, the play, as it now stands, totally lacks unity, coherence, and proportion."[3]

One approach to *The Blind Beggar*, yet untried, should lead to a more sympathetic understanding of its early appeal and some reasonable speculations on the shape of the original text, plus a clearer insight into Chapman's intent in the writing of the largely maligned comedy. This is an examination of the various folk tales and legends which are combined in the play. Such treatment is called for by the curiously "primitive" nature of the work,[4] with its romantic hero, transformations, wicked queen, prophecies, ancient Egyptian setting, magic, blind seer, picaresque roguery, and rough humor, all familiar elements in the great body of popular literature inherited by the English Renaissance.

Since *The Blind Beggar of Alexandria* is hardly one of the best-known Elizabethan comedies, a very brief summary of the plot is in order before a study of the various analogues and parallels. The noble Cleanthes has been banished from Egypt by King Ptolemy at the instigation of Queen Aegiale. One gathers that the Queen had fallen passionately in love with Cleanthes, who had rejected her advances, whereupon she had accused him falsely before the king and demanded his punishment. Rather than flee his native land, Cleanthes assumes a variety of disguises: Irus, the blind beggar; the usurer Leon; and Hermes, a mad count. His conduct during this period is that of a low-comedy rogue; he marries two sisters and then cuckolds himself by seducing each in the disguise of the "other" husband; he bilks a gullible citizen out of a sizeable sum of money through rapid-fire changes of costumes and identities; and he brings about the deaths of Prince Doricles and (apparently) Ptolemy and Aegiale. Eventually he throws off his disguises to defeat a series of invading armies and assumes the throne of his country.

Even this brief summary (which is actually much more coherent than the extant text) indicates some obvious links with folk tales and legends. For example, the relationship between Cleanthes and the wicked Queen Aegiale represents one version of the extremely popular story which has been given the title of "Potiphar's Wife." This familiar tale deals with a queen or wife of a nobleman who falls violently in love with a young man (sometimes her stepson) connected to her household. She tries to seduce him, but he virtuously rejects her, whereupon she complains to her husband that the young man has attempted to violate her honor. The helpless hero is then subjected to punishment—threatened death, banishment, or disgrace—but in the end his innocence is established and the treachery of the lady is dealt with severely, often by death.

Occurrences of this tale are extremely widespread, and it is of great antiquity. As John D. Yohannan has pointed out, "One would be hard put to find a story that has had a wider circulation among more varied audiences over a longer period of time."[5] The oldest recorded version is the Egyptian folktale of the brothers Anpu and Bata and the former's unnamed wife. In classical legend and literature, it is found in the tales of Theseus, Phaedra, and Hippolytus (put into dramatic form by Euripides and Seneca); Hyppolyte, Acastus, and Peleus; and Antea and Bellerophon. It became a popular tale in Moslem culture, appearing in such sources as the *Koran* and the verse novel, *Yusuf and Zulaikha*, by the fifteenth century Persian poet Jami. It formed the basis of several Buddhist homilies, such as "The Eyes of Kunala," dating from about the fifth century A.D. By medieval times the story had achieved very wide circulation; perhaps the most popular version—certainly the most frequently related during the Middle Ages, apart from the biblical account concerning Joseph—was included in the collection of tales called *The Book of Sindibad*, much of which was subsequently incorporated into *The Arabian Nights*.[6]

Some of the very early versions of the tale are characterized by the same primitive savagery which occasionally erupts in Chapman's *Blind Beggar*. In India, for example, where the tale was especially popular,[7] there was the story of a man named Kotač, whose daughter, Dony, is married to Kavdn. Of this couple come a son, Kamatn, and a daughter, Puy. When the son is seventeen and the daughter fourteen, their mother dies, and Kavdn takes a second wife, a sixteen-year-old girl named Menar. Kavdn has to leave town for three days. Menar becomes very desirous of her stepson, Kamatn, and attempts to seduce him. She "bit him on his cheeks and put her arms around his body," but he rebukes her: "Have you any sense at all, or have you not? What sense is there that a father's wife comes to her son and makes sport with him? Go away!" Menar subsequently complains to her husband that his son forced her to lie with him. She, her husband, and her two brothers murder the boy, and the remainder of the tale describes the revenge of Puy, his sister, who engineers the violent deaths of the four murderers.[8]

Another interesting early version occurs in "Katha Sarit Ságara." This is the story of Queen Asokavati, who becomes desperately enamored of Gunasarman, faithful minister of the king Mahasena. After Gunasarman's rejection of the queen and the false accusation which she brings against him, he escapes death in a manner vaguely reminiscent of Cleanthes' strategy in *The Blind Beggar*: "he wards off their sword cuts by his cunnings of fence, makes his way out of the palace by force, and putting on his eyes an ointment which renders him invisible, leaves the country . . . ."[9]

The best-known version of the tale and the one which gives the story its type name in Christian cultures occurs, of course, in the Old Testament. This is the story of Potiphar's wife and Joseph as told in Genesis 39.7–23. The scriptural treatment imparted to the tale an ethical bias which permanently influenced later versions. As John A. Yohannan has pointed out, the hero, in the Hebraistic tradition, came to represent the "Chosen Seed"; he was regarded as "destined by God to carry out a divine mission." His encounter with Potiphar's wife was "but one more obstacle on the road to ultimate fulfillment of the promise . . . . Joseph, of course, must resist her, be unjustly punished, later be vindicated, and finally become elevated to the high office for which he is marked . . . . About his status as the Fortunate Youth, there hangs the aura of a religious teleogy."[10]

This heightening of Joseph's character is evident in the versions of the tale of "Potiphar's Wife" which appeared in the prose fiction of medieval Europe. Summarized below are two treatments of the legend which were easily accessible to Chapman and which are notable for the dignity and nobility of the men who are maligned by treacherous females. The first occurs in the *Heptameron* of Margaret, Queen of Navarre. The Duchess of Burgundy is attracted to a young man who is a favorite of the Duke, and she reveals to him her love on several occasions. He rebuffs her advances with extraordinary decorum: "my Lord has brought me up from childhood, and made me what I am, and to save my life I could not entertain towards any wife, daughter, sister or mother of his any thought contrary to what is due from a loyal and faithful servant." The Duchess then complains to her husband that the young man has attempted to dishonor her and demands his punishment. The Duke is temporarily satisfied of his subject's innocence, but, under repeated haranguing from his wife, he makes the young man confess that, rather than being in love with the Duchess, he is engaged in a love affair with the Duke's widowed niece. (Under the rules of courtly love he is, of course, pledged to absolute secrecy.) The madly jealous Duchess wrests from her harassed husband the truth about the affair and arranges for the public humiliation of the young widow and her lover. The widow dies of a broken heart; her lover kills himself, and the enraged Duke stabs his wife.[11]

Boccaccio's version of the tale emphasizes strongly the heroic stature of the central figure. At the time the Roman empire was transferred from French to German control, the king of France and his son went to lead the French army. They leave the kingdom in the hands of the capable vicar general, Gautier, Count of Antwerp, a forty-year-old widower with two children. The wife of the king's son falls in love with him and suggests that he return her love, but Gautier,

who was a very loyal gentleman, began with the gravest reproofs to rebuke so fond a passion and to repel the princess, who would fain have cast herself on his neck, avouching to her with oaths that he had liefer be torn limb from limb than consent unto such an offence against his lord's honor, whether in himself or in another.

The lady is incensed and cries out for help, and the Count is forced to flee to England with his two children, knowing that his account of what actually happened would bear little weight with the king and the prince. The count and all his descendants are doomed to perpetual banishment, and his estate is destroyed. Then follows the placing of his two children with noble families in England and eighteen years of common labor in Ireland. Eventually the king of France dies; his son assumes the throne, and the young king's wife falls gravely ill and confesses, before her death, the injustice of her accusations against Gautier. By a series of circumstances, the Count is finally restored to his old dignity and wealth, and his children enjoy a sudden elevation to nobility.[12]

Clearly, the widespread popularity of the tale of "Potiphar's Wife" should be taken into account in any evaluation of *The Blind Beggar of Alexandria*. More will be said of this influence later. Of equal significance are a number of other folk legends and myths which would have been thoroughly familiar to Chapman's audiences and which show obvious similarities to events and characters in the play. For example, the various disguises and tricks of Cleanthes would have evoked strong associations with certain stock figures and situations from popular literature. The wily beggar, the rascal who lives by his wits, was a thoroughly familiar character; among the many examples which could be cited are the parasite in the New Comedy of Plautus and Terence; the wily servants in the later *commedia erudita* in Italy; and such English imitations as Diccon in *Gammer Gurton's Needle*, Pasiphilo in Gascoigne's *Supposes*, and Matthew Merrygreek in Nicholas Udall's *Ralph Roister Doister*. Of particular interest, insofar as Chapman's play is concerned, are those stories of a clever beggar who (like Cleanthes) assumes a variety of disguises in order to bilk his victims. One

such rogue is found in the very early *Handlyng Synne* by Robert of
Brunne. In a section celebrating the liberality and courtesy of St. John
the Almoner is found an account of a beggar who takes advantage of
the saint's charitable nature by rapid changes of costume:

> He com, and asked þe charyte,
> And seynt Ihon, þat was so fre,
> He commaundede hys seriaunte
> For to ȝyve hym syxe besaunte.
> Þys pylgrym ȝede and chaunged hys wede,
> More to aske, ȝyf he myȝt spede.
> And seyd he hadde goun many a gate,
> And to þe cyte he was com late,
> And of spensys had he non,
> So hadde he yn pylgrymage gon.
> Seynt Ihon commaundede hys aumenere
> To ȝyve hym ouþer syxe, for he had mystere.
> Þe aumener parceyved weyl þat tyme
> Þat hyt was þe same pylgryme
> Þat toke byfore þe charyte,
> And seyd, "syre, þys ys he."
> Noþeles, oþer wroth or glad,
> He ȝaf hym, þat seyn Ihon bad.
>
> Þys pylgrym eft besyde nam,
> And efte þe þryd tyme cam
>
> yn a-noþer wede þan he was ore,
> And asked at seynt Ihon ȝyt more.
> Þe aumenere was wroth þerfore,
> Þat he asked so oute of skore,
> Syn hym was ȝyve so largely,
> And ȝyt he asked, and was greedy.
> But Seynt Ihon, he was fre,
> And yn ful grete charyte
> He commaunded to hym a-none
> To ȝyve hym twelve besauntes echone . . . .[13]

The protean beggar became a popular rogue in several cultures. In
the picaresque literature of Spain, for example, there is the story of
"Juanito Malastrampos," whose chicanery includes a device found in
The Blind Beggar, pretended death. Juanito owes money to a good
many people, including a tailor who is threatening to take back a yet
unpaid-for suit. Juanito decides to play dead and is actually placed in
his coffin in church. Some thieves enter the church to rob it. Juanito
rises from his coffin; the horrified thieves flee, and he carries away the
loot they were after. He then defrauds another victim with a scheme
involving a "magic" rabbit. The victim and his fellow sufferers place
Juanito in a sack and start out to dump him in the ocean. They stop at
a tavern, leaving the sack outside, where Juanito convinces a passer-by

that he is on his way to marry the daughter of the king. The two men exchange places (and identities), and Juanito leaves with a herd of goats. Juanito shows up next day in his home town, apparently risen again from the dead, claiming that he obtained the goats from the ocean. When his victims demand proof, he parades the herd alongside the ocean, and the fools whom he has duped many times before see the reflection of the goats in the water and dive in.[14]

The quick changes of costumes and identities by Cleanthes are also related (though obviously not as closely) with a very large number of folk tales and myths dealing with rapid transformations of identity or metamorphoses involving a bewildering variety of shapes and substances. The theme is quite old. In classical legend, for example, there is the story of Herakles and Perikylmenos, one of the sons of Nereus, who tried to avoid capture by resorting to the powers of transformation which Poseidon had given him. He could change himself into a lion, snake, bee, or even gnat, but when he assumed the last form, Herakles' vision miraculously cleared so that he detected and caught him.[15]

Cleanthes' treatment of the two wives whom he marries under different disguises is related to a great variety of stories from popular literature dealing with seduction, polygamy, and other unorthodox sexual relationships. Thus, for example, his marriage to the two silly girls Elimine and Samathis in his respective disguises as Hermes and Leon is at least vaguely related to a large number of folk tales which describe the seduction of a woman by an adventurer disguised as either her husband or lover. The classic example is the seduction of Alcumena by Jupiter, disguised as her husband Amphitryon, and the consequent birth of Hercules, a story well known in the Renaissance by means of Plautus' *Amphitrou* and other sources.[16] Another typical version is found in the *Decameron*: Ricciardo Minutolo is violently attracted to Catella, wife of Filippelo Figninalfi, but she does not respond to his advances. Consequently, he pretends to be in love with someone else in order to obtain her confidence. He tells her that her husband is in love with Ricciardo's wife and has asked her to meet him at a certain bagnio in the city at noon. Catella agrees to the suggestion that she substitute herself for his loyal wife. The whole story is, of course, a fabrication, and Ricciardo greets Catella when she enters the darkened room. He enjoys her to the fullest before he reveals his identity and then blackmails her into silence by threatening to tell everyone that she agreed willingly to meet him. Eventually, she admits that she enjoyed the session, and the two continue to meet discreetly thereafter.[17]

Another group of folk tales which bear a strong resemblance to the story of Cleanthes' polygamous marriages and his subsequent double seduction of his two wives has to do with a husband who takes the place of his wife's paramour (in essence, a stunt which Cleanthes manages twice) or the wife who visits her husband's bed disguised as another woman. This "bed trick" was widely employed in sixteenth- and seventeenth-century drama,[18] as evidenced by Shakespeare's *Measure for Measure* and *All's Well That Ends Well*.[19] Further examples of the device are abundant;[20] of particular interest to a reading of Chapman's play are those tales in which the husband rather than the wife is disguised.[21]

Several other groups of stories (all showing characteristics of the *fabliau*) are more directly related to Cleanthes' sexual chicanery. These include several tales in which a husband engineers his own cuckoldry (again, a feat accomplished by Cleanthes). A good example is found in the *Heptameron*. In the country of Alletz a man named Bornet falls in love with his maid servant, who informs her mistress of his attempts to seduce her. The wife instructs her servant to agree to an assignation and then substitutes herself in the young woman's bed. After Bornet has satisfied himself fully, he sends in his close friend Sandras, who does not speak while he is cloistered with her. The wife, thinking that her husband has returned, takes it all very calmly, anticipating eagerly her later recriminations. Before he leaves, Sandras takes her ring from her finger. The next morning Bornet asks her where her ring is, and she triumphantly recounts the whole story. He has no choice but to remain silent and to plead with his friend Sandras to keep quiet about the affair. The story becomes common knowledge, however, and "men called him cuckold without imputing any shame to his wife."[22]

Another group of tales has to do with couples who become entangled in a state of mutual adultery, a situation which, in a sense, is also duplicated in *The Blind Beggar*. A typical treatment of this theme is included in Straparola's collection of tales. Messer Arthilao Sara goes out of town and asks his close friend Liberale Spinosa to look after his wife. Spinosa tells the gullible woman, who is three months pregnant, that she is carrying an incompletely formed child. He gallantly offers to "complete" it. This he does, many times. When Sara returns, his wife tells him of the assistance provided by his friend. Sara then invites Spinosa and his wife to dinner, drugs her, and steals her necklace and rings. When she wakes, he tells her that he can recover the lost articles by "fishing" for them, a plan which she readily accepts. She tells her husband of Sara's magical powers, and the two men are thereafter forced to live in a state of mutual adultery.[23]

Finally, of especial significance to a reading of Chapman's comedy are a number of tales dealing with polygamy and polyandry. In some cultures, of course, polygamous or polyandrous marriages were not uncommon and, in many cases, were acceptable rather than clandestine, as in *The Blind Beggar*.[24] Instances in folk literature of bigamous marriages arranged furtively are rarer, although they do occur. Below are two good examples, both from the Middle East. The first is an Arabian tale dealing with a woman who has two husbands, a juggler who is at home only at night and a robber who spends only days with her. The story is summarized by Victor Chauvin as follows:

Une dame du Caire a deux maris: l'un, escamoteur, n'est à la maison que la nuit; l'autre, voleur, le jour seulement; aussi ne se connaissent-ils pas. L'un et l'autre se décidant une fois à voyager, demandent des provisions à la femme; elle donne à chacun successivement un demi-gigot.

Le hasard les réunit dans un caravansérail et le gigot fair naitre en eux des soupçons qu'ils convertissent bientôt en certitude. Retournant ensemble, ils obtiennent des aveux et conviennent que celui-là seul restera marié avec elle qui aura fait le meilleur tour.

L'escamoteur enleve à un juif une bourse de cent sequins et la lui glisse de nouveau après en avoir enleve dix pièces et y avoir mis son cachet. Il le mène ensuite au cadi, qui, convaincu par l'exacte description de la bourse, la lui adjuge.

A son tour, le voleur s'introduit avec l'escamoteur dans le palais. Il trouve un page, qui, tout assoupi, chatouille la plante des pieds du roi. Il l'endort avec un flacon de narcotique, le suspend au plafond et prend sa place auprès du roi. Il lui raconte deux histoires, notamment la sienne, et lui demande lequel, de l'escamoteur ou de voleur, est le plus audacieux. Le roi se pronounce en faveur du voleur.

Il l'endort alors a son tour et s'échappe avec son compagnon. Le lendemain, le roi, voyant son page suspendu, comprend que c'est de lui qu'on a parlé. Il le nomme lieutenant de police; quant a l'escamoteur, il s'avoue vaincu.[25]

The second tale, recorded by Hans Stumme, is somewhat more pertinent to Chapman's *Blind Beggar* in that it features a husband who is married to a "day wife" and a "night wife." Two brothers, one of whom has a daughter and the other a son, sign a pact that their children will eventually marry. The brothers and their wives die while the children are still quite young, and the two are raised under the belief that they are brother and sister. One day, however, the young man finds the marriage pact and joyfully announces to his supposed sister that they are really cousins and can thus marry, which they do immediately. Sometime later, the wife tells her husband about seeing a remarkably beautiful girl, daughter of the fisherman Achmed. Intrigued, the husband seeks out Achmed and asks for his daughter's hand in marriage, stipulating, however, some unusual conditions:

Herr Achmend, ich bitte dich, mir deine Tochter zur Frau zu geben. Aber eine Bedingung ist dabei: ich brauche sie nicht in der Nacht zu besuchen, sondern bloss am Tage! Und sie muss bei dir im Hause wohnen bleiben können.

The father agrees, and the young man begins his double life, spending his days with the fisherman's daughter and his nights with his first wife. Eventually the latter becomes suspicious and trails him to his other "home," disguising herself as a poor working girl in order to be taken in as maid. Soon she works out her revenge. She tells her not overly bright mistress that she will take her to the baths, but leads her instead to her own house and pours boiling water over her, causing painful burns and the loss of her hair. The fisherman's daughter makes her way home and hides her injuries from her husband. That night the first wife mentions that Achmed's daughter has been engaged in illicit relationships with a Jew and has had her hair cut off as punishment. The husband divorces his recent bride and presumably enjoys thereafter a happy and monogamous life with his first wife.[26]

The previous discussion has, I believe, established clearly the many affinities between Chapman's *Blind Beggar of Alexandria* and widely popular folk literature. I have not intended to suggest that any of the tales cited above were immediate sources for the play, nor, indeed, that all of them were well known in sixteenth-century England. I suspect that they were available in one form or another, and I would further guess that Chapman relied primarily on two sources which combined these various themes, a romance representing one version of the tale of "Potiphar's Wife" and a *fabliau* or related story concerning a beggar who pretends to blindness and assumes a variety of disguises in order to dupe his victims.[27] This is only speculation, however, and not really germane to the primary aim of this essay, which is to offer some solutions to certain critical problems attached to the play.

For example, a study of the folk legends and myths embodied in the work may reveal a good deal about the shape of the comedy as Chapman conceived it. The extraordinary popularity of the tale of "Potiphar's Wife" and the strangely fragmentary account of the relationship between Cleanthes and Aegiale strongly suggest that the original play featured prominently the story of the wicked queen who falls violently in love with one of her husband's great warriors, is rejected by him, engineers his banishment, and is eventually punished. Parrott's hypothesis concerning the nature of Chapman's text is thus substantially strengthened:

It is plain . . . that it was the farcical scenes, in which the beggar displayed "his variable humours in disguised shapes," and not the romantic story of Aegiale and

Cleanthes, which caught the fancy of the public. It is not unlikely that the former scenes have been enlarged beyond their original form; it is certain that the latter have been cut down.[28]

A recognition of the close relationship between the play and a number of folk tales and legends also helps to explain its contemporary success, a phenomenon which has been difficult for modern readers to understand. As suggested above, the original version was likely more palatable fare than the surviving text, but, whatever the play's artistic merits, it must have appealed hugely to audiences nurtured on the romances, *fabliaux*, and other well-known tales like those combined in it. *The Blind Beggar of Alexandria* has roots which go deep into the tradition of folk literature inherited by the English Renaissance, and, as its frequent performances indicate, its characters and situations were apparently familiar to and popular with sixteenth- and seventeenth-century audiences.

The present study may also be useful in assessing the intent of the play. This and other comedies by Chapman (particularly *The Widow's Tears*) have occasioned a large measure of critical puzzlement since they seem violently antagonistic to the traditional image of the dramatist as a sober didactician. Samuel Schoenbaum has noted that the concept of Chapman as a "grave moralist" has lingered since Anthony Wood's characterization of him as a "person of most reverend aspect, religious and temperate, qualities rarely meeting in a poet."[29] This by-now stereotyped picture of Chapman as a somber philosopher-poet does not fairly reflect his comedies, which reveal, more clearly than the rest of his writings, that he was not necessarily a didactic moralist or systematic philosopher. Mr. Schoenbaum argues, "As an artist Chapman is . . . more complex than his admirers have generally been prepared to concede."[30] For example, many readings of *The Widow's Tears* evade or soften the "pervasive cynicism" of the piece. The central character, Tharsalio, who has frequently been viewed as a cautionary example of depravity, in reality

towers above the hypocrites, fools, sentimentalists, and self-deluders who comprise the remainder of the dramatis personae. There is no force to counter him; in being corrupted, Tharsalio has achieved a species of wisdom. He is the dramatist's spokesman, and his vision, terrible as it may appear, is also Chapman's vision.[31]

In my opinion, the atmosphere of *The Blind Beggar of Alexandria* in many ways anticipates the "pervasive cynicism" of *The Widow's Tears*, and Cleanthes is an early prototype of Tharsalio. If one accepts the play (as I do) as something other than "entertainment,"[32] he recognizes, despite the butchered text and frequently wretched language and plotting, the same sardonic acknowledgment and celebration of man's susceptibility to lust, greed, cruelty, and other manifestations of human depravity. Like Tharsalio, Cleanthes scornfully manipulates a parade of deeply flawed characters: in *The Blind Beggar*, the silly and hypocritical girls Elimine, Samathis, and Martia, the lust-blinded Queen Aegiale, the ineffectual King Ptolemy, Bragadino, the *miles gloriosus*, the gullible merchant Antisthenes, and a series of other minor characters. Cleanthes himself is an appropriate ruler and symbol of this seamy universe. Apparently exempt from conventional morality, he deliberately flouts those conventional human relationships which hold civilization together—the marriage bond, the rules of commerce, the law, due respect for royalty, even recognition of the sanctity of life itself. In other words, Cleanthes is more than a grotesque impersonation of Tamburlaine or a low-comedy con man; he and the play are deserving of more serious consideration than they have received.

That consideration is encouraged by a recognition of the folk traditions embodied in the work, for the attitudes found in these folk motifs and themes (whatever Chapman's immediate source or sources) provide one index of the attitudes in the play. It would be misleading to claim that they are the only criteria of judgment, but it would be equally erroneous to dismiss the force of tradition in evaluating the work.

Thus, in assessing the central figure of Cleanthes, one should take into account his associations with certain stock characters in folk literature. For example, in all earlier versions of the tale of "Potiphar's Wife," the maligned young man is the object of admiration and sympathy. He exhibits strength of character, loyalty, ingenuity (in re-establishing his reputation), and great courage. The influence of this tale on *The Blind Beggar* should be allowed, and Cleanthes should be granted some of the qualities traditionally attached to the hero of the popular legend. This is not to say that he is more "moral" than he seems—that, in the original text, he displayed the humility and purity of a Joseph—but recognition of the bonds between him and the hero of the tale of "Potiphar's Wife" makes it clear that Chapman did not visualize him as a mere caricature.

Cleanthes also derives some measure of stature and respect from his associations with the other folk tales discussed above. Such popular rogues as the protean beggar and the ingenious seducer or bigamist were inevitably admired for their resourcefulness in evading conventional codes of conduct, and Cleanthes probably evoked much the same reaction from sixteenth- and seventeenth-century audiences, largely because of his kinship to stock characterizations with which they were thoroughly familiar.

Thus, however distasteful and eccentric his behavior, Cleanthes is hero rather than clown; he is endowed with sufficient dignity and strength to function as the author's "dramatic spokesman," to borrow Schoenbaum's phrase. The apparent burden of *The Blind Beggar of Alexandria* is much like that in *The Widow's Tears*: human beings are dangerously susceptible to the most ignoble and degrading motives, and the "strong men" of society often gain power, not because of their superior virtue, but because of their superior vision. As a study of the folk tales and motifs embedded in the play helps to point out, *The Blind Beggar of Alexandria* offers a view of Chapman which has been obscured by a simplistic codification of the moral platitudes found elsewhere in his work.

NOTES

[1] *George Chapman: A Critical Study* (Toronto: Univ. of Toronto Press, 1966), 84.

[2] Charlotte Spivack, *George Chapman*, Twayne's English Authors Series, No. 60 (New York: Twayne, 1967), 60.

[2] *The Plays of George Chapman. The Comedies* (New York: Dutton, 1914), I, 673–74. Subsequent citations in the text are from this edition.

[4] Spivack, 60.

[5] *Joseph and Potiphar's Wife in World Literature* (New York: New Directions, 1968), 1.

[6] This summary is based primarily on W. A. Clouston, *Popular Tales and Fictions: Their Migrations and Transformations* (Edinburgh and London: Blackwood and Sons, 1887), I, 9–10 and II, 449–502; Yohannan, *passim*; and the *Dictionary of Folklore, Mythology and Legend*, ed. Maria Leach (New York: Funk and Wagnalls, 1949), I, 497. A closely related and equally widespread tale is "The Precepts and Uriah Letter," described in Antti Aarne, *The Types of the Folktale*, 2nd rev. ed., trans. and enl. by Stith Thompson, Folklore Fellows Communications, 74, No. 184 (Helsinki: Suomalainen Tiedekatemis, 1961), 315 (Type 910K). The hero in this story accidentally observes the queen engaged in an intrigue and is slandered by her, even though he does not reveal her treachery. He is eventually exonerated. An excellent example of this tale is summarized by Clouston (II, 448–50) from the Arabian romance of the "Seven Vazirs."

[7] R. C. Temple says in "The Folklore in the Legends of the Panjab," *Folk-Lore* 10 (1898), 391: "Versions of Potiphar's wife are common in Indian and all Oriental folklore."

[8] Murray B. Emeneau, *Kota Texts*, Univ. of California Publs. in Linguistics (Berkeley: Univ. of California Press, 1944–46), III, 171–79. See also "The Prince and the Spirit Horse" in Lucas King, "Folktales from the Panjab. IV," *Folk-Lore* 35 (1924), 87–91, and the references in Stith Thompson and Jonas Balys, *The Oral Tales of India*, Indiana Univ. Folklore Series, No. 10 (Bloomington: Indiana Univ. Press, 1958), K2III.

[9] Clouston, II, 500–502.

[10] Yohannan, 14. In the Moslem tradition, says Yohannan (158–59), "Yusuf

became the very symbol of the great monotheistic idea of Abraham, who is, of course, the fountainhead of Islam as of Judaism and Christianity. Yusuf was, besides, a type of ideal beauty, the Adonis of his world, as the Moslem poets never tire of reiterating."

11 *The Heptameron of the Tales of Margaret, Queen of Navarre*, trans. George Saintsbury (London: Society of English Bibliophilists, 1894), v, 175–213 (tale 70). Saintsbury points out (v, 175) that the story was likely borrowed from an old *fabliau* known as *châtelaine de Vergy*.

12 Giovanni Boccaccio, *The Decameron*, trans. John Payne (1925; rpt. New York: Liveright, 1943), 131–40 (eighth story, second day). The tale is found frequently in Italian literature; Dominic Peter Rotunda, in his *Motif-Index of the Italian Novella in Prose*, Indiana Univ. Folklore Series, No. 2 (Bloomington: Indiana Univ. Press, 1942), lists in K2111 analogues by Heliodorus, Bandello, Orologi, and Sansovino. Cf. K2111.1: "*Woman makes vain overtures to stepson and falsely accuses him of murder*. She tries to poison him but her own son accidentally takes the beverage and apparently dies. Plot is revealed when doctor states that he had substituted sleeping potion for the poison." This closely related tale is found in Ariosto's *Orlando Furioso*, Ser Fiorentino Giovanni's *Il Percorone*, and Francesco Sansovino's *Cento Novelle Scelte da più Nobili Scrittori della Lingue Volgare*.

13 Frederick J. Furnivall, ed., *Robert of Brunne's "Handlyng Synne,"* EETS (London: K. Paul, Trench, and Trübner, 1901), ll. 6849–78. Brunne's work was largely a translation of the Anglo-French treatise, *Manuel des Pechiez*, by William of Wadington.

14 Aurelio M. Espinosa, *Cuentos Populares Espanoles* 174 (Madrid: Consejo Superior de Investigaciones Cientificas Institutio Antonio de Nebrija, 1947), 443–46. See also "The Old Beggar and the Robbers" (Aarne–Thompson, 436, Type 1526), in which a beggar dresses up in fine clothes in order to obtain credit. For other examples of the protean beggar, see Stith Thompson, *Motif-Index of Folk Literature*, rev. and enl. ed. (Bloomington: Indiana Univ. Press, 1955), IV, K237 ("Trickster disguises himself and escapes notice of his creditors"); IV, K1834 ("Multiple disguise: one person disguising successively seems to be many"); IV, K1982 ("Ubiquitous beggar. In disguise obtains alms three times from the same person"); II, D611 ("Protean beggar"). See also Thompson-Balys, D612 and K1834.

15 Louis H. Gray, ed., *The Mythology of All Races* (Boston: Marshall Jones, 1916–32), I (William Sherwood, *Greek and Roman*, 1916), 92. See also the accounts of the magical powers of transformation possessed by Nereus (I, 87) and Thetis (I, 122); and "The Magician and the Pupil," Aarne-Thompson, 113 (Type 325).

16 These are summarized by Örjan Lindberger, *The Transformations of Amphitryon*, Stockholm Series in History of Literature, No. 1 (Stockholm: Almqvist and Wiksell, 1956).

17 *The Decameron*, 197–203, (sixth story, third day). See also the *Heptameron*, II, 141–52 (second day, fourteenth tale); *Decameron*, 79–86 (second day, third story). Seduction of a woman by a man who approaches her in the identity of her husband is a common theme in ancient Irish and Celtic legend. See, for example, "The Cycle of Mongan Son of Fiachna and Brandub Son of Eochu" (A.D. 624) in Myles Dillon, *The Cycle of the Kings* (London and New York: Oxford Univ. Press, 1946), 50; Louis H. Gray, ed., *The Mythology of All Races* (Boston: Marshall Jones, 1916–32), III (John Arnott MacCulloch, *Celtic*, 1918), 51, 56, 184; Tom Peete Cross, *Motif-Index of Early Irish Literature*, Indiana Univ. Folklore Series, No. 7 (Bloomington: Indiana Univ. Press, 1952), D658.2. See also Rotunda, K1310, K1311.0.1, K1311.1, K1317.7, K1569.7; Thompson-Balys, K1311; Thompson, IV, K1311.1; Inger M. Boberg, *Motif Index of Early*

Icelandic Literature, Bibliotheca Arnamagnaeana, No. 27 (Copenhagen: Munks-gaard, 1966), K1311, K1315, and D658.2.

[18] See William R. Bowden, "The Bed Trick, 1603–1642: Its Mechanics, Ethics, and Effects," *Shakespeare Studies* 5(1969), 112–23.

[19] An excellent discussion of the widespread popularity of the "bed trick" is provided in the study of *All's Well That Ends Well* by William W. Lawrence, *Shakespeare's Problem Comedies,* 2nd ed. (New York: F. Ungar, 1960), 32–47. Lawrence examines analogues in the folk literature of India, Turkey, Norway, Iceland, and France, and in the later treatments of Paynter and Boccaccio. Omitted from Lawrence's survey is a very old tale from India summarized by G. A. Grierson, *Linguistic Survey of India* (1908; rpt. Delhi: Motilal Banarsidass, 1967), IX (1), 707–708.

[20] See also *The Facetious Nights of Straparola,* trans. W. G. Waters (London: Lawrence and Bullen, 1894), III, 5–28 (seventh night, first fable); Rotunda, K1814 ("Woman in disguise wooed by her faithless husband": Bandello, Corna-zano, Degli Arienti); K1834.2 ("Wife takes mistress's [servant's] place in her husband's bed": Bandello, Poggi, Malespini, *Cent Nouvelles Nouvelles*); Thompson–Balys, K1814 ("Woman in disguise wooed by her faithless husband").

[21] Rotunda, K1569.7 ("Husband takes place of paramour": Bandello, Giraldi, Malespini); Thompson, IV, K1813 ("Disguised husband visits his wife"); Thomp-son–Balys, K1813.

[22] *Heptameron,* II, 1–8 (first day, eighth tale). Cf. Rotunda, K1844.1.1 ("Hus-band has servant substitute in bed. Instructed not to deceive him while he is calling on mistress. Instructions are not followed."); K1843.2.2 ("Wife takes mistress's place in husband's bed: but is deceived in turn. Husband has tired of the mistress and had previously substituted servant.")

[23] Straparola, III, 283–314 (sixth night, first tale). Cf. *Heptameron,* I, 65–78 (first day, third tale).

[24] See Mary Frere, *Hindoo Fairy Legends: Old Deccan Days,* 3rd ed. (New York: Dover, 1967), 60–70 ("Little Surya Bai"); Leslie Milne, *Shans at Home* (London: John Murray, 1910), 230–37 ("The Story of Twelve Sisters"); Thompson-Balys, T145, T145.1.2, T145.1.3; Boberg, T145 and T146; and Cross, T145.

[25] *Bibliographie des Ouvrages Arabes ou Relatifs aux Arabes Publiés dans l'Europe Chrétienne de 1810 à 1885* (Liége: H. Vaillant-Carmanne, 1892–1922), V, 254.

[26] Hans Stumme, *Marchen und Gedichte aus der Stadt Tripolis in Nordafrika* (Leipzig: J. C. Hinrichs, 1898), 149–63.

[27] Parrott suggests (*Comedies,* I, 674) that the main source was an (unidenti-fied) late Greek romance. Emil Koeppel, *Quellen Studien zu den Dramen George Chapman's, Philip Massinger's, and John Ford's,* Quellen und Forschungen zur Sprachund Kulturgeschichte der germanischen Völker, No. 82 (Strassburg: K. J. Trübner, 1897), 2, argues that some elements of the plot, such as the multiple disguises of the hero, were Chapman's own inventions. I believe that the present study contradicts both conclusions.

[28] *Comedies,* I, 674.

[29] "*The Widow's Tears* and the Other Chapman," *Huntington Library Quar-terly* 23 (Aug. 1970), 321. The quotation from Wood occurs in *Athenae Oxon-iensis,* ed. Philip Bliss (London: F. C. and J. Rivington, 1815), II, 576.

[30] Schoenbaum, 337.

[31] Schoenbaum, 334.

[32] Criticism of the play has, I believe, distorted Chapman's original intent, however useful some of it may have been in defining limited aspects of the work. Several critics, for example, have suggested that the play is a parody of Marlowe's "superman drama"; they include Ennis Rees, "Chapman's *Blind Beggar* and the

Marlovian Hero," *JEGP* 57 (1958), 60–63; Jean Jacquot, *George Chapman, sa vie, sa póesie, son theâtre, sa pensée*, Annales de l'Université de Lyon, Troisième Série, Lettres, Fascicule 19 (Paris: Société d'Édition les Belles Lettres, 1951), 81; MacLure, 85; Spivack, 62–63. There are several Marlovian echoes in the play, but they are of neither such frequency nor significance to warrant the conclusion that it is simply a spoof of *Tamburlaine*. Paul Kreider, in his *Elizabethan Comic Character Conventions as Revealed in the Comedies of George Chapman*, Univ. of Michigan Publs. in Lang. and Lit., No. 17 (Ann Arbor: Univ. of Michigan Press, 1935), 71 ff., examines the influence of conventional comic characterization on the work, but a cataloguing of dramatic "types" tells one very little about the nature of the play. Helen A. Kaufman, "*The Blind Beggar of Alexandria*: A Reappraisal," *PQ* 28(1959), 101–106, accounts for the confused nature of the play by suggesting that it is a specimen of *commedia dell'arte*, a hypothesis which fails to take sufficiently into account what appears to have been wretched treatment of the original text.

The University of Tennessee, Knoxville

RENÉ E. FORTIN

HAMLET AND THE MYTHIC HYPOTHESIS

The various archetypal approaches to *Hamlet*, which see Hamlet's mission as essentially a ritual purgation of his society, are generally satisfying in that they at least suggest reasons for the play's incomparable power. But they are nonetheless disappointing in that they fail to account adequately for the surface features of the play. The problem lies, I think, in our premature identification of Hamlet as a full-fledged mythic hero while ignoring the ironies that surround the several mythic actions he attempts.[1]

The key to Shakespeare's ironic strategy in this play is suggested by Robertson's familiar description of Hamlet as a "supersubtle Elizabethan" stranded in a primitive, barbaric setting.[2] Although Robertson attributed the dual time-frame of *Hamlet* to Shakespeare's difficulties with his intractable source materials, more recent studies consider the anachronisms as deliberate strategies rather than an accident of composition. Peter Alexander, for example, sees as a central feature of the play the confrontation of two ages, each with its distinct claim upon the hero: "Wittenberg, the University, is face to face with the heroic past."[3] Similarly, Willard Farnham has argued that Hamlet stands "between whole worlds of truths in our culture: between the world of an uncivilized heroic past going back even behind Christianity and that of a civilized present; between the world of medieval faith and otherworldliness and that of modern doubt and this-worldliness."[4]

It might be said, therefore, that Hamlet's mighty opposites are time and history, that Hamlet's problem is that he is asked to take on a mythic task—to renew the kingdom—in an anti-heroic age that is unresponsive to myth. His frustrated quest for heroic identity, I shall try

49

to demonstrate, is reflected in the structure of the play, which consists of several mythic patterns which are projected and then ironically distorted as Hamlet fails to give life to his mythic roles.

Modern mythic studies of Hamlet begin with Gilbert Murray's analysis of the affinities between Orestes and Hamlet. Above and beyond their general situations, the revenge mission imposed upon them, Murray points out such other parallels as the hostile or latently hostile mother-relationships, the madness which afflicts both heroes, the misogyny which obsesses them, and finally their tendency to assume the role of fool.[5] The parallels were, for Murray, too striking to be dismissed as sheer coincidence; he concluded rather that they pointed to some universal psychic intuition:

> we finally run the Hamlet-saga to earth in the same ground as the Orestes-saga: in that prehistoric and world-wide ritual battle of Summer and Winter, of Life and Death, which has played so vast a part in the mental development of the human race .... Hamlet also, like Orestes, has the notes of the Winter about him. Though he is on the side of right against wrong he is no joyous and triumphant slayer. He is clad in black, he rages alone, he is the bitter Fool who must slay the King.[6]

The shared venture of Hamlet and Orestes is therefore the re-enactment of a vegetation ritual, depicting the killing of the Summer King by the Winter King in order to bring about the restoration of Nature's vitality or, alternately, the killing of the Year King by a wintry slayer who "weds the queen, grows proud and royal, and then is slain by the Avenger of his predecessor."[7]

The Hamlet-Orestes parallels are susceptible to other interpretations, such as the existential one proposed by Jan Kott. Kott sees the tragic myths as dramatizations of the human condition, enforcing a decision between two orders,

> the order of action, whose measure is efficacy, and the order of value, in which all gestures count and in which a gesture dearly bought by death gives meaning to fleeting human existence. The dramatic world of Hamlet-Orestes contains all human situations in which choice is enforced by the past, but has to be made on one's own responsibility and on one's own account.[8]

Hamlet and Orestes, then, share in the existential agony of moral decision in the face of necessity (or, in Kott's term, "prediction"), but Hamlet responds to this situation in a way that is in keeping with his Elizabethan situation. The quality of his response, as we shall see, is markedly different from that of Orestes.

Hamlet's affinities with Oedipus, his other heroic prototype, have been more extensively studied. Freud and Jones are, of course, foremost among the critics who have traced Hamlet back to Oedipus, both finding the Hamlet story to be a version of a fundamental sexual myth.[9] According to this view Hamlet is a victim of sexual repression, paralyzed by his suppressed guilt over an infantile incest-wish. His inability to kill Claudius results specifically from his feelings of complicity, from his unconscious identification with the person who has consummated his most secret wishes, to kill his father and wed his mother. Among more recent critics, Fergusson grants at least a partial validity to the Freudian reading but concludes that the sexual myth is too restrictive. Instead he locates the center of the Oedipus-Hamlet stories in the scapegoat roles to which both heroes are driven:

The themes of *Oedipus* are, from many points of view, strikingly similar to those of *Hamlet*. . . . it is clear that in both plays a royal sufferer is associated with pollution, in its very sources, of an entire social order. Both plays open with an invocation of the well-being of an endangered body politic. In both, the destiny of the individual and of society are closely intertwined; and in both the suffering of the royal victim seems to be necessary before purgation and renewal can be achieved.[10]

Thus Oedipus begins as hero, as priest-king of his society, but because of his uncovered guilt and consequent suffering, he becomes a "scapegoat, a witness and a sufferer for the hidden truth of the human condition."[11] And Hamlet, in Fergusson's reading, follows the same general pattern, though admittedly more obscurely, and achieves some sort of purgation for himself and Denmark by his tragic ordeal.[12] Certainly the parallels are suggestive; moreover, their shared obsession for the knowledge that plunges them into tragic experience warrants our giving serious thought to the ties between Oedipus and Hamlet.

But Hamlet's mythic credentials do not establish him exclusively as a hero. Lord Raglan has pointed out as a recurrent pattern in literature and myth the strange symbiosis between hero and fool, an observation that seems especially pertinent to *Hamlet*.[13] Murray, without pursuing the point, noted vestiges in Hamlet of the Amloði figure of the sources and expressed wonder that Shakespeare had created "his greatest hero out of a Fool transfigured."[14] Later critics have developed this hint; Fergusson finds the Fool figure prominent in the improvisational activities of Hamlet, who is at times clown-and-ritual-head of state, gag-man and royal victim, and finally a Fool figure with unmistakable religious overtones.[15] Levin, while also sensitive to the archetypal implications of the Fool, sees Hamlet especially as a distant echo of the classical *eiron*, "the Socratic ironist whose ignorance concealed a deeper wisdom"; more immediately, he conjectures that Shakespeare was dramatizing in the Hamlet-Fool the humanistic critique of the intellect "in the grand Erasmian manner."[16] Both agree, in any case, that there is within Hamlet a peculiar coalescence of two antithetical mythic figures, the Hero and the Fool.

The archetypal accretions of the Fool figure considerably enrich the significance of Hamlet's tragedy, for the fool in antiquity was widely recognized as a central figure in ritual; the fool, after reigning for a time as mock-king, served as the scapegoat to be killed as a surrogate of the king.[17] Chambers emphasizes the importance of the fool's madness in the scapegoat ritual; though originally the fool's primary qualification for the role seems to have been his dispensability, "the common belief in madness or imbecility as a sign of divine possession may perhaps have contributed to make the village fool or natural seem a particularly suitable victim."[18] The fool, therefore, precisely because of his madness, is surrounded by a religious aura; in this identity the fool comes to be associated with the Saint, the Poet, and the Seer.[19]

This murky but rich mythic background accounts in part for our difficulty in denoting Hamlet truly; if we are attentive to the archetypal suggestions of the play, Hamlet emerges as a character of many masks, encompassing in his mythic dimensions the Winter-king, the incest-driven Oedipal son, the royal victim, the Fool, and the existential striver for Truth who defies fate in the name of humanity. The guises are many, but they all seem to be directed toward a single mythic function, the restoration of a social order, either by ritual sacrifice or by revelation of a healing truth.

A general review of the plot of *Hamlet* suggests at first that the hero successfully lives up to his mythic responsibilities. Returning from a prolonged stay at Wittenberg, Hamlet finds a kingdom suffering a spiritual disease, the cause of which, he is told by the Ghost, is a murder "most foul, strange, and unnatural" (I.v.28).[20] The murder is, in fact, a regicide, which makes Hamlet's mission a public as well as private responsibility. He must, that is, do nothing less than cleanse the state of pollution: "Let not the royal bed of Denmark be / A couch for luxury and damned incest" (I.v.82–83). Claudius is more than a murderer: he is the usurper of the kingship, an institution that in Elizabethan times was regarded with religious awe, having absorbed some of the "holy and religious fear" (III.iii.8) formerly accorded the Pope and the Church. The rightful monarch—in this case, presumably Hamlet— was to be the ruler, high-priest, and father of the community; he was to be the person on whom, as Laertes states, the "sanity and health of this whole state" would depend (I.iii.21), or, in the figure used by Rosencrantz, the "massy wheel . . . To whose huge spokes ten thousand lesser things / Are mortised and adjoined" (III.iii.17–20).[21]

Hamlet's activities in the play must therefore be seen in the context of his royal status, and, more specifically, of the preemption of his royal office by Claudius. He accepts the "sacred" mandate to set right the time, but finds that, unlike his heroic prototypes, he cannot act decisively. And early indication of Hamlet's discomfort with his heroic role is expressed in his first soliloquy, when he describes Claudius as "my father's brother, but no more like my father / Than I to Hercules" (I.ii.152–53). The reference to Hercules has far-reaching implications, indicating the persistence in the Renaissance of primitive concepts of heroism. Hercules, according to one side of the tradition, is the simple man of deeds, representing "a core of primitive strength never completely transmuted by the refining power of more civilized ideals";[22] thus Hamlet's reference to Hercules hints at a nostalgia for the primitive heroic situation that would make the deed of blood accessible to him. Later, finding his revenge machinery stalled, Hamlet recalls Pyrrhus, son of Achilles, again a simple-minded warrior "roasted in wrath and fire" (II.ii.449) and unwaveringly committed to violence.

It is significant in this context that Hamlet voices admiration for Fortinbras, the man of "unimproved mettle hot and full," (I.i.96) for his audacity in war. Fortinbras, Hamlet perceives, is capable of venturing "all that fortune, death and danger dare, / Even for an eggshell" (IV.iv.52–53) and will "find quarrel in a straw / When honour's at the stake" (IV.iv.55–56). But Hamlet's admiration is tempered by his awareness of the horrible pointlessness of Fortinbras' Polish campaign, waged "to gain a little patch of ground / That hath in it no profit but the name" (IV.iv.18–19). Fortinbras, in short, is the simple man of action that Hamlet, given a less critical temperament, might have been. But Hamlet cannot accept the simple soldierly code of Fortinbras, for it belongs to another, simpler age. As soldier-hero in the mold of Fortinbras, Hamlet would be able to fulfill without hesitation the command of the Ghost; but Hamlet cannot evade the subtleties of his predicament: the command, as many have observed, results in an extraordinary confusion of two moralities, the pagan Teutonic and the Christian, and there is no reconciling middle ground. Where the revenge code would enjoin Hamlet, in the name of honor and filial piety, to avenge his father's death, the Christian code expressly prohibits revenge. Thus Hamlet is inhibited by "craven scruples" (IV.iv.40) and finds that "conscience does make cowards of us all" (III.i.83).

Unable to bring himself to commit the cleansing act of killing Claudius, Hamlet is forced progressively to isolate himself from the polluted society whose center he, as rightful ruler, should normally have been. As Holloway describes it, Hamlet has assumed a role which "takes him from being the cynosure of his society to being estranged from it, and takes him through a process of increasing alienation to a point at which what happens to him suggests the expulsion of a scapegoat or the sacrifice of a victim, or something of both."[23]

It is in this isolation that Hamlet resorts to the role of fool, where he serves as counter-image or "shadow" to the King. His riddles and quibbles link him with the abusive fool of mythology, who characteristically confounds the wisdom of the king by his cunning simplicity.[24] Moreover, riddles in antiquity were often thought of as reflecting preternatural knowledge, and the Hamlet sources reveal that this mythic residue is present in the Hamlet story. Saxo credits his hero with "a wisdom too high for human wit under a marvellous disguise of silliness," while Belleforest, granting Hamlet powers of divination, agonizes at some length over their origin—even considering it probable that "the minister of Sathan therein played his part."[25]

In any case, the fool role is immensely suggestive; Hamlet, finding himself incapable of the heroic deed, resorts to the instrument of the fool, the ironic (or prophetic) word. It could be said, in fact, that the tension between word and deed, which many have noted in Hamlet, is at least partially understandable as the result of a tension between two conflicting mythic roles: the royal prince and the fool. Because he is dispossessed by Claudius, Hamlet must express his somber truths by indirection, and the abusive clown seems increasingly to assume the religious identity of an inspired madman or prophet. As Fergusson has stated:

if Hamlet is the joking clown, he is also like those improvising Old Testament prophets who, gathering a handful of dust or of little bones, or a damaged pot from the potter's wheel, present to a blind generation a sudden image of their state.[26]

Through the first part of the play, therefore, the language of Hamlet is remarkably dominant as the play's center of interest. Having assumed his antic disposition, Hamlet is in a position to use language as an instrument of exploration, of concealment, or of correction. His language is used to taunt Polonius, to thwart the spying of Rosencrantz and Guildenstern, to instruct the players (largely about the proper use of language!), to castigate Ophelia, to chastise Gertrude with "words [that] like daggers enter in mine ears" (III.iv.96), and to "unkennel" the "occulted guilt" of Claudius (III.ii.77–78). But the word finally yields to the deed, in Hamlet's sudden killing of Polonius.

The first phase of Hamlet's ordeal ends with his "casual slaughter" of Polonius, an act which results in his being sent to England. This sea-voyage is for many critics fraught with archetypal implications; it is seen as a symbolic death-rebirth pattern, and the Hamlet who is "set naked on your kingdom" (IV.vii.43) has evidently undergone a sea-change, being finally reconciled to his task.[27] Significantly, both Saxo and Belleforest seem to attach great symbolic significance to the voyage, for in both narratives the hero before his departure instructs his mother to arrange "pretended obsequies" for him on the anniversary of his departure, and it is at this mock-funeral that Hamlet—in a symbolic rebirth of sorts—makes his appearance.[28]

The apparent transformation of Hamlet is manifested by the serenity of his disposition and the religious tone of his language, which communicate that Hamlet is now sure of his way, acquiescent in all things to the will of God. He is by his own testimony the man of "perfect conscience," (v.ii.67) reliant upon the "divinity that shapes our ends" (v.ii.10). Moreover, because of his newly acquired faith in a "special providence," he is ready to "defy augury" (v.ii.208–209), explicitly linking his powers of divination, which he hinted at earlier,[29] to heavenly guidance.

Thus, according to the mythic script, Hamlet is then guided darkly to his martyrdom, the death that he must suffer in order to cleanse Denmark. There is, asserts Maud Bodkin, a powerful "spiritual power" in Horatio's invocation of "flights of angels" (v.ii.349) over the body of Hamlet,[30] and many respond with a similar exultation to the promise of the "soldiers' music and the rites of war" (v.ii.388) which will attend Hamlet's passage. Miss Bodkin has observed that

our exultation in the death of Hamlet is related in direct line of descent to the religious exultation felt by the primitive group that made sacrifice of the divine king or sacred animal, the representative of the tribal life, and, by the communion of its shed blood, felt that life strengthened and renewed.[31]

Such readings are admittedly quite moving, but how consistent are they with the facts of the play? Recent criticism has demonstrated the need for delicacy and tact in approaching myth in Shakespeare;[32] caution, I suggest, is particularly essential in *Hamlet* since the principle of this play seems to be to outline bold patterns only to expose them as ultimately abortive. Specifically, *Hamlet* apparently evokes images of mythic heroism only to point out the inability of its hero to perform as mythic hero, to provide, that is, either the sacrificial cleansing or the healing revelation. Fergusson himself, despite his final acceptance of the mythical *Hamlet*, calls attention to the ironic distortions of Hamlet's role:

In *Hamlet* it is as though every one of these [mythic] elements had been elaborated by a process of critical analysis. Hamlet himself, though a prince, is without a throne; though a sufferer for the truth, he can appear in public as a mere infatuated or whimsical youth. . . . Shakespeare provides many ironic parallels to his story—and to this I may add that it takes both Hamlet and Claudius to represent the royal victim of the tradition.[33]

The essential feature of a mythic action is its social impact, but the redemptive act of Hamlet has been widely questioned precisely because of its inefficacy. Even Fergusson, while affirming the final integrity of the mythic pattern, seems nevertheless sensitive to the dubious success of the hero: "He feels his way toward [his martyr-like death], not with public sanction, but with the faithless worldliness of the Danes."[34] Other critics are less able to overcome their doubts: Tillyard finds in *Hamlet* "no great revelation or reversal of direction, or regeneration"; Knights finds that Hamlet, unlike Lear, cannot break out of the closed circle of self-contempt and loathing . . . . the awareness that he embodies is at best an intermediate stage, at worst a blind alley"; Vyvyan similarly denies that there is any renewal, insisting that *Hamlet* is a "study of degeneration from first to last."[35] Finally, Kott points out that Hamlet differs crucially from Orestes in resisting the choice that he must make: "Unlike all the Orestes of antiquity, Hamlet will not accept this choice (to kill or not to kill). He will be forced to make it, forced by others."[36] The existential affirmation that we expect is never made, and the final scene is for Kott extremely bleak:

The return of legality is without any motivation, deprived even of any semblance of necessity. It does not mean anything. It follows from the very logic of a structure, without any justification, without reference to any hierarchy of values.[37]

It is hardly astonishing that many critics fail to see any religious or quasi-religious affirmation in Hamlet's final moments, however devoutly such a consummation might be wished.[38] For above and beyond Hamlet's general fumbling, we must face the strongest evidence of all, the fact that Hamlet, despite his alleged reconciliation with Heaven, is utterly unrepentant—in fact, quite cavalier—about sending Rosencrantz and Guildenstern to their deaths "not shriving time allowed" (v.ii.47). It is perhaps the one major action in the play that cannot be explained away, even by appealing, as Cruttwell does, to the fact that Hamlet is literally at war with Claudius.[39] The return of the ambassadors from England with news of the killing of Rosencrantz and Guildenstern is *dramatically* unnecessary and therefore seems to be a pointed reminder that Hamlet's order for their execution is to have an important bearing on our final estimate of him. We must come to the inescapable conclusion that Hamlet's insistence on killing their souls as well as their bodies is an appalling act in any moral context.[40]

Despite Horatio's invocation of the flights of angels, what we witness, if we look with our judgment rather than with our eyes, is a scene of stark desolation, of almost random slaughter. It takes something like an act of faith to feel exultation in Hamlet's death and in the deaths for which he is directly or indirectly responsible. And if we are unable to bring ourselves to perform this act of faith, we are merely following the precedent of Horatio, who himself finally abandons his religious language to interpret the action in wholly secular terms:

> ... let me speak to th'yet unknowing world
> How these things came about; so shall you hear
> Of carnal, bloody, and unnatural acts,
> Of accidental judgments, casual slaughters,
> Of deaths put on by cunning and forced cause ....
> (v.ii.368–72)

It is a dreary catalogue of human fallibility that Horatio recites, and there is precious little indication that any good will come from the disaster which burdens the stage. If new life is to germinate from death, this new life is most inauspiciously embodied in Fortinbras, who, by whatever standard one measures him, seems unequal to his destiny. This, the cession of the kingdom to Fortinbras, the man of "unimproved mettle hot and full" (I.i.96), is the upshot of Hamlet's mythic activity: as Winter King, as scapegoat or royal victim, Hamlet accomplishes little.

The other side of Hamlet's mythic function, serving as prophet of a healing truth, is fulfilled no more adequately. It is obvious that the sexual myth, first of all, is not brought to its completion, for what seems to be crucial in this myth is a process of recognition of guilt, leading to remorse, and eventually to a growth of insight into the human condition. On this plane, the hero must come to terms with the radical ambivalence of the parent-son relationship. Thus Miss Bodkin traces in the sufferings of Oedipus a progression from unconscious guilt to a "final expression of respect and loyalty" to the parent-figures; in *Hamlet*, however, she can appeal only to a vague "intuitive apprehension" in the hero (and, by extension, in the onlooker).[41] And Freud's own uneasiness about the reticence of Hamlet can be inferred from his treatment of the two heroes:

As the poet brings the guilt of Oedipus to light by his investigation, he forces us to become aware of our inner selves, in which the same truths are still extant, even though they are suppressed .... In *Oedipus Rex* the wish-fantasy of the child is brought to light and realized as it is in dreams; in *Hamlet* it remains repressed, and we learn of its existence—as we discover the relevant facts in a neurosis—only through the inhibitory effects which proceed from it. In the more modern drama, the curious fact that it is possible to remain in complete uncertainty as to the character of the hero has proved to be quite consistent with the overpowering effect of the tragedy.[42]

The *Oedipus* plot, in short, is therapeutic, liberating us from the dark demons of the unconscious by exposing repressed impulses to the light of consciousness, but *Hamlet* has that within that passeth show; it fails to dramatize the repressed life of its hero, lacking—in Eliot's famous dictum—the objective correlative of Hamlet's emotion. Hamlet, it can be convincingly argued, achieves neither self-knowledge nor revelation.

A brief review of the main outlines of the Oedipus story underscores the great distance between the two heroes as vessels of truth. The fate of Oedipus is inextricably bound with the experience of knowing: it is through his sagacity in answering the riddle of the Sphinx that Oedipus is called to be sacred king of Thebes and is revered almost as a god. But because of his unrelenting pursuit of truth, Oedipus then discovers the guilt of his marriage, and, with this advance in knowledge obtained at great personal cost, takes upon himself the guilt of his society, effecting its purgation by suffering in exile. In *Colonus*, finally, his guilty knowledge is transformed into prophetic wisdom, and Oedipus emerges from his tragic ordeal as seer and saint, favored of the gods.[43]

In Hamlet too there is promise of the truth that saves, but where Oedipus gains renown as the solver of riddles, Hamlet is best known as the *creator* of riddles. And, although these riddles suggest, as Dover Wilson has observed, "unfathomed and unfathomable depths,"[44] what they most clearly disclose is the fatal ignorance of a hero whose ultimate revelation is the vision of death in the graveyard scene, a confrontation with the ultimate riddle:

Where be your gibes now? Your gambols, your songs, your flashes of merriment, that were wont to set the table on a roar? Not one now to mock your own grinning? Quite chop-fallen? Now get you to my lady's chamber, and tell her, let her paint an inch thick, to this favour she must come. (v.i.177–82)

In this part of the play what we are invited to witness is the failure of language. Having just experienced the degradation of the word in his dialogue with the gravedigger ("We must speak by the card, or equivocation will undo us"—v.i.128–29) and about to meet Osric, whose foppish language he will contemptuously burlesque, Hamlet here meditates upon the death of the fool, "a fellow of infinite jest" (v.i.173), and ultimately upon the death of language. "The rest is silence" could, in fact, be borrowed from its more familiar context to serve as a commentary on this scene.

Hamlet has much to say about language in the course of the play, instructing the players, for example, to "suit the action to the word, the word to the action" (III.ii.16–18) and to "let those that play your clowns speak no more than is set down for them . . . " (III.ii.37–38). But the decorum and moderation in language that he pleads for is precisely what Hamlet is himself unable to achieve. Despite Horatio's rebuke about his "wild and whirling words" (I.v.133), Hamlet indulges continually in linguistic extravagance, in a verbal hypertrophy that constantly damages his cause.[45] He eventually reproaches himself about his lack of discipline:

> This is most brave,
> That I, the son of a dear father murdered,
> Prompted to my revenge by heaven and hell,
> Must like a whore unpack my heart with words,
> And fall a-cursing like a very drab,
> A stallion!
>
> (II.ii.568–73)

Something of this verbal extravagance is seen in the nunnery scene, when he castigates Ophelia; in the closet scene, when he "roars so loud and thunders in the index" (III.iv.53); and in the burial scene, when he tries to out-rant Laertes. In each of these scenes we note that Hamlet, far from using language to convey the privileged wisdom of the fool-prophet, succeeds only in venting his ineffectual passion or his cynicism. The language of Hamlet, we must conclude, is a flawed instrument which simply thickens the darkness of his world and leaves us at last as the "yet unknowing world." And the fool-prophet lapses finally into silence.

It is evident, I think, that the mythic patterns elaborated by several critics are integral parts of the play's structure and must find a place in any critical consideration of the play. It seems, however, equally evident that the critic must be extremely discriminating in his handling of the patterns, for Shakespeare's handling of myth in this tragedy is profoundly ironic. Hamlet does indeed try to perform mythic actions, but a careful analysis of the consequences of his actions indicates that he fails dismally in his mythic roles. In an age which had already been considerably demythologized, Shakespeare's hero searches racial memory for a mythic conception of heroism that would give significance to his life. His tragedy, precisely, is that his life, and death, are meaningless: the society that he entrusts to Fortinbras is neither renewed by his death nor in possession of any saving truth.

NOTES

1 For a sensitive study of the ironies surrounding Hamlet's quest for heroism, see G. K. Hunter, "The Heroism of Hamlet," in *Stratford-Upon-Avon Studies 5: Hamlet*, gen. eds. John Russell Brown and Bernard Harris (London: Edward Arnold, 1963), 90–109.

2 J. M. Robertson, *The Problem of Hamlet* (New York: Harcourt, Brace and Howe, 1920), 74.

3 Peter Alexander, *Hamlet, Father and Son* (Oxford: Clarendon Press, 1967), 35.

4 Willard Farnham, "Introduction," Pelican *Hamlet*, in *The Complete Pelican Shakespeare*, gen. ed. Alfred Harbage (Baltimore: Penguin Books, 1969), 932.

5 Gilbert Murray, *Hamlet and Orestes: A Study in Traditional Types* (New York: Oxford Univ. Press, 1914). Israel Gollancz refers to an earlier interpretation of the Hamlet story as a nature myth by A. Zinzow (Halle, 1877) in *The Sources of Hamlet* (1924; rpt. New York: Octagon Books, 1967), 35.

6 Murray, 20–21.

7 Murray, 17; he points out that two distinct patterns are often confused.

8 Jan Kott, "Hamlet and Orestes," *PMLA* 82 (1967), 313.

9 Sigmund Freud, *The Interpretation of Dreams*, tr. A. A. Brill (New York: Macmillan, 1913), 225; Ernest Jones, *Hamlet and Oedipus* (Garden City, N.Y.: Doubleday, 1954). See especially 77–79.

10 Francis Fergusson, "Hamlet, Prince of Denmark: The Analogy of Action," in *The Proper Study: Essays on Western Classics*, eds. Quentin Anderson and Joseph A. Mazzeo (New York: St. Martin's Press, 1962), 348. The essay first appeared in *The Idea of a Theater* (Princeton: Princeton Univ. Press, 1949) and has been reprinted in several collections.

11 Fergusson, 354.

12 Ibid., 361–62.

13 Lord Raglan, *The Hero: A Study in Tradition, Myth, and Drama* (London: Methuen, 1936), 213.

14 Murray, 7.

15 Fergusson, 351, 357.

16 Harry Levin, *The Question of Hamlet* (New York: Oxford Univ. Press, 1959), 124–25.

17 E. K. Chambers, *The Medieval Stage* (Oxford: Clarendon Press, 1925), I, 136; Enid Welsford, *The Fool: His Literary and Social History* (1935; rpt. Gloucester, Mass.: P. Smith, 1966), esp. 68–73.

18 Chambers, I, 137.

19 Welsford, 76 ff.; inevitably a Christian culture would also recall St. Paul's description of the Christian as a "fool for Christ" in I Corinthians 4.10.

20 All references are to *The Complete Pelican Shakespeare*, gen. ed. Alfred Harbage (Baltimore: Penguin Books, 1969).

21 See Fergusson, 353; for the symbolic importance of kingship, see Harold Toliver, "Shakespeare's Kingship: Institution and Dramatic Form," in *Essays in Shakespearean Criticism*, eds. James Calderwood and Harold Toliver (Englewood Cliffs, N. J.: Prentice-Hall, 1970), 58–82.

22 Eugene M. Waith, *The Herculean Hero in Marlowe, Chapman, Shakespeare, and Dryden* (New York: Columbia Univ. Press, 1962), 17. Cf. also Hamlet's reference to "the Nemean lion's nerve" (I.iv.83). Although the Hercules references seem to focus on Hercules as the man of action, the Hercules myth is much richer. See Marcel Simon, *Hercule et le christianisme* (Paris: Société d'Editions, 1955). Simon shows how Hercules was transformed into a symbol of

virtue, and even into a pagan "type" of Christ. But Hamlet's allusions do not seem to evoke this part of the tradition.

²³ John Holloway, *The Story of the Night* (London: Univ. of Nebraska Press, 1961), 135.

²⁴ Welsford, 88–89.

²⁵ Gollancz, 131; 237–45.

²⁶ Fergusson, 357.

²⁷ This interpretation is by now almost critical dogma. For typical readings, see Maynard Mack, "The World of Hamlet," *The Yale Review* 41 (1952), 521–22, an essay also available in several collections; and Paul N. Siegel, *Shakespearean Tragedy and the Elizabethan Compromise* (New York: New York Univ. Press, 1957), 112–13.

²⁸ Gollancz, 117–27; 231–51.

²⁹ These hints of preternatural insight include Hamlet's references to his "prophetic soul" (i.v.41) and his statement to Claudius: "I see a cherub that sees them [the plans of Claudius]" (iv.iii.47).

³⁰ Maud Bodkin, *Archetypal Patterns in Poetry* (1934; rpt. London: Oxford Univ. Press, 1968), 20–21.

³¹ Bodkin, 31.

³² See Robert G. Hapgood, "Shakespeare and the Ritualists," *Shakespeare Survey 15* (1962), 111–23, for a judicious appraisal of myth criticism.

³³ Fergusson, 354.

³⁴ Ibid., 362.

³⁵ E. M. W. Tillyard, *Shakespeare's Problem Plays* (London: Chatto and Windus, 1957), 26; L. C. Knights, *Approach to Hamlet* (Stanford: Stanford Univ. Press, 1961), 90; John Vyvyan, *The Shakespearean Ethic* (London: Chatto and Windus, 1959), 55.

³⁶ Kott, 312.

³⁷ Ibid.

³⁸ I am not intimating that the *play* lacks affirmation; Hamlet's point of view is not necessarily Shakespeare's.

³⁹ Patrick Cruttwell, "The Morality of Hamlet—'Sweet Prince' or 'Arrant Knave,' " in *Stratford-Upon-Avon Studies 5: Hamlet*, 128.

⁴⁰ The point has been made elsewhere; see, for example, Harold Skulsky, "Revenge, Honor, and Conscience in *Hamlet*," *PMLA* 85 (1970), 86.

⁴¹ Bodkin, 14.

⁴² Freud, 224–25; Freud implies that *Oedipus Rex* is more explicit in its handling of the theme because it is the product of an earlier and less self-conscious age.

⁴³ Louis Martz, in "The Saint as Tragic Hero," *Tragic Themes in Western Literature*, ed. Cleanth Brooks (New Haven: Yale Univ. Press, 1955), 166–67.

⁴⁴ John Dover Wilson, ed., *New Cambridge Hamlet* (Cambridge, Eng.: Cambridge Univ. Press, 1936), xxxix.

⁴⁵ Brents Stirling has a perceptive discussion of Hamlet's language and its relation to his "madness" in *Unity in Shakespearean Tragedy* (New York: Columbia Univ. Press, 1966), 91–94.

Providence College

CARL DENNIS

THE VISION OF *TWELFTH NIGHT*

More than most of Shakespeare's comedies, *Twelfth Night* is so rich in meaning that no single critical perspective seems to be able to encompass and unify all the issues that the play raises. In recent years, however, some very illuminating attempts at interpretation have been made. Perhaps the most convincing total view is presented by Joseph Summers in his essay, "The Masks of *Twelfth Night*."[1] For Mr. Summers the play is about the masks or guises which men assume, consciously or unconsciously, that prevent the discovery or expression of their real natures. Most of the masking here is the result of self-deception. Orsino may believe that he is really in love, but his stylized melancholy as a lovesick suitor suggests that he is more intrigued with the idea of being a lover than with any particular woman, that he confuses a conventional role with real emotion. Olivia may believe that her grief for her dead brother is sincere, but her extravagant plans for mourning suggest more a determination to fulfill some social ideal of the grieving lady than a need to express a grief she actually feels. And Sir Andrew and Malvolio, seduced by cruder notions of ideal upper-class behavior, make pretensions to a cultivation of manners and nobility of character which are bathetically crude and unjustified. The wisest characters in the play, Mr. Summers argues, avoid self-deception by consciously adopting their masks as necessities. Viola must adopt the disguise of a boy to protect herself, having been cast ashore friendless in a foreign country. And Feste, although he wears no motley in his brain, must assume the professional role of the fool to make his living in the world, using the license of his role to point out the various self-deceptions in the other characters. None of the masks are fully

63

removed until the romantically magical appearance of Sebastian, which undeceives the Duke and Olivia and makes Viola's mask no longer necessary. But even then Malvolio and Sir Andrew are unreformed, and Feste, yielding to the demands of his vocation, must preserve his role to the end.

I have summarized Mr. Summers' position here not to refute it but to build upon it, for I agree with most of his contentions. What I want to do in this essay is to place the self-deceptions of the characters in more specifically moral terms, to talk about the kinds of self-centeredness that underlie the confusion of feelings with social conventions. This approach will help make more clear the close relations between the major and the minor characters, and will finally bring into prominence the religious dimensions of the play that are often neglected.

In discussing the delusions of the major characters, Mr. Summers asserts that the causes of Orsino's role-playing are "boredom, lack of physical love, and excessive imagination."[2] Though all of these causes are operative, the play also encourages us to judge his posturing in moral terms as a kind of self-glorification. Orsino is vain. He loves in the grand style because he wants to display to others the exquisiteness of his own emotions. All his actions, all his words are public. Never speaking once in soliloquy, he usually has as an audience for his moodiness all the retainers of his court. Even when he goes off to muse in quiet about love, at the end of the first scene, he makes it clear that his courtiers are to accompany him:[3]

> Away before me to sweet beds of flowers.
> Love thoughts lie rich when canopied with bowers.
>
> (I.i.39–40)

Apparently even his silent reveries are meant to impress others. If he prefers Cesario above the other courtiers, the reason seems again to be vanity. For he sees in the delicate and sensitive boy, in whom "all is semblative a woman's part" (I.iv.34), a particularly appreciative audience for his polished refinement as a lover. On one occasion, in fact, just before sending Cesario on his second mission to Olivia, he tells the boy specifically to follow the example of his master when he falls in love:

> Come hither, boy. If ever thou shalt love,
> In the sweet pangs of it remember me;
> For such as I am all true lovers are,
> Unstaid and skittish in all motions else
> Save in the constant image of the creature
> That is beloved.
>
> (II.iv.15–20)

The irony here is that the pupil to whom Orsino pretentiously offers instruction is a far better lover than the teacher. For the selfless woman beneath the boy's clothes loves humbly in complete secrecy, not vainly in the public eye, and proves her love not by words but by deeds, serving Orsino by aiding his suit to another woman.

When the role-playing of Orsino is seen as a function of his vanity, one notices a specific connection between him and Olivia's other declared suitor, Sir Andrew Aguecheek. The disparity between Sir Andrew's oafishness and his expectations of becoming a complete gentleman only magnifies the disparity between Orsino's actual self-involvement and his extravagant claims to suffer the emotions of real love. Both men are prompted by a vain desire to impress the world with their refinement. And their both being rejected as suitors by Olivia suggests an even closer connection in their deficiencies as lovers. What makes Sir Andrew ridiculous as a suitor is not only his boorish stupidity but also his obvious unconcern with the woman he is pursuing. He pays court to Olivia simply to fulfill the role of the gentleman, not because he is emotionally attracted to her, and thus is ready to "accost" and "board" Maria the minute Sir Toby suggests it. For if the aim of courtship is only to polish one's manners, almost any woman will do. In this way he helps make it more obvious that Orsino is attracted not to Olivia but to some disembodied image of a woman in his mind, an image which he creates only to stimulate impressive poses in himself.

Both men are thus encapsulated by their imaginations. They pay court to Olivia, it should be noticed, not directly but through intermediaries, Sir Andrew through Sir Toby and Orsino through Viola. For direct contact might have the painful effect of forcing them to subordinate their ideal programs to the dictates of a real lady. Too engrossed in perfecting their own images for public approval, they cannot relate at all to people around them. Sir Andrew's self-imprisonment is more grossly obvious since the discrepancy between his view of himself and the view others have of him is so tremendous, but he only exaggerates aspects of Orsino's isolation. As Sir Andrew is mocked consciously by his friend Sir Toby, so Orsino is exposed unconsciously by his servant Cesario, who gives him a real object of love whom he is too self-engrossed to perceive. Indeed, in his treatment of Cesario, Sir Andrew appears no more foolish than the Duke. Where Andrew admiringly writes down Cesario's rhetoric for future use, awed by terms like "odours," "pregnant," and "vouchsafed" (III.i.100), Orsino compliments his servant on his "masterly" speech (II.iv.23), seeing in it a proof that the boy can appreciate his master's professional love-longings. And where Sir Andrew wants to frighten off his supposed rival Cesario in a duel, Orsino for one moment at the end of the play wants to kill Cesario in cold blood, when his vanity is hurt by the boy's apparent marriage to Olivia. It is hard to tell here who is more shut off from reality. Only when the Duke decides to give up the woman who doesn't love him for the woman who does can he be said to move out of the mental prison which his vanity has constructed.

Like the Duke's posturings as a lover, Olivia's exaggerated grief for her dead brother is motivated by a vain desire for displaying her sensibilities; but since she is soon cured of her affectation by Feste's wit and by falling in love with Cesario, it may at first be difficult to see her as being as self-involved as Orsino. Yet if we look closely at her love for Cesario, we find that it is not a natural attraction ousting artificial ideals, but a reflexive relation in which Olivia loves an image of herself. The fact that Cesario is really a woman disguised as a man suggests not only that Olivia has been "charmed" by a mere "outside," as Viola says (II.ii.19), but also that she is engaging in a form of narcissism. She loves someone of her own sex because she is too self-involved to love an object that is totally distinguished from herself. That particular aspect of herself which she finds mirrored in Cesario seems to be her proud imperviousness to love. In Cesario's resistance to her charms, in his courteous but plain-spoken criticisms of her character, she finds an ideal image of her own haughtiness to Orsino. In loving him she therefore pays tribute to the beauty of her own Petrarchan detachment. Thus the more scornful Cesario becomes, the more she dotes on him. "Oh, what a deal of scorn looks beautiful / In the contempt and anger of his lip," she exclaims as her advances are rebuffed on one occasion (III.i.157–58), charmed by the kind of disdain in which she herself has taken pride. This reflexiveness of her love for Cesario is emphasized overtly in a symbolic way by the fact that the names "Olivia" and "Viola" are anagrams, each containing the same letters. For to Olivia, Viola is not a separate person but an anagram of herself, a reflected compendium of her own imagined virtues. To the reader, of course, Viola is more of a moral contrast to Olivia than a moral complement. With no taint of narcissism, she loves a man generously and selflessly without any hope of immediate return.

Olivia's narcissism is mirrored in an exaggerated way by the narcissism of her steward Malvolio, who is "sick of self-love" (I.v.97). Whereas Olivia loves an object who represents herself, Malvolio, still more involuted, loves only grandiose fantasies of his own greatness.

More proud than vain, more self-involved than either Orsino or Sir Andrew, Olivia and Malvolio do not even require an appreciative audience to further their self-esteem. They are their own audience. Olivia can therefore live somewhat apart from the life of her retainers, unlike the Duke; and Malvolio can afford to offend the retainers with his prudish spleen. To both, the world outside their imaginations is only a distraction. Thus Malvolio's rudeness is often only an extension of his mistress's. He is discourteous to Cesario partly because he has no respect for anyone but himself, but he also is following his mistress's proud orders to turn away all missions of courtship. And Viola includes both mistress and steward when she asserts, "The rudeness that hath appeared [in me] have I learned from my entertainment" (i.v.230–31). In the same way Malvolio is following orders when he tries to quiet the merry-making of Sir Toby. If the noise offends his inflated dignity, it also disturbs his mistress's self-indulgent grief and her subsequent self-worshiping love for Cesario. This connection is reinforced later when Olivia points out the similarity of her own melancholy and Malvolio's apparent madness, after he appears before her smiling without cause: "I am as mad as he, / If sad and merry madness equal be" (iii.iv.14–15).

For the reader, of course, the common denominator of their disorders is not madness but pride. Such parallelism is underscored by the introduction of the device of the anagram in the trick played on Malvolio. For the name that Maria's letter gives to Malvolio's inflated idea of himself is MOAI, and, as Malvolio says, "every one of these letters are in [my] name" (ii.v.153). His proud identification of himself with the MOAI of the letter, with the darling of his mistress and the Fates, is a grotesque image of Olivia's reflexive love for her anagram Viola. And Malvolio's name itself tells us of his relation to his mistress. For "Malvolio" suggests not only "bad will" but, anagrammatically, "bad Olivia."[4] Malvolio represents what Olivia might become if she had no sense of humor, no ability to detach herself from her own follies. Not until Olivia marries Sebastian can she be safely said to repudiate the Malvolio within her, and even this event may at first appear to be more of an accident than a sign of inner change. But Sebastian seems to defend the reality of her growth when he asserts that "nature" moved her to marry him and not Cesario (v.i.267). Presumably her instincts are able to distinguish the man from the woman even though her conscious wits are befuddled. Nature seeks its complement, not its reflection. Poor Malvolio, however, does not change. Sir Toby and his friends try in a comic way to exorcise his pride by exorcising from his possessed mind the father of pride, the Devil; but he is too immured in his self-love to be shaken by this humiliation.[5]

Because "nature" helps Olivia to break out of her self-involvement, we may be inclined to see the greatest contemner of unnatural ideals in the play, Sir Toby Belch, as the wisest man in Illyria. His celebration of the demands of the flesh and the simple joys of conviviality is an effective antidote to the excesses of artificial love that betray his niece and the Duke. Toby is too committed to the pleasures of food, drink, and social merriment to be drawn into the solipsistic worlds of vanity and narcissism, and his joke on Malvolio is a fitting reprisal against all unnatural forms of delusive self-involvement. And yet with all his naturalness, Toby never achieves any deep attachment to the world of men around him. If he is taken in by no grandiose images of himself, he is nevertheless thoroughly selfish. Living mainly to satisfy his physical wants and willing to manipulate others for his own comfort, he is just as self-involved and self-confined as the more introverted protagonists. Surely in his role as a go-between for Sir Andrew to Olivia he is opposed in every way to selfless Viola as she exhorts Olivia to love the Duke. Viola serves because she loves Orsino, Toby because he wants Sir Andrew's money. Viola disguises her love and engages in a service that if successful will spoil her happiness; Toby disguises his contempt for his declared friend in order to dupe him more thoroughly. His opposition to Viola is emphasized overtly when he tries for his own amusement to discomfit her and Sir Andrew by arranging a duel between them. This plan is frustrated, it should be noticed, by the appearance of another moral foil to Sir Toby, Antonio, who has risked his life in coming to Illyria in order to accompany and protect his beloved friend, Sebastian. To be sure, Toby's Sir Andrew may not deserve such dedication, and he is partly responsible for his own duping. But Toby aggravates his friend's vanity by his constant praise, encouraging him to pursue Olivia even when Sir Andrew wants to give over the enterprise. And Toby treats his niece poorly as well. Though he knows Sir Andrew is a fool, he is willing to bother Olivia with Andrew's troublesome courtship, and perhaps is even willing to have her marry him, if it will further his own comfort. Though we can call Toby a clear-sighted rogue who never deceives himself about his own intentions, we cannot finally overlook his egotism. Even his shrewdness is qualified toward the end of the play when his mistaking Sebastian for Cesario leads to his being beaten. The world proves too mysterious to be approached simply through practical intelligence.

It is particularly fitting that Sir Toby has his head cracked by Sebastian; for Sebastian, along with his sister Viola, embodies a way of life which is opposed to Toby's and which is finally vindicated in the play as the truest and most productive attitude to the world. Viola and Sebastian are genuine givers and receivers. They love each other and their friends, and, more generally, they love life in a way that enables them to maintain a receptive openness to all experience. Thus they confront the world directly, cut off from men and events neither by the appetitive selfishness of Sir Toby nor by the fantasy-loving self-involvement of Olivia, Orsino, and their comic doubles. Sebastian is, of course, somewhat mystified by the world of Illyria, where he is mistaken for Cesario; but the confusion is more the Illyrians' than his own. And when a rich and beautiful noblewoman throws herself mysteriously at his feet, his surprise does not prevent him from gladly accepting the lady's offer, from throwing himself completely into the experience. Avoiding the kind of wit that tries to manipulate the world for practical advantage, avoiding the self-centered fantasizing that prefers the inner world to the outer, Sebastian discovers a realm that is more beneficent and miraculous than the ego-ridden characters could ever imagine. The right attitude to the world is centered neither in the natural wants of the flesh nor in the artificial constructs of the imagination, but in a religious awe before the unearned bounty which the world bestows on man, an awe akin to man's perception of God's grace.

The key word in the play for this religious perception is "wonder," and though at times the marvels it discloses make it seem akin to madness, Sebastian is careful to distinguish the two states of mind:

> This is the air, that is the glorious sun,
> This pearl she gave me, I do feel't and see't.
> And though 'tis wonder that enwraps me thus,
> Yet 'tis not madness.

(IV.iii.1–4)

Although Sebastian goes on to say that the strangeness of events tempts him to call himself mad, his very ability to marvel at his experience is a sign of his sanity. For to be wise is to perceive the miraculousness of the world. This distinction between madness and wonder is crucial in *Twelfth Night* because those characters whose self-involvement prevents their wonder at life are shown to be tainted with various kinds of madness. Orsino declares his madness openly, for living in the irrational world of whim is part of the lover's code. His fancy, he boasts at various times, is "full of shapes," "unstaid and skittish," "giddy and unfirm" (I.i.14; II.iv.18, 34). Olivia too acknowledges that her love is irrational. When she falls in love with Cesario, her mind seems diseased:

> Even so quickly may one catch the plague?
> Methinks I feel this youth's perfections
> With an invisible and subtle stealth
> To creep in at mine eyes.
> (I.v.314–17)

And Malvolio, with his fantastic ambition aggravated by Maria's letter, engages in antics that prove him the victim of "very midsummer madness," as Olivia says (III.iv.61), and require his mock incarceration. Even Sir Toby, who is free of self-deluding fantasies, is mad in one sense. In abandoning himself to his appetites he makes his life chaotic, rejecting, as Maria says, "the modest limits of order" (I.iii.9); and when he enters drunk to tell of Cesario's arrival, Feste makes it clear that Sir Toby is "like a drowned man, a fool, and madman" (I.v.139). His self-indulgence, like that of Orsino, Olivia, and Malvolio, shuts him off from reality.

The religious awe which the loving person feels at the miraculous bounty of the world often takes the specific form of a particularly trusting attitude to fortune. Although Sebastian has been wrecked at sea and apparently lost his sister forever, he does not regard his good fortune in Illyria as a just compensation for previous misfortune but rather as the working of fate whose generosity is above and beyond his ken. His experience is an "accident and flood of fortune" that "exceed[s] all instance, all discourse" (IV.iii.11–12). And in trusting fortune here he is repeating what his sister has already done. When Viola is first cast ashore friendless, she has as much reason as her brother to curse the cruelty of chance. But instead she puts herself in a hopeful frame of mind, believing that chance may have saved Sebastian:

> Viola: Perchance he is not drowned. What think you sailors?
> Captain: It is perchance that you yourself were saved.
> Viola: Oh, my poor brother: And so perchance may he be.
> (I.ii.5–7)

Later, Viola shows the same kind of hope with regard to her frustrated love for Orsino. As she contemplates the apparently hopeless tangle of misplaced affections, she gives up any attempt to resolve the confusion herself, and decides to rely on the power of time to bring about a happy conclusion:

> O Time, thou must untangle this, not I!
> It is too hard a knot for me to untie!
> (II.ii.41–42)

Brother and sister, then, regard fate as a power outside their control which they must trust to right in the future, whatever inadequacies appear in the present. The less generous, more self-involved characters, however, show themselves to be incapable to making this leap of faith. They all fail to trust fortune, though they fail in different ways.

The trouble with Orsino's attitude to fortune is that he identifies it with the vagaries of his own moods, instead of regarding it as an independent power. Because of his self-centeredness the events of his world seem confined to the activities of his own imagination, and the shifts of fortune become indistinguishable from the shifting contents of his mind. Instead of trusting in external fate, he simply abandons himself to "the spirit of love" which resides within:

> O spirit of love, how quick and fresh art thou!
> That, notwithstanding thy capacity
> Receiveth as the sea, naught enters there,
> Of what validity and pitch soe'er,
> But falls into abatement and low price,
> Even in a minute! So full of shapes is fancy
> That it alone is high fantastical.
>
> (I.i.9–15)

For Orsino the sea of love that swallows all experience is not the sea of time to which all events are subject, but the inner sea of fantasy.[6] His abandoning himself to love is therefore not a reliance on fate to bring about his union with his beloved but a reliance on his fancy for the entertainment that results from continuous change.

Olivia's lack of humble trust in fortune is perhaps less easy to perceive. For when she finds herself suddenly in love with Cesario, she appears to believe that her fate lies in the hands of powers outside of her control:

> I do I know not what, and fear to find
> Mine eye too great a flatterer for my mind.
> Fate, show thy force, ourselves we do not owe.
> What is decreed must be, and be this so.
>
> (I.v.327–30)

What makes one suspicious about this statement of submission is that fate here is not so much an external force as another name for the strongest desire within Olivia. In naming fate as her master, she is simply trying to avoid responsibility for yielding to feelings which she knows to be suspect. Her apparent trust in fortune is thus really only an expression of her self-centeredness. Like Orsino she is too self-involved to think of fate as something separate from her own inner life. She confuses fortune with her own whims, with her reluctance to fight against her narcissism. Only when fortune miraculously helps to change her reflexive love for Cesario into real object-love for Sebastian does she become aware of its independent power. Then she can perceive in awe that her fate is "most wonderful" (v.i.232).

A more gross example of pride with regard to fortune is found in Malvolio's self-delusions. Malvolio, it should be noticed, sprinkles his ambitious fantasies of preferment with casual references to the power of fortune and the gods. In the crucial scene where his ambition allows him to be gulled by Maria's letter, he enters musing " 'Tis but fortune, all is fortune," that his mistress should admire him and want to marry him (II.v.27); after reading the letter and applying its praises to himself, he exclaims, "Jove and my stars be praised" (II.v.186–87); and even when Olivia has called him mad to his face, his self-infatuation allows him to exclaim smugly, "Well, Jove, not I, is the doer of this, and is to be thanked" (III.iv.91–92). Behind all these pious bows to fortune lies Malvolio's belief that he owes his supposed rise not to luck but to his irresistible merit. Though he is told in the letter that "some are born great, some achieve greatness, and some have greatness thrust upon 'em" (II.v.156–58), he is too self-loving for the "thrusting" to seem anything but an inevitable reward for his superlative talents; and indeed he has imagined the contents of the letter before he receives it. Because he is so certain of his unqualified worth, it is impossible for him to see fate as miraculous at all. A truly religious perception of the bounty of the gods is accessible only to the man who knows that he is not all-deserving, who is humble enough to see gifts as gifts, not as rewards, and so can wonder at the world's graciousness. As a result of his pride, the only fortune that Malvolio encounters is a bad one, the misfortune of his being mocked and imprisoned as a madman. Feste's taunting moral on this occasion, "And thus the whirligig of time brings in his revenges" (v.i.384–85), makes clear that fickle fortune always is ready to discomfit those who assume that time is their servant, a point he makes emphatically again at the end of the play in his song about the inevitability of "the wind and the rain" befouling "swaggerers."

After dealing with characters who identify fate with their own moods or their own merits, one turns with relief to Sir Toby's practical demands on life. Making no attempt to subjectify fate, Toby is content if fortune allows him the simple pastimes of the immediate present. And yet Toby's belief that he can live for the moment suggests finally a limitation of imagination, a somewhat casual dismissal of fortune as a power not finally relevant to his own life. This skepticism seems to be articulated most directly when he discusses Sir Andrew's dancing talents in terms of astrological influences:

Sir Toby: I did think, by the excellent constitution of thy leg, it was formed under the star of a galliard.

. . . .

Were we not born under Taurus?
Sir Andrew: Taurus! That's sides and heart.
Sir Toby: No, sir, it is legs and thighs. Let me see thee caper.
(I.iii.140–42, 146–49)

Toby's astrological references here are so patently flippant, so clearly introduced merely to puff up Sir Andrew's vanity, that they suggest just the opposite of superstition, a naturalism that views man as subject to no influences at all beyond his own control. It is obvious to Toby that he alone, and not the stars, manipulates Sir Andrew. But Toby's proud confidence that he can control people and events to satisfy his simple demands is rudely jolted at the end of the play by the miracle of Sebastian's appearance. Fortune cannot be anticipated. Wonder, not practical shrewdness, is the only adequate response, and Toby's reliance on his manipulative powers makes that wonder impossible.

A somewhat more experienced and self-critical form of naturalism is expressed at the end of the play in Feste's final song. This song is often taken as an expression of a healthy realism about the workaday facts of life which must be acknowledged after holiday wish-fulfillment, but a closer look suggests a different meaning. The misfortunes that befall the subject of the song are the results not of impractical idealism but of sensual self-indulgence. The song is a prodigal's confession, a gloomy tale of the childish man who expects the world to satisfy his appetites.[7] The speaker lives the life of a swaggering boaster and a drunkard, an extreme mixture, perhaps, of Malvolio and Sir Toby; and the misfortunes of "the wind and the rain" which he encounters "everyday" are less an expression of the hostility of fate than the result of his own actions. There is more than enough wind in his boasting and wet in his drink to give him all the trouble he encounters, and this is all he can ever expect to encounter by confronting the world on the level of sensual demands. Feste's song recognizes the practical limits of such childish indulgence, but its earthly prudence is not the final standard of the play; for it cannot do justice to the large and open world of giving and faith where Sebastian and Viola dwell. The alternative offered to the song's perspective is not simply the temporary joy and release of secular festival but a religious wonder that reveals an existence more real, more complete, and of a higher order than common life. This is the vision man attains once he is able to break out of the confining walls of the self.

NOTES

1 Joseph Summers, "The Masks of *Twelfth Night*," *University of Kansas City Review* 22 (Oct. 1955), 25–32.

2 Ibid., 26.

3 Citations from *Twelth Night* in this essay are to *The Complete Works*, ed. G. B. Harrison (New York: Harcourt, Brace and World, 1968).

4 The anagram isn't perfect since "Volio" contains no "a"; but "Volio" and "Volia" are similar enough to suggest that the likeness is not accidental.

5 The special relation of the Devil to pride is specifically made clear with reference to Olivia. When Viola looks at Olivia's uncovered face she says, "I see what you are, you are too proud; / But if you were the Devil, you are fair" (I.v.269–70).

6 The reference to the sea of time in this passage has been pointed out by D. J. Palmer in his interesting essay, "Art and Nature in *Twelfth Night*," *Critical Quarterly* 9 (1967), 201–12. In discussing several passages dealing with fortune, Mr. Palmer contends that the notion of fortune's power is central to the play's meaning. His approach differs from mine in that he sees fortune simply as the fragility and mutability of human affairs; I contend that fortune is a beneficent force and that the characters can be discriminated morally by the degree of their receptiveness to its agency.

7 Leslie Hotson makes the interesting suggestion that the "foolish thing" of the first stanza should be taken in the sexual sense, and that the song catalogues the three vices of drunkenness which correspond to the three ages of man, lechery, wrath, and sloth (*The First Night of Twelfth Night* [New York: Macmillan, 1955], 170–71). Mr. Hotson, however, regards the song primarily as a caution against Saturnalian excesses, and so he does not attempt to place it in the context of those values in the play which are higher than prudence.

State University of New York at Buffalo

JAMES QUIVEY

RHETORIC AND FRAME: A STUDY OF METHOD IN THREE SATIRES BY MARVELL

Along with Samuel Butler and a scant few lesser Restoration poets, Andrew Marvell stands as a transitional figure in the history of English verse satire. Like Butler, Marvell was a guidon for the new directions established in the Restoration period, directions leading away from the direct declamatory satire of the Renaissance and seventeenth century toward the more sophisticated and infinitely more entertaining forms of indirect satire that reached near perfection a half century later in Pope's polished *Rape of the Lock*. Though a major figure in the transition, however, Marvell wrote relatively early in the period before the directions were clearly in focus; consequently, it is not surprising that his satires are strikingly uneven in quality and, correspondingly, that the limited amount of critical commentary they have elicited is disproportionately uncomplimentary.

A general reaction to Marvell's Restoration satires, epitomized, perhaps, by T. S. Eliot's dismissal of them as "random babbling,"[1] is that they are confusingly formless and inordinately difficult to read. The most frequently cited specific reasons for this want of readability are the rapidity and ellipticity with which the poet introduces great numbers of subjects and the obscure topicality of many of the subjects. To these reasons should be added three more. The two negative features that most distinguish Marvell's satires, and especially his most famous satire, are his seemingly patternless shifting of modes of discourse, for example, shifts from narration to indirect dialogue and back, and his inattention to rhetorical matters that relate less directly to poetry per se than to basic communication, such as consistency of point of view and

75

tense. Among the most distinguishing positive features of Marvell's satires, on the other hand—but still inextricably a part of the reading problem, because sufficient attention is seldom devoted to their functions and effects in the poems—are the clever and varied frame devices that the poet employs.

Unquestionably rhetorical shifts and inconsistencies are confusing to the reader and ostensibly are artistically indefensible. Yet, like other unattractive generic qualities of satire—crude language, for instance—these characteristics are well within the traditions of formal verse satire, traditions that continued to influence Restoration satirists despite their interest in the new burlesque. Further, these shifts and inconsistencies, and the ellipticity and topicality too, are probably deliberate elements of Marvell's method, and they are largely consonant with and justified by the frame techniques Marvell uses. Examination of Marvell's method, his rhetorical modes of presentation and development and his frame techniques, reveals the very limited extent to which the political satires *are* distractingly formless and confusing, if read closely, as well the extent to which these qualities, real or imagined, can be justified on grounds other than, or in addition to, tradition.

Three satires whose reputations can benefit from such an examination are "Last Instructions to a Painter," "The Loyall Scot," and "A Dialogue Between the Two Horses."[2] These are likely the best known of Marvell's satires. All are of sustained length, all exhibit some of the features in question, and all utilize frame devices. Because a satiric frame clearly establishes an internal dramatic situation, rhetorical shifts or flaws in frame poems may be *less* distracting than in non-frame poems since the dramatic situation and personae are adequately defined, and meaning is thus relatively unlikely to be obscured. But, conversely, rhetorical flaws in frame poems may prove *more* distracting for virtually the same reason: with the dramatic situation and personae clearly set, any rhetorical flaws only more obviously violate propriety.

The most significant of Marvell's satires is "Last Instructions to a Painter" (1667), a long parody of Waller's panegyric, "Instructions to a Painter, For the Drawing of the Posture and Progress of His Majesties Forces at Sea, Under the Command of His Highness Royal, Together with the Battel and Victory Obtained over the Dutch, June 3, 1665," which appeared in 1666. Marvell's "Last Instructions," one of a series of opposition responses to Waller's poem,[3] is a wide-ranging denouncement of both the public and private conduct of members of court and Parliament that provides us as no other poem of the period does with intimate details of the ineffectuality of Parliament and with equally intimate personal details concerning little-known Parliamentary figures. Though the poet distributes his barbs freely in "Last Instructions," his two major focal points are the debates in Parliament late in 1666 over broadening the excise tax in order to secure additional revenue for the Second Dutch War and the military mismanagement of that war, permitting the Dutch to embarrass England's navy in Chatham Harbor the following spring.

As the longest and best of Marvell's satires, "Last Instructions" has received considerably more critical attention than any of the others, and the common complaint is that the poem is difficult to read.[4] John Wallace attributes the difficulty to a "discursive structure";[5] biographer-critic Pierre Legouis blames the elliptical portraits and the scatter-shot approach that permit Marvell to include eighty-four subjects in 990 lines in comparison with twenty-seven in 1,030 lines of Dryden's *Absalom and Achitophel*;[6] similarly James Sutherland finds fault with the "plethora of material" and the "constant shifting of the attack to a fresh victim."[7] Further, Legouis, although not speaking in a context of rhetorical modes, criticizes qualities in the poem that clearly are related to expositional structure. He finds no clear order of presentation in the portraits, no clear "pecking order" of importance, and he is disconcerted by the fact that some of the minor figures receive more attention than major figures.[8] Although all of these factors contribute to an impression of confusion and artlessness, a more important contributor may be the relatively minor and purely rhetorical difficulties that occur to some extent throughout the poem, but manifest themselves most obviously in the first thirty lines:

> After two sittings, now our *Lady State*,
> To end her Picture, does the third time wait.
> But er'e thou fal'st to work, first *Painter* see
> It be'nt too slight grown, or too hard for thee.
> Canst thou paint without Colours? Then 'tis right;
> For so we too without a Fleet can fight.
> Or canst thou dawb a Sign-post, and that ill?
> 'Twill suit our great debauch and little skill.
> Or hast thou mark't how antique Masters limn
> The Aly roof, with snuff of Candle dimm,
> Sketching in shady smoke prodigious tools,
> 'Twill serve this race of Drunkards, Pimps, and Fools.
> But if to match our Crimes thy skill presumes,
> As th' *Indians*, draw our Luxury in Plumes.
> Or if to score out our compendious Fame,
> With *Hook* then, through the *microscope*, take aim
> Where, like the new *Controller*, all men laugh
> To see a tall Lowse brandish the white staff.
> Else shalt thou oft thy guiltless Pencil curse,

Stamp on thy Pallat, nor perhaps the worse.
The Painter so, long having vext his cloth,
Of his Hound's Mouth to feign the raging froth,
His desperate Pencil at the work did dart,
His anger reacht that rage which past his Art;
Chance finisht that which Art could but begin,
And he sat smiling how his Dog did grinn.
So may'st thou perfect, by a lucky blow,
What all thy softest touches cannot do.
Paint then St. *Albans* full of soup and gold,
The new *Courts* pattern, Stallion of the old.
                                        (1–30)

These lines constitute the frame introduction plus two lines of the initial portrait; and they show clearly the rhetorical shifts that mar the poem to a small degree. Apparently the first two lines are designed to provide exposition for the dramatic situation, to establish that a painter is about to complete a portrait of England. As such—and because they are not dialogical and because the intelligence they convey is certainly already obvious to the painter—they are public discourse; that is, they are directed at the reading audience, an audience outside the internal dramatic situation involving the two personae, the painter and his loquacious patron. The next eighteen lines, lines 3 through 20, are private or dramatic discourse, spoken by one character in the dramatic situation and directed at the other. That they are directed at the painter is clear enough from the direct address in line 3; rhetorically, however, there are no distinctions between the poem's first two lines and the next eighteen lines to establish that the *speakers* are different. Assumedly, the speaker in the first two lines is Marvell, detached from the dramatic situation, whereas the speaker in the drama is a persona. So a shift in speaker occurs here, but Marvell provides no rhetorical signals to indicate the shift.

A parallel speaker shift occurs at line 21 where Marvell interrupts the persona's monologue to interject six lines of descriptive narration (ll. 21–26) which reveal the painter's working up sufficient rage to do justice to the portraits he must paint. Then follow two more lines of frame, here moralistic exposition rather than narration, before the actual instructions begin in line 29. The frame includes the first two lines plus lines 21 through 28 and consists of Marvell's remarks to the general audience. That the persona's monologue is interrupted by external comment is not in itself distracting; but in this case the grammatical subject of the public discourse shifts from the Lady State of the first two lines, and tense shifts from present to past to future. Hence, within the space of but a few lines, the reader of the poem must contend with shifts in mode of discourse, in speaker, in audience, in subject, and in tense.

This artlessness, however—if, indeed, it is artlessness—simply underscores the poem's formal verse satire ancestry. In her widely known essay on the design of formal verse satire, Mary Claire Randolph notes that such satires are often confusing:

When the conversation begins abruptly and jerkily, as it usually does, and continues elliptically, broken and interrupted here and there ... frequently without either Satirist or Adversary being clearly identified as the speaker, the uninitiated reader is apt to feel thoroughly lost. One of the most common editorial and critical accusations against formal verse satire is that its lack of clarifying guidewords and transitions results in extreme confusion of dialogue.[9]

Although this statement does not describe exactly the condition of Marvell's "Last Instructions," it does establish that a degree of rhetorical freedom was a part of the tradition that informed Marvell and that, consequently, any rhetorical artlessness in "Last Instructions" is somewhat justified by tradition.

Once the poem is well underway, its presentation levels out considerably. The speaker remains the patron persona, and the painter is his silent companion throughout the main poem to the epilogue. In presenting the verbal portraits Marvell utilizes a variety of discourse modes, but here the shifts are not distracting. The portraits, related historically to the tradition of the Theophrastian prose character, are developed through narration, description, and exposition, in proportions varying with Marvell's intentions. The instructions-to-a-painter frame, rather than binding the writer to a particular developmental method such as chronological narration, allows for considerable freedom and variety. In addition, this frame device permits the poet to focus immediately on those qualities of his subject that he wishes to exploit. The first two portraits, for example, of Henry Jermyn, ambassador to the French Court (ll. 29–48), and Clarendon's daughter, Anne Hyde (ll. 49–78), are heavily descriptive; the third portrait (ll. 79–104) contains description also, but since it is here the randy Lady Castlemaine's promiscuity that Marvell wishes to exploit, and since only so much can be said of promiscuity through description, he shifts to a primarily narrative mode in lines 81–102 and offers a ruinous account of her affair—at least Marvell alleges such an affair—with a footman:

> She through her Lacquies Drawers as he ran,
> Discern'd Love's Cause, and a new Flame began.
> Her wonted joys thenceforth and *Court* she shuns,
> And still within her mind the Footman runs:

His brazen Calves, his brawny Thighs, (the Face
She slights) his Feet shapt for a smoother race.
Poring within her Glass she re-adjusts
Her looks, and oft-try'd Beauty now distrusts:
Fears lest he scorn a Woman once assay'd,
And now first, wisht she e're had been a Maid.
Great Love, how dost thou triumph, and how reign,
That to a Groom couldst humble her disdain!
Stript to her Skin, see how she stooping stands,
Nor scorns to rub him down with those fair Hands;
And washing (lest the scent her Crime disclose)
His sweaty Hooves, tickles him 'twixt the Toes.
But envious Fame, too soon, begun to note
More gold in's Fob, more Lace upon his Coat
And he, unwary, and of Tongue too fleet,
No longer could conceal his Fortune sweet.
Justly the Rogue was whipt in Porter's Den:
And *Jermyn* straight has leave to come agen.
                                                    (81–102)

At line 105 the persona broadens his horizons from individuals to
Commons, and it is here, apparently, that for many the poem begins
to deteriorate. After requesting the painter to paint the two political
parties and the Speaker of the House (ll. 105–16), the persona ad-
dresses him again: "Here Painter rest a little, and survey / With what
small Arts the publick game they play" (ll. 117–18). For the next 514
lines—to line 632—the persona orders no sustained individual portraits and, except for a parenthetical address in line 148—("And
Painter, wanting other, draw this Fight)"—seems entirely to disregard
the painter. The rhetorical mode in this long section, which includes
both the mock-heroic battle of the excise and the hilarious burlesqued
account of the Chatham Harbor debacle, is primarily narration. The
portraits are no longer really portraits but frequently are little more
than passing remarks which, taken together, make up a huge composite
of British leadership. The following passage is typical:

Then the Procurers under *Progers* fil'd,
Gentlest of men, and his Lieutenant mild,
Bronkard Loves Squire; through all the field array'd,
No Troop was better clad nor so well pay'd.
Then march't the Troop of Clarendon, all full,
Haters of Fowl, to *Teal* preferring *Bull*.
Gross Bodies, grosser Minds, and grossest Cheats;
And bloated *Wren* conducts them to their seats.
                                                    (ll. 173–80)

Marvell's method here has not found a very receptive audience. Sutherland says of the instructions frame and of Marvell's adaptation of it:

The form was not suggested by the content, but was simply imposed upon it. It should be added, too, that so far as "Last Instructions" go Marvell forgot about his painter for long periods, and indeed made comparatively little use of such advantages as his vehicle gave him. Later when Waller's poem was no longer topical and was only half remembered, the effectiveness of any parody of it was largely destroyed.10

In an equally negative vein, Legouis says:

If we consider that two of the satires are addressed to an imaginary painter whose pencil they pretend to direct, we shall wonder at the small number of full-length portraits. When we think that Marvell is going to make a character sit for him he passes on at once to the story of his life, of his deeds. The physical description is often picturesque but the moral one remains summary.11

While these are honest and partially just criticisms, they can be answered in several ways. In the first place, "Last Instructions" *is* a parody, and it can be effective only if it follows Waller's poem closely enough to be recognized as a parody. A justification for Marvell's 514-line abandonment of his painter, then, lies in the very simple fact that in his much shorter 336-line poem Waller abandons his painter between lines 65 and 287. Waller uses the patron-painter situation to establish the necessary exposition and then resorts to descriptive narration to render the account of the Duke of York's naval victory. Marvell does essentially the same thing with respect to both of the battles his poem treats. That "Last Instructions" has become a less effective parody as the details of Waller's poem have faded is hardly a debatable statement, but such a criticism might be leveled at any parody. No parody can be fully appreciated unless its reader is acquainted with the prototype.

With respect to the comments that Marvell fails to take advantage of his frame and that he offers too few sustained portraits, perhaps precisely the opposite is the case in both instances. He does use the frame to advantage, and he does provide enough full portraits. A poem consisting of eighty-four fully drawn portraits would be unmanageable and incalculably boring, even if well executed. Rather than attempting anything so foolhardy, Marvell uses only as many sustained portraits near the beginning and ending of the satire as the instructions-to-a-painter frame demands. In the middle of the poem, then, he uses the frame to great advantage in that the patron persona's monologue allows Marvell to cover a vast array of material while the painter rests, a situation that is neither unnatural nor distracting. The persona has a legitimate opportunity to ramble at will. Further, in a sense, the middle portion of the poem does present sustained portraits, not of individuals, but of composites of Commons, the court, and the navy. These bodies were composed of insignificant as well as significant persons and were marked by small as well as great vices. That the persona introduces these people in a rapid-fire, seemingly orderless fashion is entirely consistent with the tenor of the events he is describing. Surely the English did not present a very orderly picture at Chatham Harbor. Thus, whether or not the form of the poem is suggested by its content, certainly the form is wholly consonant with the content. The rhetorical shifts, the vast quantity of subjects—always moving, many faceless, and many faces without character—are qualities which, while perhaps temporarily distracting and suggestive of poor craftsmanship, are nonetheless perfectly compatible with the big, burlesqued battle motif that orders the long middle section of the poem and are justified by the advice-to-a-painter frame.

The epilogue, "To the King," which mirrors a similar appendage in Waller's poem, approaches Marvell's lyrics in control and craftsmanship. It gains consistent focus from a series of tight analogies proclaiming Charles's greatness—"And you, *Great Sir*, that with him Empire share, / Sun of our World, as he the Charles is there" (ll. 955–56)—and analogies establishing the insidious destructiveness of Charles's courtiers:

> Not so does Rust insinuating wear,
> Nor Powder so the vaulted Bastion tear;
> Nor Earthquake so an hollow Isle overwhelm,
> As scratching *Courtiers* undermine a *Realm*.
> (ll. 975–78)

The crisp analogies and a few balanced couplets (rare in Marvell's decasyllabic satires), such as "(But *Ceres* Corn, and *Flora* is the Spring, / *Bacchus* is Wine, the Country is the *King*)" (ll. 973–74), surely indicate that Marvell was in full command of his poetic powers when he wrote "Last Instructions"; and they reinforce the supposition that much that appears formless and artless in the poem is the poet's deliberate attempt to recreate in satiric verse the confusion of a government working at cross purposes, as the Restoration government so often did. Regardless of Marvell's intentions, about which we can only conjecture, "Last Instructions" is a big poem treating what for Marvell and Restoration England, especially the opposition, were big matters. The great number of subjects and the apparent lack of system in their presentation are details contributing to the poem's most striking quality and perhaps its greatest virtue, its vastness.

The total effect of "Last Instructions" can be underscored dramatically by comparing it briefly with Marvell's other painter poem, "Further Advice to a Painter" (1670). Operating with the same instructions frame but on a markedly smaller scale (it has only sixty-four lines), "Further Advice" is flawless where critical opinion has judged "Last Instructions" flawed. In it the patron persona does not desert his painter; the portraits, though all composites, are small in dimension and proceed in an orderly fashion; the entire discourse is a dramatic monologue with no confusion as to speaker or audience; and the total number of subjects is limited. Yet, precisely for all of these reasons, because it is so obviously controlled in form and subject and because it contains none of the "flaws" found in "Last Instructions," "Further Advice" lacks the tremendous scope and satiric vigor that characterize the longer poem, and by comparison it is dull and static. Possibly the most dynamic scene in "Further Advice" is the one which describes the attack on Sir John Coventry:

> Draw me a Champion mounted on his steed,
> And after him a brave Bregade of Hors
> Arm'd at all points ready to reinforce
> The body of foot that was to have the van
> In this Assault upon a single man.
>
> (ll. 40–44)

These lines compare very unfavorably with the kind of passage from "Last Instructions" that Legouis and Sutherland would find most objectionable:

> *Carteret* the rich did the Accomptants guide,
> And in ill *English* all the World defy'd.
> The *Papists*, but of those the House had none:
> Else *Talbot* offer'd to have led them on.
> Bold *Duncombe* next, of the Projectors chief:
> And old *Fitz-Harding* of the Eaters Beef.
> Late and disorder'd out the Drinkers drew;
> Scarce them their Leaders, they their Leaders knew.
>
> (ll. 203–10)

Although this passage is no better than mediocre in relation to the finest passages in "Last Instructions," its rapid pace, emphatic force, masculine vigor, and punning wit make it rhetorically interesting. Like the lines from "Further Advice," these describe a prelude to battle; but the two passages offer few other similarities.

The instructions-to-a-painter frame, designed by Waller to proffer praise, is used by Marvell in "Last Instructions" (and "Further Advice") for satiric comment. In "The Loyall Scot" (1669), on the other hand, Marvell, basing his parody on John Cleveland's scathing denunciation of the Scots, "The Rebel Scot" (1644), praises the heroics of a Scottish-born officer named Archibald Douglas who died for the English cause at Chatham Harbor, and produces a moderate, didactic poem that, outside its frame context, is not explicitly satiric.[12] The frame serves only as a vehicle in the painter poems, but in "The Loyall Scot" the satire evolves from and is dependent upon the frame. For the most part, the poem is explicitly satiric only because its praise of Captain Douglas and its plea for rationality are articulated by the Scot-hating Cleveland persona; the same words voiced by Marvell would not be satiric because of his well-known pro-Scots feelings. Outside the Cleveland frame the poem is implicitly satiric, but only subtly so and only in the broad sense that had England's government been in proper command of itself, Douglas' death at Chatham Harbor would not have been necessary.

The first fourteen lines of the poem establish the frame. Cleveland's shade is selected by his heavenly peers to deliver the welcoming address to Douglas' shade, which has arrived from the sunken ship in Chatham Harbor. In these lines Marvell justifies Cleveland's selection for the honor and neatly condemns the anti-Scots sentiments featured in Cleveland's original "Rebel Scot":

> Much had hee Cur'd the Humor of his vein:
> Hee Judg'd more Clearly now and saw more plain.
> For those soft Airs had temper'd every thought,
> And of wise Lethe hee had took a draught.
>   Abruptly he began disguising art,
>   As of his Satyr this had been a part.
>   (ll. 9–14)

At this point the Cleveland persona takes over and begins his two-part address. Both the mechanics of the transition to a new voice and its effect are clever and should discourage charges of artlessness. The transition from the poet's voice to the Cleveland persona's is indicated graphically by indentation and also by the intelligence of line 13; nothing in the persona's initial words, however, indicates that a shift in voice has occurred, and the monologue seems to begin in the middle of nowhere:

> Not so brave Douglass, on whose Lovely Chin
> The Early down but newly did begin,
> And modest beauty yet his sex did vail,
> Whilst Envious virgins hope hee is a Male.
>   (ll. 15–18)

Marvell's design here, as lines 13 and 14 indicate, is not to write a satire but to rewrite Cleveland's, to add his own version of Cleveland's monologue to "The Rebel Scot" as an integral part of that poem so that, after vehemently denouncing Scotland, he concludes:

> A Voider for the nonce!
> I wrong the Devill, should I picke the bones.
> That dish is his: for when the Scots decease,
> Hell like their Nation feeds on Barnacles.
> A Scot, when from the Gallow-Tree got loose,
> Drops into *Styx* and turnes a Soland-Goose.[13]

"The Rebel Scot" will suddenly reverse position with "Not so brave Douglass" and proceed systematically to recant all of the anti-Scot expression of its first 126 lines. Thus, rather than having to attack and refute Cleveland's popular poem, Marvell simply lets Cleveland destroy it himself.

The recantation is in two rhetorical parts. Up to line 62 the persona narrates the heroic death of Douglas on the burning ship and establishes his matchless virtues, which contrast with the diseased beastliness of Scotsmen as they are presented in "The Rebel Scot." With the existence of superior Scots thus before his audience, the Cleveland persona can shift to persuasive exposition at line 63 and appeal to both reason and emotion in an effort to rid the Scots and English of their reciprocal hatred and to unite them. The final lines of the monologue, addressed directly to Douglas, refocus attention on the frame and totally obliterate "The Rebel Scot" sentiments as the Cleveland persona says, "My former satyr for this verse forget" (l. 276). The dramatic situation is concluded at this point, and it remains only for Marvell, in his own voice, to report Douglas' response to the welcome:

> Here Douglas smileing said hee did Intend
> After such Frankness shown to bee his friend,
> Forwarn'd him therefore lest in time he were
> Metemsicosd to some Scotch Presbyter.
> (ll. 282–85)

These two couplets unite the Scots and the English.

The two-part monologue structure of "The Loyall Scot" is Marvell's response to a similar structure in the parodied poem and illustrates his ability to make the most of the advantages afforded by a frame. Because Cleveland's poem first makes every effort to discredit the Scots and then expresses a plea for their ostracism, Marvell's poem must first praise the Scots and then plead for Scottish-English unity. In this context the sustaining images of the Cleveland poem must be negated by the major images of Marvell's poem. Just as the first part of Cleveland's poem is unified by repeated images of beasts—"A *Scot* within a beast is no disguise" (l. 36), by images of dishonor—"Unmask them well;

their honours and estate, / As well as conscience, are sophisticate"
(ll. 105–106), and images of disease—"Scotland's a Nation Epidem-
icall" (l. 70), the Douglas section of Marvell's poem is unified by
repeated images of beauty, honor, and wholesome purity. Most obvious are the images of beauty that make Douglas a "modest beauty"
(l. 17) "on whose Lovely Chin / The Early down but newly did begin" (ll. 15–16) and the images of honor that make him a "valiant
Scott" (l. 62). Perhaps more significant structurally, however, are the
images of fire which provide the element of purification and which, in
addition, introduce the concept of melding which then becomes the
central image in the second part of the persona's discourse. The first
hint of the concept occurs in a water rather than in a fire context: "Oft
as hee in Chill Eske or Seyne by night / Hardned and Cool'd those
limbs soe soft, soe white" (ll. 21–22). Despite the total absence of fire
here, "Hardned and Cool'd" elicits a picture of fire-heated metal tempering into perfect form. That young Douglas' limbs must be shaped
by "Chill Eske or Seyne" rather than by fire is dictated by the image
of generation by water in the final line of Cleveland's poem: "A Scot,
when from the Gallow-Tree got loose, / Drops into *Styx*, and turns a
Soland-Goose." Thus, the opening phrase of the persona's monologue
in Marvell's poem—"Not so brave Douglas" (l. 15)—is intended to
negate the image of the solan goose by replacing it with one of beautiful, noble Scottish youth. Considerably more overt fire imagery appears in line 26, "That flyst loves fires reserv'd for other flame?" and
such imagery becomes concentrated as Douglas' death on the burning
deck is described. Particularly significant is the fact that the fire imagery continues to suggest the tempering process, largely because fire
images continue to appear in conjunction with images of form. Lines
45–46, for example, reinforce the relationship between fire and per-
fected form: "His shape Exact which the bright flames enfold / Like
the sun's Statue stands of burnisht Gold." Similarly, in line 52 the
flames cause "his Altered form and sodred Limbs to Melt," and the
molten metal slides into the English harbor where symbolically it alloys
Scotland and England. The Douglas section ends at this point (l. 62),
but images of flame and molten metal continue to appear; hence, these
images become a major link between the two sections of the discourse.
Also, these images continue to reinforce the unity concept which, re-
iterated in several different metaphorical contexts, sustains the second
part. Perhaps the most effective image of unity, and one that utilizes
molten metal, occurs in lines 71–74:

> Mixt in Corinthian Mettall at thy Flame
> Our nations Melting thy Colossus Frame,
> Shall fix a foot on either neighbouring Shore
> And Joyn those Lands that seemed to part before.

By using "The Rebel Scot" and his frame situation to full advantage and by manipulating images, Marvell squelches the bitter anti-Scots sentiments of the parodied poem and unifies his own poem as well.

"A Dialogue Between the Two Horses" (1675), as Professor Sutherland notes in one of the few published commentaries on the poem, combines two traditional satiric vehicles, dialogue and beast fable, and it develops an original comic effect because of the fact that the beasts are only statues of beasts.[14] Because the poem consists of a formally defined frame introduction and conclusion plus direct dialogue in the dramatic situation, there is little possibility of confusion as to speaker or unexpected and distracting rhetorical shifts. Special attention must be devoted to the frame, however, and especially to the final eight lines which Margoliouth believes to have been added after manuscript copies were already in circulation.[15]

"A Dialogue Between the Two Horses" is a follow-up satire to two written slightly earlier, "The Statue in Stocks-Market" and "The Statue at Charing Cross," the former prompted by the equestrian statue of Charles II and the latter by a similar statue of Charles I, both erected in London during Charles II's reign. The third poem in the series brings the two statue horses together for a consideration of the vices and failings of their respective masters. The poet's ostensible task in the frame, both in the introduction and in part of the conclusion, is to convince his audience of the credibility of the framed dramatic situation; but Marvell also takes advantage of the frame to render some satiric comment in his own voice. He makes his talking statues credible by providing examples of similar phenomena and, in the process, he takes some shots at English Catholics. He first cites examples from pagan lore, then moves directly to examples from Catholic tradition; we can suppose that he expected the significance of proximity to be noted. He says:

> All Popish beleivers think something divine,
> When Images speak, possesses the shrine:
> But they that faith Catholick ne're understood,
> When Shrines give Answers, say a knave's in the Roode;
> Those Idolls ne're speak, but the miracle's done
> By the Devill, a Priest, a Fryar, or Nun.
> If the Roman Church, good Christians, oblige yee
> To beleive men and beasts have spoke in effigie,

> Why should wee not credit the publique discourses
> Of a Dialogue lately between the two Horses?
>
> (ll. 15–24)

It is also in the frame, its conclusion, that the one couplet that surpasses everything else in Marvell's satires as an unqualified expression of contempt for the Stuart monarchy appears: "But I should have told you, before the Jades parted, / Both Gallopt to Whitehall and there Horribly farted" (ll. 167–68).

Regardless of Margoliouth's feeling that the final eight lines of the frame were added after the rest of the poem had already appeared, both the frame and the total satire can assume full dimension only if these lines are read as part of the poem. In a context of the entire poem, the final lines in no way seem tacked on. A speech motif begins to develop in the first couplet of the frame ("Wee read in profane and Sacred records / Of Beasts that have uttered Articulate words"), and evidence of the motif appears in nearly every couplet thereafter of both the introduction and conclusion through line 180.[16] In addition, the framed dramatic situation is a dialogue consisting primarily of criticisms of England's government, her Stuart monarchy in particular, and of predictions of the dismantling of that monarchy. At one point in the dialogue, Charing, the first Charles's horse, judiciously cautions his fellow statue against seditious speech:

> Enough, dear Brother, for tho' we have reason,
> Yet truth many times being punisht for Treason,
> We ought to be wary and Bridle our Tongue;
> Bold speaking hath done both man and beast wrong.
>
> (ll. 97–100)

Thus, the two concepts of rebellious speech and official suppression of free speech are obvious, if perhaps somewhat unstable, components of the poem's meaning before they finally crystalize in the appended section. The last six lines before the appended portion read:

> Tho' Tyrants make Laws which they strictly proclaim
> To conceal their own crimes and cover their shame,
> Yet the beasts of the field or the stones in the wall
> Will publish their faults and prophesy their fall.
> When they take from the people the freedome of words,
> They teach them the Sooner to fall to their Swords.
>
> (ll. 175–80)

Then following these heavily didactic lines is the poet's reasoned appeal to Charles to rescind his order closing the coffee houses:

> Let the Citty drink Coffee and Quietly groan
> They that Conquered the Father won't be slaves to the Son:

'Tis wine and Strong drink makes tumults increase;
Chocolet Tea and Coffee are liquors of peace.
No Quarrells or oathes amongst those that drink 'um;
Tis Bacchus and the Brewer swear Dam 'um and sink 'um.
Then, Charles, thy edict against Coffee recall;
Theres ten times more Treason in Brandy and ale.

(ll. 181–88)

Read in its entirety and with proper attention to the frame, "A Dialogue Between the Two Horses" is a closely knit satire that integrates frame and dramatic situation exceptionally well. The statues' rather aimless and unsystematic criticisms of King and court in the dialogue, ranging from family relationships to petty governmental bribery to gross monarchial tyranny, though significant satiric points in themselves, serve primarily to illustrate the frame statement that an unhappy people will object. Marvell's message to Charles is that words are less painful than swords. The final eight lines concretize the entire poem and, despite the range of issues covered in the dialogue, focus attention on a single issue. The satirist shows the King one small way in which he can stem the tide of resentment increasingly rising against him in the years following the first glory of the Restoration.

Close reading of these three satires, with particular attention to the functions and effects of their frame devices, reveals them to be more skillfully constructed than is commonly supposed. Because Marvell's frame techniques permit him to use multiple voices and multiple modes of discourse, they give him a degree of freedom from the rigid demands of internal consistency. Thus, the rhetorical flaws that appear, especially in "Last Instructions," are not particularly objectionable, not only because they are justified in terms of their formal verse satire antecedents, but also because the instructions-to-a-painter frame allows the poet this luxury. Further, the rhetorical flaws, like the elliptical portraits and the scatter-shot presentation, contribute to the poet's effort to suit form to subject. "The Loyall Scot" derives virtually its entire satiric thrust from its frame and cannot be read rewardingly unless this is taken into account and unless the reader is intimately familiar with Cleveland's "Rebel Scot." Similarly, and finally, "A Dialogue Between the Two Horses," too, can be read properly only with close attention to the frame. The unordered discourse of the statue personae, their "random babbling," becomes ordered and meaningful when it is recognized to be controlled by the speech motif advanced in the frame.

NOTES

1 "Andrew Marvell," *Selected Essays* (New York: Harcourt, Brace, 1950), 260.

2 The attribution problem is severe in Marvell's case. His major editor, H. M. Margoliouth, regards eleven of the satires variously attributed to Marvell as likely to be his: "Clarindon's House-Warming," "Upon His House," "Upon His Grand-Children," "The Last Instructions to a Painter," "Further Advice to a Painter," "The Loyall Scott," "*Bludius et Corona*," "*Scaevola Scoto-Brittannus*," "The Statue in Stocks-Market." "The Statue at Charing Cross," and "A Dialogue Between the Two Horses." See "Commentary" in *The Poems and Letters of Andrew Marvell*, 2nd ed. (Oxford: Clarendon Press, 1952), I, 213, 263, *passim*. In his recent edition of the poems, George deF. Lord, who expresses more faith in the Bodleian MS. volume (Eng. poet. d. 49) than Margoliouth, rejects "Upon His House," "Upon His Grand-Children," "Further Advice to a Painter," "A Dialogue Between the Two Horses," and "*Scaevola Scoto-Brittannus*," but adds to the canon "The Vows," "Upon the Citye's Going in a Body to Whitehall," "The Second Advice to a Painter," and "The Third Advice to a Painter." See "Introduction" to *Andrew Marvell: Complete Poetry* (New York: Random, 1968), xxx–xxxii. At the risk of error, the present study will, like the vast majority of Marvell studies since the publication of Margoliouth's first edition in 1927, accept Professor Margoliouth's authority and assume with him on the basis of internal evidence that "A Dialogue Between the Two Horses" is Marvell's. All quotations of Marvell's verse will be drawn from Margoliouth's second edition.

3 See Mary Tom Osborne, *Advice-to-a-Painter Poems* (Austin: Univ. of Texas Press, 1949), a finding list.

4 Exceptions to this reaction are those of Earl Miner, "The 'Poetic Picture, Painted Poetry' of *The Last Instructions to a Painter*," *MP* 63 (May 1966), 288–94, who, in an article devoted to an examination of the instructions genre, concedes "careful artistry and planning" to the poem (294); George deF. Lord, "Two New Poems by Marvell?" *Bulletin of the New York Public Library* 62 (1958), 551–70; and Ephim Fogel, "Salmons in Both, or Some Caveats for Canonical Scholars," *Bulletin* 63 (1959), 223–36. The latter two are attribution studies that use Marvell's painter techniques as a basis for establishing authorship of other painter poems.

5 *Destiny His Choice: The Loyalism of Andrew Marvell* (Cambridge, Eng.: Cambridge Univ. Press, 1968), 157.

6 *Andrew Marvell: Poet, Puritan, Patriot*, 2nd ed. (Oxford: Clarendon Press, 1968), 169.

7 "A Note on the Satirical Poetry of Andrew Marvell," *PQ* 45 (Jan. 1966), 47.

8 *Andrew Marvell: Poet, Puritan, Patriot*, 170.

9 "The Structural Design of Formal Verse Satire," *PQ* 21 (Oct. 1942), 372–73.

10 "A Note on the Satirical Poetry of Andrew Marvell," 51.

11 *Andrew Marvell: Poet, Puritan, Patriot*, 169.

12 Early editions of "The Loyall Scot" carry nearly 150 lines that both Margoliouth and Lord regard as spurious. Margoliouth's text carries the spurious lines, but in reduced type; his text also carries the eight-line English version of "*Bludius et Corona*" as a part of "The Loyall Scot." Because considerable doubt exists as to the propriety of the inclusion of these eight lines in the poem, neither they nor the spurious lines are here considered part of "The Loyall Scot"; line references, however, are to the text as it appears in Margoliouth.

13 Brian Morris and Eleanor Withington, eds., *The Poems of John Cleveland* (Oxford: Clarendon Press, 1967), ll. 121–26. Subsequent "Rebel Scot" quotations are from this source.

14 "A Note on the Satirical Poetry of Andrew Marvell," 51.

15 See Margoliouth, 317–18.

16 The following speech-related words all appear in the poem's frame, not in-

cluding the appended lines: (l. 2) "uttered," "Articulate," "words"; (l. 3) "Mag-pyes," "Parratts," "cry"; (l. 4) "talke"; (l. 5) "windpipe," "Lungs"; (l. 6) "spoken," "Tongues"; (l. 7) "tells," "story"; (l. 8) "Bellow'd"; (l. 9) "tell"; (l. 10) "roar"; (l. 11) "spoke"; (l. 12) "reprov'd"; (l. 13) "Delphos"; (l. 14) "Questions," "oracular," "Answers"; (l. 16) "speake"; (l. 18) "Answers," "say"; (l. 19) "speake"; (l. 22) "spoke," "effigie"; (l. 23) "discourses"; (l. 24) "Dia-logue"; (l. 26) "told," "truths"; (l. 30) "agreed"; (l. 33) "Salutes"; (l. 34) "dis-coursed," "disputes"; (l. 163) "Speech"; (l. 164) "presage"; (l. 165) "swear"; (l. 166) "declare"; (l. 167) "told"; (l. 169) "portended"; (l. 170) "spoken"; (l. 171) "Delphick," "oracular," "speeches"; (l. 172) "say"; (l. 173) "words"; (l. 174) "Prophecy"; (l. 175) "proclaim"; (l. 178) "prophesy"; (l. 179) "words."

Eastern Illinois University

CHARLES SCRUGGS

"SWEETNESS AND LIGHT": THE BASIS OF SWIFT'S VIEWS ON ART AND CRITICISM

Unlike most Augustans, Jonathan Swift distrusted literary criticism and critical terminology, and thus some recent scholars have felt that he contributed almost nothing to the critical thinking of his age. Compared with the incisive documents of Pope and Addison, J. W. H. Atkins says, Swift's critical writings are "somewhat disappointing," and he "has little to offer in the way of constructive theories or appreciations."[1] Harold D. Kelling voices the same opinion: "only a very thin *Ars Poetica* could be collected from his pronouncements."[2] Kelling's remark, however, should be revised to read "overt pronouncements," for the bee-spider episode in *The Battel of the Books* is one of the most exciting aesthetic statements made in the eighteenth century. Curiously enough, the great critical works on matters of aesthetics— *The Mirror and the Lamp* (M. H. Abrams) and *From Classic to Romantic* (W. J. Bate), for instance—have chosen to ignore it. Perhaps the reason is that this beast fable (or "le mythe animal," as Pons calls it) is more suggestive than analytical. Perhaps another reason is that Swift used the allegory to discuss literature in general and not specifically imaginative literature. Still the utterances of the bee and the spider's retort *do* reveal aesthetic principles which are quite consistent with other opinions expressed in Swift's letters, prose satires, essays, and poetry. Moreover, we can construct a substantial *Ars Poetica*, together with certain implications for the function of criticism, from this famous allegory and from observations made elsewhere in the Swiftian canon.

My approach to Swift's aesthetic principles is quite simple. I wish to prove that he belongs to the tradition of Renaissance-Augustan humanism which, in the words of W. J. Bate, "seeks to find a significance in art which transcends technical criticism."[3] For Swift, as for Sir Philip Sidney, the "end of all earthly learning" is "vertuous action."[4] Art moves us to such action because it delights as it instructs. The bee in *The Battel of the Books* is Swift's primary metaphor for art. It also conditions his view of the literary artist and the response of the reader.

In *The Battel of the Books*, the bee-spider episode interrupts the preparation for battle between the Ancients and Moderns, and, as Aesop observes, it at once defines the source and nature of their literary disagreements. The spider, like the Moderns, "Spins and Spits wholly from himself, and scorns to own any Obligation or Assistance from without."[5] He considers himself to be a more authentic creator than the bee, because the bee is dependent upon nature for the materials of his art. He tells the bee,

What art thou, but a Vagabond without House or Home, without Stock or Inheritance; Born to no Possession of your own, but a Pair of Wings and a Drone-Pipe. Your Livelihood is a universal Plunder upon Nature; a Freebooter over Fields and Gardens; and for the sake of Stealing, will rob a Nettle as readily as a Violet.   (231)

What the spider never learns is that the results of such thefts are honey and wax, or rather, sweetness and light. Also, the true artist can turn nettles into violets. As a principle of art (and especially the satiric art), this ability of the artist to transmute his materials means that nettles as well as flowers may be used as grist for the artistic mill. Like Aristotle and John Keats, Swift was excited by the idea that art can change something negative into something positive, and many of the remarks in his letters, though sometimes contradicted by his own writings, seem to substantiate this idea. In a letter to Pope in 1716, he talked of bad writers as "Tools in my opinion as necessary for a good writer, as pen, ink, and paper."[6] Later in 1725 he rallied Pope about the underground passage to his garden: "I have been long told by Mr. Ford of your great Atchivements [sic] in building and planting and especially of your Subterranean Passage to your Garden whereby you turn a blunder into a beauty which is a Piece of Ars Poetica."[7]

Turning "a blunder into a beauty" belongs to a classical conception of art, but the idea is often qualified by those eighteenth-century critics devoted to literary decorum. Addison, for instance, would persuade us that a disgusting subject like a dunghill can please if it is dressed up "in an apt description!"[8] That is to say, the dunghill gives us pleasure only "if the image be represented to our minds by suitable expressions."

For Addison, "suitable expressions" are elegant, whereas for Swift, "suitable expressions" are less a matter of literary propriety than a matter of moral propriety; a vulgar word like "s———" at the end of *Cassinus and Peter* reveals the vulgarity and moral danger in man's illusions about women and love.

Swift was careful to point out that transmuting something into art does not change its essence or destroy its truth. The bee may visit "all the Flowers and Blossoms of the Field and the Garden," but his flights leave no "Injury to their Beauty, their Smell, or their Taste." Or to translate the bee's remarks into aesthetic terms:

> For, though the Muse delights in Fiction,
> She ne'er inspires against Conviction.
> *(To Dr. Delany*, ll. 105–106)

> Unjustly Poets we asperse;
> Truth shines the brighter, clad in verse;
> And all the Fictions they pursue
> Do but insinuate what is true.
> *(To Stella*, ll. 57–60)

The bee, then, is a craftsman whose product is a mirror of reality, but of a reality transfigured and made more perfect by his craft. In this light, Swift reminds us of Sidney's *Apologie For Poetrie* and the golden world which the imitation of nature can create.

Swift's metaphorical bee comes into clearer focus when compared with the respective bees of Sir William Temple and Alexander Gerard. Swift may have agreed with many of Temple's aesthetic beliefs, but he separated himself from his patron on one important issue. For instance, in *Of Poetry* Temple's bees stress the saccharine side of art. It is true they "work up their Cells with Admirable Art," yet they also "extract their Honey . . . and sever it from the Wax . . . ."[9] No doubt Temple's Epicureanism is responsible for such severing; in this essay he sees poetry as keeping us "humor'd a little," until life's hardships are over. On the other hand, an "original genius" critic like Alexander Gerard can use the bee to express a subjective view of art. In *An Essay on Genius* (1774), he illustrates the spontaneous response of the artistic imagination by comparing it to the actions of a bee:

As the bee extracts from such flowers as can supply them juices which are proper to be converted into honey . . . so true genius discovers at once the ideas which are conducive to its purpose, without at all thinking of such as are unnecessary or would obstruct it.[10]

Gerard's insect, we notice, looks inward ("ideas" . . . "thinking"). That of Swift first looks outward toward the fields and gardens and then inward toward the imagination; he is a cosmopolitan creature as opposed to an insular one. Also, as a symbol of artistic excellence, he suggests a point of view beyond the pettiness of topical quarrels about theories of art. Swift may have felt that antiquity produced greater artists than had his modern age, but he never would have denied the possibility of the present and future generations matching the past.[11] The reason the brunt of mock-heroic satire falls upon the Moderns (*The Battel of the Books*) is that the Moderns claim to have equaled or surpassed the Ancients, whereas in reality they have not done so. It is the Modern author, as "miles gloriosus," whom Swift attacks and not the modern author per se.

When the spider criticizes the bee as a homeless vagabond, the bee, instead of offering a rebuttal, translates the spider's criticism into other terms. The bee does not see his travels as an indication of poverty but rather as the cause of his artistic wealth. His opulence is not dependent upon the acquisition of things; all he claims for his own are his "Wings and . . . Voice" (231). Such a statement is only a half-truth, because it implies that the talent which the artist brings to his materials is minimal. As we shall see, Swift never separated the artist's talent from the material he uses. One aspect of his talent is his ability to select his material, in short, his "Flights" (231).

Swift's correspondence with John Gay often explains, indirectly, what he meant by the word "Flights." Time and again Swift asked Gay to produce more plays and fables. "I wonder you will doubt of your genius," he mildly rebuked Gay:

The world is wider to a Poet than to any other Man, and new follyes and Vices will never be wanting any more than new fashions. Je Donne au diable the wrong Notion that Matter is exhausted. For as Poets in their Greek Name are called Creators, so in one circumstance they resemble the great Creator by having an infinity of Space to work in.[12]

The man of genius, then, is more sensitive to the sources of art than are other men, for his knowledge of the world enlarges his area of artistic research; like the bee, he has "an infinity of Space to work in." Unlike a Romantic poet, he is less sensitive to the complexities of feeling in the individual than to the varieties of subject matter in nature.

In his artistic advice to his friends, Swift stressed the importance of new material for the creation of original works of art. He chastised Gay for merely rewriting *The Beggar's Opera* in his new plays, *Polly* and *Achilles*, and he lamented Pope's restriction of his genius to translations when he should be writing poetry.[13] Earlier in his life, when Swift was on speaking terms with Ambrose Philips, he wrote the pastoral poet traveling in foreign lands and encouraged him to lay in "new Stocks to revive [his] Poetical Reputation."[14]

But diversity for its own sake is useless unless the subjects chosen have intrinsic merit. "I take that to be a part of the Honesty of Poets," confessed a youthful Swift to his cousin Thomas, "that they can not write well except they think the subject deserves it."[15] And his opinion did not change as he grew older. For instance, in 1732, Swift expressed a preference for John Milton over the eighteenth-century poet James Thomson; the preference reflected this same concern for a worthy subject. Thomson's *Seasons* are interesting, Swift wrote Charles Wogan, but "they are all Description, and nothing is doing, whereas Milton engages me in Actions of the highest Importance . . . ."[16] Thus it is the moral importance of subject matter, however diversified when embodied in separate artistic constructs, that is the essential ingredient of the work of art. And appropriately, an artist's "Flights" involve an imagination that can see beyond itself.

After an artist has selected his subject, how does he handle his material and what is the result of his efforts? Swift avoided a definitive treatment of these issues, but in his *Proposal for Correcting the English Tongue*, he does say that a true genius is "one, who upon a deserving Subject, is able to open new Scenes, and discover a Vein of true and noble Thinking, which never entered into any Imagination before."[17] In short, originality ("new Scenes") must be consistent with Truth ("true . . . Thinking") just as sweetness must not conflict with light. Also, the effect of the art object should give the reader pleasure through the novelty of the experience ("never entered into any Imagination before"), but the novelty itself must convey truth. That is, art should force readers to look at old subjects in new ways or to recognize new subjects in terms of traditional (true) values.

The idea of genius consists of an interrelationship between subject matter and artist (flowers and bee); neither artist nor material asserts a primacy over the other. In this respect, Swift's definition of genius is similar to Pope's definition of true wit (". . . Nature to advantage dressed / What oft was thought, but ne'er so well expressed") if we remember that "what oft was thought" does not suggest banal subject matter and that "ne'er so well expressed" means more than a felicitous style. It means expression which transmutes subject matter so that nature appears in her best light or, as Swift puts it, so that "Truth shines the brighter." Although Samuel Johnson was wrong in claiming that Pope "reduces it [wit] from strength of thought to happiness of language," Johnson's redefinition of the term is in line with the mainstream

of classical aesthetic thinking: "If by a more noble and more adequate
conception that be considered as Wit which is at once natural and new,
that which though not obvious is, upon its first production, acknowledged to be just . . . that, which he that never found it, wonders how he
missed."[18] Both Johnson and Pope described wit as the poet's ability
to create an art object which is natural (faithful to nature) but new
(that is, one which looks at the normal in a way that is novel but does
not distort the truth). Swift no doubt would have applauded these defi-
nitions; they also defined his conception of true genius.

What is striking about Swift's aesthetic attitudes is the enormous
freedom they give the artist. First, he has an unlimited space in which
to search for his materials and, second, he is encouraged to discover
new insights in the materials he finds. In these two ways, Swift defined the artist as a creator. We often think of Swift as a highly controlled craftsman, and it is surprising to discover his pleas for artistic
inspiration and imaginative flights. In his *Ode to Congreve*, he tells the
playwright:

> Beat not the dirty paths where vulgar feet have trod,
> But give the vigorous fancy room.
>
> (ll. 205–206)

And in a letter to his cousin Thomas, Swift spoke of his own poetic
process: "I do not believe my self to be a laboriously dry writer because if the fitt comes not immediatly I never heed it but think of something else . . . ."[19] Again, a young Swift was expressing these views, but
the views did not change as he grew older. Even late in his life, Swift
could remark to Lord Orrery: "I believe the first thoughts on a Subject
that occurs to a Poets imagination are usually the most natural."[20]

But sometimes the poetic fit does not come; sometimes a fertile
thought turns out to be a bubble. As he said to Gay, still trying to
convince his friend to write a new play or poem:

Scheams [sic] are perfectly accidental; some will appear barren of hints & matter,
but prove to be fruitfull; and others the contrary. And what you say is past doubt,
that every one can best find hints for himself; though it is possible, that sometimes a friend may give you a lucky one just suited to your own imagination.[21]

Good art is not simply a question of inspired genius working upon a
worthy subject. The subject must also be congenial to the artist's temperament. What is suited to one man's genius may not be suited to another's. In other words, the artist must have self-awareness: he must
know the limits of his talent; he must know what subjects he can safely
and successfully handle. In *Epistle to a Lady*, Swift comments upon the

limits of his own talent. The sublime style is out of his range, he tells
the lady who wishes him to praise her in heroic strains:

> Shou'd I lofty Numbers chuse,
> E'er I reach'd Parnassus Top
> I shou'd burst, and bursting drop.
> (ll. 260–62)

Swift would never play the fool by dabbling in the sublime, but he
would use such overreachers as material for his own comic art.

In summary, Swift encouraged originality and diversity in art, but
the originality and diversity were controlled by long thought on a worthy
subject. What is worthy, of course, depends in part upon sheer chance
and in part upon the artist's ability to choose a subject which does not
transcend the bounds of his self-imposed limits. However, to a man of
genius the world is wide, and no one loved its expansiveness more than
Swift. "I am against Monopolyes [in wit]," he told Pope.[22] In a letter
to Gay, he enthusiastically praised the plays and poems of his friends
at his own expense: "The Beggers Opera hath knockt down Gulliver.
I hope to see Popes Dullness knock down the Beggers Opera . . . ."[23]
Only fresh wits and original works of art could make possible a flour-
ishing literary scene. "I hate to have any new Witts rise," he told Stella
in his journal, "but when they do rise I would encourage them . . . ."[24]

When Matthew Arnold borrowed Swift's phrase (via Horace),
"sweetness and light," in *Culture and Anarchy*, he was inadvertently
summing up what Swift considered to be the best qualities in a critical
point of view—candor and taste. Both men wished to see the literary
object as it really is, to react to it in their reading with taste, and to
present it in their criticism with urbanity. In *Remarks upon Tindall's
"Rights of the Christian Church,"* Swift insists that if a critic cannot
give pleasure in the distribution of his critical wares, he must learn to
follow Horace's rule for poets: "Quae desperes tractata nitescere posse,
relingues."[25] (Abandon that which you cannot make attractive with
your touch.) To pile quotation upon quotation is not only dull reading
but uninformative, since pedantry in itself reflects a misunderstanding
of that which it attempts to explicate. Like art, criticism is organic: it
must be entertaining at the same time that it is instructive.

The orthodox opinion of Swift is that he hated all critics and criticism, but the truth is that Swift was less sceptical of criticism as a legitimate employment than he was aware of the difficulty of being a good
critic. His standards for criticism were rigorous: "to answer a Book
effectively," says the satirist in the "Apology" to the *Tale*, "requires

more Pains, and Skill, more Wit, Learning, and Judgment than were employ'd in the Writing it" (10). Also, the *Tale* proper provides two positive attitudes towards critics. First, it restores "Antient Learning from the Worms, and Graves, and Dust of Manuscripts" (93). Second, Swift ironically condemns a certain kind of critic because the avant-garde no longer holds him in esteem:

> By this Term [critic] was understood such Persons as invented or drew up Rules for themselves and the World, by observing which, a careful Reader might be able to pronounce upon the productions of the learned, form his Taste to a true Relish of the Sublime and the Admirable, and devide [sic] every Beauty of Matter or of Style from the Corruption that Apes it.   (92)

Unlike the Modern critic who enjoys wallowing in literary abuses, this critic observes corruptions only so that he may avoid them. Negative criticism is a necessary but not an enviable duty; it is a service performed only to distinguish "Beauty . . . from the Corruption that Apes it." In addition, the passage just quoted suggests that the rules drawn up by critics guide a reader's taste but by no means enslave it. Swift, apparently, would allow the "careful Reader" to come to grips with the aesthetic material. It is enough that the critic helps the reader to see clearly, that he educates those qualities needed to appreciate and evaluate good literature.

We must return to the "Apology" (*Tale*) to find the qualities Swift admired in a perceptive reader. Implicit in this defense against uncharitable critics are the criteria for making an accurate literary judgment. Those who criticize his work, the satirist says, "have neither Candor to suppose good Meanings, nor Palate to distinguish true Ones" (4–5). These two qualities, candor and taste, are repeated later in the "Apology" when Swift attacks William Wotton's *Observations upon The Tale of a Tub*. That gentleman's criticism of the *Tale*, observes Swift, "forces Interpretations which never once entered into the Writers' [sic] Head, nor will he is sure into that of any Reader of Tast [sic] and Candor" (12). Taste and candor in the reader are the counterparts to sweetness and light in the artist. For clarity of vision (light), the reader substitutes honesty of understanding; for urbanity (sweetness), the reader substitutes an acute perceptiveness. No doubt Swift believed the man of genius to be the only reader who has developed this sense of taste to its fullest. At least he recognized this authority when applied to his own work. "One thing, I confess, would still touch me to the quick," he said in a letter to Reverend Henry Jenney; "I mean, if any person of true genius would employ his pen against me."[26] Also, good taste appears to be a refinement upon common sense. It is not the sensitive, delicate perception of the late eighteenth-century aesthete but rather the educated, rational response of the gentleman.

It must be emphasized that honesty (candor) and common sense (or taste) are not separate qualities. The artist's knowledge is urbane; it is neither the bare fact (pedantry) nor the sugar-coated pill (the Romance). Similarly, both taste and candor are integrated elements of one faculty, man's literary judgment. Swift has given us two satirical portraits of literary artists who have violated his aesthetic code: the Grub street narrator of the *Tale* and Lemuel Gulliver. The former's devotion to Epicurean ethics (the famous digression on madness) leads to a view of art that is all sweetness and no light. "As Mankind is now disposed," he says at one point, "he receives much greater Advantage by being Diverted than Instructed" (124). To be sure, he boasts of kneading up "a Layer of Utile and a Layer of Dulce" throughout his treatise, but in this case instruction merely proves to man that diversion is the only good he can hope for. Lemuel Gulliver insists that his only concern in his *Travels* is the presentation of truth. In the first three voyages, when Gulliver speaks of "truth" he usually means the literal fact. Consequently, he says of his work: "I have been chiefly studious of Truth, without affecting any Ornaments of Learning, or of Style."[27] Gulliver claims to be an honest man who narrates a plain tale with candor.

In the fourth voyage (the author's life among the Houyhnhnms), Gulliver's concern for the literal truth takes on another dimension. He never loses his journalistic touch for reporting the factual situation, but now the plain facts have a moral impact on his own life. His encounter with the virtuous Houyhnhnms and the despicable Yahoos shocks him into recognizing human depravity as it exists in himself and in his fellow Europeans. At this point, his devotion to the literal truth acquires the tinge of moral enthusiasm. Swift's irony soon becomes apparent. Incensed by Yahoo duplicity and disguise, Gulliver declares that "Truth appeared so amiable to me, that I determined upon sacrificing every thing to it" (258). Critics have made much of Gulliver's single-mindedness as it affects his personality, but this passion for truth also explains the character as artist, the man who writes up his journeys for the sole purpose of educating mankind.

In the concluding chapter Gulliver discusses his aim in publishing his *Travels*. Repeating his interest in truth instead of ornament and his dislike of "strange improbable Tales," Gulliver goes on to tell his readers that the "principal Design was to inform, and not to amuse . . ." (291). Likewise, it does not seem to matter if people like his book as long as they reform their lives. As he says to cousin Simpson, "I wrote for their Amendment, and not their Approbation" (8). Such earnestness, of course, leads to Gulliver's angry disappointment with the public's reaction to his work:

> Instead of seeing a full Stop put to all Abuses and Corruptions, at least in this little Island, as I had Reason to expect: Behold, after above six Months Warning, I cannot learn that my Book hath produced one single Effect according to mine Intentions.   (6)

This indifference confirms Gulliver in his misanthropy. It again proves to him "that the Yahoos were a Species of Animals utterly incapable of Amendment by Precepts or Examples."[28]

The Grub Street writer's view of art provides a sharp contrast to that of Gulliver. He desires a philosophy which will conceal the truth, so that man is protected from looking over the edge of the abyss. Art must project the same illusion. Romances and children's tales avoid the moral dilemmas of life in an attempt to prove to us that tinsel trappings are the only reality. In this way art can give us as much pleasure as our deluding imaginations. According to Gulliver, art must not only embody the brute fact; it is the brute fact. Instead of avoiding the moral issue, the author should force it upon the reader in much the same way that Sir Robert Walpole threatened Ireland with Wood's half-pence: he promised to cram that brass down Irish throats.

As many critics have observed, the identification of Swift with his personae results in a misunderstanding of his artistry. This same identification, we might add, also leads to certain misconceptions about Swift's aesthetic attitudes. His ridicule of eccentric aesthetic theories (the modern writer's Epicureanism, Gulliver's didacticism), which are rigidly narrow because of the jaundiced view of life they espouse, is indicative of Swift's flexibility, not his limited view of the human condition. At times, Swift's moral realism may be as unrelenting as Gulliver's, but one difference between the character-author and the Dean appears in their respective approaches to art. From his travels, the bee in *The Battel of the Books* brings back both honey and wax. Gulliver, in contrast, greets his readers (as well as his wife) with moral awareness divorced from human understanding. Like William Wotton, who mistakes caviling for criticism, Gulliver mistakes ideas for art. His proud desire to instruct mankind in the moral truth lacks the art of pleasing and thus loses its effectiveness. However, behind the mask of Gulliver-author lurks the satirist Swift whose smiles indicate that moral realism, in art or in life, is not enough unless it be tempered by urbanity.

NOTES

¹ J. W. H. Atkins, *English Literary Criticism: 17th and 18th Centuries* (London: Methuen, 1951), 173.

² Harold D. Kelling, *The Appeal to Reason: A Study of Jonathan Swift's Critical Theory and Its Relation to His Writings,* Diss. Yale 1948, 4.

³ W. J. Bate, *From Classic to Romantic: Premises of Taste in Eighteenth-Century England* (New York: Harper, 1946), 60. It is generally recognized today that Swift belongs to a Renaissance tradition, this thesis having been given recent expression in Paul Fussell's excellent study, *The Rhetorical World of Augustan Humanism* (Oxford: Oxford Univ. Press, 1965). Still Fussell discusses Swift's aesthetic views only indirectly.

⁴ Philip Sidney, "An Apologie For Poetrie," in *English Literary Criticism: The Renaissance,* ed. O. B. Hardison (New York: Appleton-Century-Crofts, 1963), 108. I am aware of Swift's supposed attack on Sidney in *Advice to a Young Poet.* However, Herbert Davis seriously questions Swift's authorship of this piece. See *The Prose Works of Jonathan Swift,* ed. Herbert Davis, IX (Oxford: Oxford Univ. Press, 1968), xxiv–xxvii—hereafter cited as *Prose Works.* Davis' views themselves have been questioned by Louis Milic, *A Quantitative Approach to the Style of Jonathan Swift* (The Hague: Mouton, 1967), 237 ff., but the issue is still very much unresolved.

⁵ *A Tale of a Tub,* ed. A. C. Guthkelch and D. Nicol Smith (Oxford: Oxford Univ. Press, 1958), 234. For the sources of Swift's beast fable, see Irvin Ehrenpreis, *Swift and his Contemporaries* (London: Methuen, 1962), 231–36. Two possible sources which Ehrenpreis does not mention are John Heywood's "The Spider and the Flie" and Ben Jonson's *Timber.* Jonson says that when a poet imitates another author, he should not imitate servilely but should "draw forth out of the best and choicest flowers with the bee, and turn all into honey, and work it into one relish and savour . . . ."

⁶ *The Correspondence of Jonathan Swift,* ed. Harold Williams, II (Oxford: Oxford Univ. Press, 1965), 214—hereafter cited as *Correspondence.*

⁷ *Correspondence,* III, 103.

⁸ "The Pleasures of the Imagination," in *Eighteenth-Century Critical Essays,* ed. Scott Elledge (Ithaca: Cornell Univ. Press, 1961), I, 65—hereafter cited as *Critical Essays.*

⁹ *Of Poetry,* ed. J. E. Spingarn (Oxford: Oxford Univ. Press, 1909), 54.

¹⁰ *Critical Essays,* II, 886.

¹¹ Emile Pons made this point as early as 1925: "Son imagination l'a élevé si haut au-dessus de la querelle qu'il n'aperçoit plus, ou ne veut plus apercevoir, les deux armées en présence; il ne voit que la multitude dessordonnée et hurlante, avide et rageuse, qui englobe toutes les especes—et les confond." *Les Années De Jeunesse et Le "Conte Du Tonneau"* (Oxford: Oxford Univ. Press, 1925), 284. Also see Philip Pinkus, "Swift and the Ancients-Moderns Controversy," *UTQ* 29 (Oct. 1959), 50.

¹² *Correspondence,* III, 360.

¹³ *Correspondence,* III, 380–81, 41. Cf. Swift's remarks to Pope: "I have often chid Mr. Gay for not varying his Schemes, but still adhering to those that he had exhausted." *Correspondence,* IV, 133.

¹⁴ *Correspondence,* I, 153.

¹⁵ *Correspondence,* I, 8.

¹⁶ *Correspondence,* IV, 53.

¹⁷ *Prose Works,* IV, 19.

¹⁸ *The Life of Cowley,* in *Samuel Johnson; Rasselas, Poems, and Selected Prose,* ed. Bertrand Bronson (New York: Holt, Rinehart, and Winston, 1952), 470.

19 *Correspondence*, I, 8.

20 *Correspondence*, IV, 124.

21 *Correspondence*, III, 495.

22 *Correspondence*, III, 117.

23 *Correspondence*, III, 278. Cf. his remarks to Pope: "You talk of this Dunciad, but I am impatient to have it volare per ora—there is now a vacancy for fame: the Beggars Opera hath done its task, discedat uti satur." *Correspondence*, III, 286.

24 *Journal to Stella*, ed. Harold Williams (Oxford: Oxford Univ. Press, 1948), 512.

25 *Prose Works*, II, 79.

26 *Correspondence*, IV, 26.

27 *Prose Works*, XI, 94.

28 Despite his statement to Pope before *Gulliver's Travels* was published that his intention was "to vex the world rather than divert it," Swift himself was delighted with, and often amused by, the diverse responses to his book. See *Correspondence*, III, 102, 187–91. Also, unlike Gulliver, he could transform his anger into art.

University of Arizona

HUGO M. REICHARD

THE SELF-PRAISE ABOUNDING IN SWIFT'S *VERSES*

Self-praise figures so much in the closing section of the *Verses on the Death of Dr. Swift* that for centuries admirers have strained to save Swift from disgrace. They have summarily discounted or even excised peccant parts of the poem.[1] They have declared him lavishly ironic or incipiently senile for blowing his own horn.[2] They have sublimated the object of his tributes from a flesh-and-blood person into a disinterested "spirit" or a "topic of history."[3] They have left the self-praise intact but have linked it to some more imposing position of Swift's, as a sign of weakness "necessary to complete his thesis that all mankind is egotistical, selfish and proud"; or as a "form of exemplary behavior, which distinguishes him as a human being whose natural vanity has not suffered the corruption of mind"; or as a mark of surpassing "trust in God."[4] Understandably but unduly, such endeavors have engrossed our attention. Let us now concentrate on determining as fully as possible how, within the poem, the self-praise is stated, suggested, veiled, sweetened, and ultimately used.

It may, I think, help to start by recalling that at least two authors very familiar to Swift—Plutarch and Montaigne—have marveled at the challenge (rather than boggled at the odium) involved in discoursing of oneself, and especially in praising oneself.[5] Plainly, *Verses* is a poem in which Swift discourses of himself. While only a handful of other characters (chiefly Pope and Gay, Arbuthnot and St. John, Cibber and Chartres) ever reappear at all, he recurs. He is in the title above the poem, in the by-line of the early London editions ("Written by Himself"), and in each of the three scenes of the poem proper—the dispute of the opening, the focal deathbed of the middle, and the club

105

monologue of the close. If it is striking that many words in the poem are superlatives or absolutes, it is even more remarkable that many words, from start to finish, are Swiftian—nouns (Swift, Dean, Drapier) to some extent, but pronouns preponderantly.[6] In the close of the poem, plainly, there is praise as well as discourse. But does it occur earlier? When Murry deplored the "amount of self-eulogy" in the poem, he was thinking exclusively of the 186-line scene at the club as "an incongruous addendum to what has gone before"; such an "unqualified eulogy" was "in flat contradiction" to the earlier sections of the poem (455, 457). It is indeed only too easy, when verbalizing one's impressions of the whole, to report that in the middle of the *Verses* Swift seems rarely to be complimented when he is discussed (as he is extensively), and that in the opening he seems to be treated unfavorably without qualification. Under scrutiny, however, the poem proves to have—early as well as late, as a whole as well as by parts—even more self-eulogy than Murry and many others have thought to be in question. The self-praise, plain and hidden, leads us to see better the artistry and benignity of the poem.

The proem provides by way of both presumption and self-disparagement something tantamount to self-praise. Swift enters as an *enfant terrible*, who calmly proposes to vindicate one of La Rochefoucauld's most shocking dicta, a remark so objectionable that it was dropped from the published text of the duke's maxims. This is Swift daring to try the "patience" of his readers, and indeed venturing to champion single-handedly a repugnant doctrine against the world; evidently he is pontifically damning "mankind." He is willing to display spite as well as contumacy, as he avows envy for persons both unknown and renowned (ll. 17–20, 43–70). Dr. Johnson unmasked such derogation: "Then, all censure of a man's self is oblique praise. It is in order to show how much he can spare. It has all the invidiousness of self-praise, and all the reproach of falsehood."[7] Illustratively, when Swift repines at being outdone by friends in one new kind of writing after another, he is saying that he led the way and that he runs second to nobody but the friends named; he is also demonstrating, in the phrasing and rhyming, and in the shamming (of pique and surrender), that as an encomiast of individuals, no less than as a censurer of mankind, he commands undepleted expertise. This is part of the self-aggrandizement in the opening seventy-two lines of the poem. There is a little more to it. While making a spectacle of himself for La Rochefoucauld, apparently the speaker is assuming that everybody else in the world is just as bitter a competitor as he declares himself, and he

is implying that nobody else is as brave and forthright in either arraign-
ment or confession. While providing a partial rationale for the following misbehavior of others, the speaker's introduction also gives off
intimations of self-flattery.

The middle of the poem (ll. 73–298), which is likewise focused
elsewhere (on diverse responses to the imagined death of Swift), includes a wealth of accolades to Swift himself, in a variety of modes. A
few of these—acknowledging that the man was once a "fav'rite of
Apollo" (l. 249) and a celebrity (ll. 263–64)—are quite direct, if not
undimmed. Many are covert and subliminal. To posit a decline in the
intellectual and artistic powers of the old man is to grant that the fire
and fancy of the man in "his prime" were quite high (ll. 79–104). To
show him as unpopular with admirers of Cibber, Duck, Henley, and
Woolston is to leave him honored (ll. 245–98). When Swift is crassly
condemned for willing his estate to public uses (rather than to rela-
tives or cronies), his magnanimity shines the brighter (ll. 154–64).
Eminence is attested by the numbers, locations, and stations of those
who take notice of his last illness and his death. The illness prompts
numerous visits, inquiries, predictions, and conversations (ll. 109–46),
and the death, almost instantly reported over half the town (ll. 151–
52), is major news in two capitals (l. 177), for both the high and the
low, for socialite and sovereign, for publisher and statesman, for scrib-
bler and man of letters. He is so prominent that average citizens take
an interest in his will (ll. 153–64, 202), the doctors in attendance (if
not the entire local medical society) feel obligated to defend their handling of the case (ll. 169–76), high churchmen serve as pallbearers
(l. 231), the wits of Grub Street "are all employ'd" in grinding out
elegies and obituaries (ll. 165–68), a publisher rushes to market with
volumes of apocrypha (ll. 197–204), and ladies of fashion devote to
him half their talk at the card table (ll. 225–42). His end is noticed
by some of the most illustrious persons in the land, the queen (ll. 178–
88), the prime minister (ll. 189–96), four of the greatest living writers
(ll. 205–10). In short nearly every blow against contemporaries of
Swift is accompanied by a tacit salute to him. Like the proem, the
middle of the *Verses* croons the speaker's praises, which the protracted
conclusion resumes.

But the speaker is eulogized not only in a succession of discrete passages but also, massively, in several overall developments of the poem.
In one view of developments, the argument stars Swift in a series of
scenes, first as the devil's advocate, then as the dying old master glori-
fied by crowds of scoffers, and finally as a hero (by pen and principle)

in great struggles of the past. In another view, the argument amounts to casting Swift as an unusual being who can console himself for his infirmities by considering his congeners as even worse, and who can furthermore console himself for his mortality by conjuring up the homage that might be occasioned by the supreme distress of the very best of friends (oneself). In a third view, if we follow Waingrow at a distance, the argument of the poem as a whole amounts to a rather large qualification of the idea in the epigraph and the introduction: it turns out that there is at least "one person who does not take comfort in the distresses of others" (517). So long as Swift alone appears to be such a person, in this poem as in Pope's second *Moral Essay* an entire category of beings seems cheerfully sacrificed to the greater glory of a single member.

The extensiveness of the self-praise in the *Verses* is variously concealed and cushioned by a range of expedients and consequences. For one thing, the tenor is carried in each of the three sections of the poem by an altogether unlikely vehicle. The first section is so far from seeming panegyric that it looks misanthropic and forensic from start to finish, and seems to show the speaker as little mercy as anybody else. Similarly, the middle of the poem strikes the satiric note and sticks to it, in one comic dialogue after another, among wellwishers descended from Job's comforters, among will-watchers, among lady gamblers, between prime minister and henchman, queen and favorite, bookseller and customer. The end of the poem does not long sustain the pretense that it is simply recording an "impartial" characterization. But at least it begins with the viewpoint of "one quite indiff'rent in the cause." To the degree that the pretense persists, which is to say, to the degree that we notice when Swift drops the mask (ll. 317–18, 372, 378, 459–62), the self-praise is late as well as early carried out by indirection.

The self-praise is screened by equally distracting shifts of ostensible emphasis, alike within and between the three sections of the poem. The introduction passes from pleasure to pains; the middle shuttles among close friends, casual acquaintances, and out-and-out enemies; and the close, of course, veers from alleged impartiality to de facto favoritism. Between the start and the middle, there are changes in the gravity of the distress (from minor to mortal), in the mode of discourse (from illustrated brief to collection of vignettes), in the tense and person (from now to the future, from others' distress to mine), and in jurisdiction (from mankind at large to some current urban types). Between the middle and the close, similarly, there are changes, from prospect to retrospect, from fiction to biography and history. For many readers the most disturbing of shifts is in theme. When they try to take the theme—à la Rochefoucauld—to be set for the entire poem in the opening lines, they are very strenuously occupied in fitting the middle and the close into the design. In any event, the consequence of such shifts, large and little, is to draw the reader's attention away from the underground of self-praise which eventually surfaces in the third segment of the *Verses*.

Distraction is provided also by the comedy of the poem, most conspicuously in the earlier segments, in the much-savored rhymes, dialogues, ironies, and exaggerations. There is a more intellectual kind of comedy at work at the same time, in a series of logical acrobatics, analogy, question-begging, *ipse dixit*, factitious instances, and undeclared redefinitions of terms and issues. The flights of fallacy in the *Verses* are from *if, then,* and *but,* as those in Marvell's *To His Coy Mistress* are from *if, but,* and *so:* (*if*) suppose that men revel in a friend's misfortune; (*then*) on that supposition, my surviving acquaintances may someday enjoy running me down without mercy, somewhat like this . . . ; (*but*) say, I am not as bad as you just heard them claiming, on the contrary . . . . In the process of evolving some such fantastic sophistry (alongside other overall arguments), the *Verses* fabricate a look of fair play, as if to affirm: since so much has been spoken against me (after my death at that), it is only right that something be offered in my behalf. By such a reverse form of the synthetic justice which rationalizes the denunciations of the Brobdingnagian king, the man at the club seems authorized somewhat to heap great praise upon Swift. Such comic effects lend warrant as well as charm and shade to the tributes which the poet abundantly and artfully pays himself.

Sooner or later, the self-praise which is more or less hidden manages to take effect. The staggered impacts help make the poem look like one of those works that husband resources with which to pay us for rereading them. Screened and mitigated, in varying degrees eventually released, the self-praise keeps surprises in store for the reader. Here, one sees or senses, is a man engaged, of all things, in patting himself on the back, publicly at that, and indeed at the oddest times (while knocking himself, pushing an idea, saluting friends). Whatever else this is, it is jarring, disturbing. The jolts, with their accompanying uncertainties, recall the recurrent Swiftian enterprise of pleasurably vexing, if not edifying, the world by departures from custom in the treatments of many subjects such as dawns, rains, hereafters, boudoirs, honored generals, one-year-olds, dissenters, scribblers, and gray stallions. The jarring self-praise suits a poem full of other dissonances, as the speaker coolly pictures himself as a goner whose acquaintances cannot wait to dance on his grave, as he toys with progressive digression as well as varied shifts, as he helps a variety of ladies to contradict themselves charmingly. The surprising combinations add to the plenitude, diversity, and cognitive eventfulness of the total composition.

If we appreciate the eventful profusion of self-praise in the *Verses*, two other kinds of achievement in the poem rise into view. One is so obvious that it is in danger of escaping mention. Swift's poem performs a singular feat of self-praise. The tour de force is, to be sure, hardly unflawed: the neutral who speaks up for Swift in the close is only a distant ancestor of Sairey Gamp's Mrs. Harris. Yet in a century which creates elegies in praise of lost ladies and undiscovered men, the author and subject of "the greatest epitaph in history" provides a novel specimen of the elegy for oneself.

The second achievement is unobvious. The poet's treatment of himself is at bottom linked to his treatment of his kind. As Swift goes, within the bounds of the poem, so goes the human race. Initially, he offers himself as the test case, and he never retracts or reneges. In the first section of the poem, as he gaudily sinks himself, he seems to take mankind down with him. But just as he inconspicuously manages to buoy himself up there, so he contrives stealthily to hold humanity's head above water, by strokes in several directions. For one thing, the "fault" which is charged there to "mankind" seems (like a "corrupted mind") to be an acquired rather than an inherited characteristic of human "nature." For another thing, the reported outcries against La Rochefoucauld point to a prevalent inclination to respect and defend the good name of mankind. The distresses which men everywhere can observe their friends suffering imply not only the vulnerability of human beings but also their capacity for friendship, not to mention consolation and renewed effort. Again, the awards of honors in literature and even warfare suggest a widespread ability both to use and to judge talents aright. The basis for the very discussion of La Rochefoucauld's moot dictum is the premise that men are sufficiently like Socrates to decide even prickly issues by "reason and experience" (l. 12).

In the close of the poem, even more than at the outset, Swift shares the applause, though not the limelight, with his fellows in the human race. Undoubtedly much censure is meted out in the club scene to culprits particular (like Whigs, Whig judges, biennial Irish squires) and culprits general (knaves, fools, slaves, flatterers, factions), existing in the "thousands" (l. 462). Yet there is at least as much scope to the commendations of well-behaved people. Among the commended are mere individuals (Pope, Gay, St. John, Oxford, Ormond). Others are groups. Some of the groups, such as the "wits in dirty shoes" (l. 322), may be small. Others, "the wise and good" (l. 333), are indeterminate. But still other groups would seem to be of considerable magnitude. There are, for example, the "numbers" who embodied "virtue in distress" (ll. 335–37). There are many persons who, despite threat and pressure, "still were true"; these would include the citizens of two kingdoms, among whom "not a traitor cou'd be found, / To sell him for six hundred pound" (ll. 351–54). There are, furthermore, those persons who, until the recent sway of baleful ministry, managed to uphold religion, government, law, parliament, kingship, and old England's glory (ll. 383–88). To some extent people of all other times were wholesome, inasmuch as "no age could more deserve" satire than the present age (l. 458); and to some extent people of all other places are wholesome, inasmuch as "no nation wanted" an asylum for fools and madmen so much as Ireland (l. 482). It is especially notable that Ireland constitutes an extreme case: even there, in "the land of slaves and fens," among "a servile race in folly nurs'd," in Swift's time of grave distress, "the grateful people stand his friends" (ll. 396–97, 426).

To the end the protagonist of the poem remains determined "to cure the vices of mankind," and he stays convinced that "all mortals may correct" their vices (ll. 314, 464). Folly too seems to him remediable: he "taught fools their int'rest how to know" (l. 409). He believes not only in the corrigibility of man but also in the dignity of man, for he sees the service of mankind as the source of his own worth: it is an accomplishment to leave Ireland "his debtor," not by the criterion of one-up-manship, but in the light of his summum bonum, to "merit well of human kind" (ll. 362, 483). In short, the *Verses* may be described as another of Swift's mock presentations, not a mock encomium this time nor a mock proposal nor a mock brief, but a mock defense of a cynical remark, a mock belittlement of Swift himself, and a mock denigration of mankind. For all the talk, starting from the highest authority, about affinities between Swift and La Rochefoucauld, this poem is no more a footnote to the *Maxims* than it is a fulfillment of the Grub Street plan for a "panegyric on the world." It looks, rather, like a much-tempered compliment to human nature produced, with underlying unity and other surprises, in an elegy for a lively satirist.

NOTES

[1] The discounting is illustrated by John Middleton Murry, *Jonathan Swift: A Critical Biography* (London: Cape, 1954), 457–59. The excisions, made by friends of Swift, are traced in the headnote to the text of the *Verses* used here:

Harold Williams, ed., *The Poems of Jonathan Swift* (Oxford: Clarendon Press, 1937), II, 551–72.

2 The diagnoses are rendered, respectively, by Barry Slepian, "The Ironic Intention of Swift's Verses on His Own Death," *RES* 14 (1963), 249–56; and Murry, 455–62.

3 The sublimations are made, respectively, by Ronald Paulson, *The Fictions of Satire* (Baltimore: Johns Hopkins Univ. Press, 1967), 193–94; and Edward W. Said, "Swift's Tory Anarchy," *ECS* 3 (1969), 61–66.

4 These are the interpretations, respectively, of Slepian, 256; Marshall Waingrow, "*Verses on the Death of Dr. Swift*," *SEL* 5 (1965), 513–18; and John Irwin Fischer, "How to Die: *Verses on the Death of Dr. Swift*," *RES* 21 (1970), 422–41.

5 See "On Praising Oneself Inoffensively," in *Plutarch's Moralia*, tr. P. H. De Lacy and B. Einarson (Cambridge, Mass.: Harvard Univ. Press, 1959), VII, 115–67. Montaigne's comments are instanced in "Of Training," "Of Presumption," "Of Giving the Lie," "Of Repentance," "Of the Art of Conversing," and "Of Experience." Professor Clayton D. Lein has pointed out to me that Bacon, who was read by Swift, also calls attention to the fine art of self-praise—in the *Essays* (especially "Of Friendship," "Of Discourse," "Of Praise," and "Of Vain-Glory") and in *The Advancement of Learning* (Book VIII, ch. ii).

6 "The amazing total of 122 words are superlatives or absolutes," Slepian says on 254. He notes that "all"—"perhaps the key word in the poem"—occurs 41 times. By contrast, according to my count, pronouns referring to Swift occur 189 times; "he" alone occurs 61 times.

7 Boswell, *Life of Johnson*, ed. R. W. Chapman and C. B. Tinker (London: Oxford Univ. Press, 1960), 972 (Tuesday, 28 April 1778). Waingrow (513) pioneered in relating Johnson's analysis to the *Verses*.

8 This side of the poem was originally noticed, under the rubric of balance, by Maurice Johnson, "*Verses on the Death of Dr. Swift*," *N&Q* 199 (1954), 474.

Purdue University

G. DOUGLAS ATKINS

THE EVE OF ST. AGNES RECONSIDERED

In the 150 years since its publication, *The Eve of St. Agnes* has elicited a broad spectrum of response. Since the Victorian period, when the poem was widely thought to be simply "a gorgeous gallery of poetic pictures" and to "mean next to nothing,"[1] interpretation and assessment of Keats's "enchanting" stanzas have undergone a series of major volte-face. Until the early 1950s, though, the Victorian assessment went largely unchallenged, with twentieth-century commentators for the most part content to discuss the poem in terms of its treatment of young love or as autobiographical, particularly in light of Keats's infatuation with Fanny Brawne; much effort, in addition, was spent trying to pinpoint sources and identify echoes. Then appeared Earl Wasserman's powerfully written essay,[2] which invigorated Keats studies and turned the tables almost completely on previous approaches. Wasserman sought to establish once and for all the poem's deep intellectual content by positing a metaphysical interpretation of the work as an analogue of speculations appearing in the letters; specifically, he argued, *St. Agnes* is a poetic demonstration "of the truth of Imagination—What the Imagination seizes as Beauty must be truth."[3] In 1961, in a widely influential essay, since reprinted at least three times, Jack Stillinger[4] tried, with considerable success, to recover the poem from the highly improbable reading given and the dubious methods employed by Wasserman. From a validation of the visionary imagination the poem suddenly became a repudiation of the visionary imagination, with Madeline now seen as a hoodwinked dreamer and Porphyro as a rapist. Only recently has this equally improbable reading been seriously challenged. That challenge came in a suggestive essay by Stuart M.

113

Sperry, Jr., "Romance as Wish-Fulfillment: Keats's *The Eve of St. Agnes.*"[5] Sperry's general reading of the poem, if not his conclusions and interpretative methods, was as inevitable as it was necessary. In what amounts to a kind of synthesis of the directly antithetical views of Wasserman and Stillinger, Sperry argues that

> the poem has no meaning that can be reduced to a simple theme or statement . . . , but lies rather in a state of mature realization. One might say that realization concerns, more than anything, the infiniteness of human desire, the wish-fulfilling power of the imagination, and the beauty as well as the tenuousness and insecurity of the spell that power casts.   (43)

With Sperry's help we may finally have reached the point where succeeding interpretations will not have to appear as polar opposites of the one(s) they are attempting to correct or overturn.

The basic thrust of Sperry's essay is surely correct; we must not reduce *St. Agnes* "to the value of a simple thesis, a representation of the imagination as either good or bad, truth or deception" (28). And just as surely, the interpretations of the poem offered by Wasserman and Stillinger, in which these conflicting views appear, are too simplistic, indeed one-sided, to do justice to the complexity of Keats's thought and art. Stillinger's reading of *St. Agnes* is no more adequate than Wasserman's. If against Wasserman we point out, for example, that St. Agnes' Eve is no "transcendent occasion" but, more humbly, a time when the superstitious believe they may, by force or certain ceremonies, gain a glimpse of their future husbands; that there is no textual support for the claim that Madeline is at heaven's bourn, nor that spiritual grace has made such an achievement possible; that Porphyro is led to seek out Madeline's chambers through his physical desire for her, not because "knowledge of Madeline's intention to experience the spiritual repetition of earthly happiness awakens the thinking principle within him" (120), knowledge he could not in any case have had; that Porphyro's supposed spiritualization in his ascent through the castle proves short-lived since in the bedchamber he becomes "Beyond a mortal man impassion'd far" (316);[6] and finally that the poem presents at the climactic point, not a spiritual repetition of earthly pleasures, but rather an earthly repetition of imaginative pleasure—if we must insist on these crucial errors committed by Wasserman, we must also draw attention to the misreadings in Stillinger's interpretation. Stillinger is surely right to point to Keats's tough-mindedness, though the proper understanding of it, I believe, eludes both him and Sperry. Clearly, there is no textual warrant for viewing Porphyro as a villain, despite Stillinger's claim. Both Angela and the narrator are drawn to him; from the very beginning (when the narrator is fearful of Porphyro's safety: "let no buzz'd whisper tell: / All eyes be muffled, or a hundred swords / Will storm his heart" [82–84]) to the climactic moments in the bedchamber ("Now prepare, / Young Porphyro, for gazing on that bed" [196–97]), there is virtually no distance between narrator and this supposed villain.

Further, if we go outside the poem for a moment, we can be assured that Keats not only sympathized, and perhaps identified, with Porphyro but also expressed approval of the sexual consummation which is at the center of the poem. On September 7, 1819, Richard Woodhouse reported Keats's personal views on the sexual act in *St. Agnes* to the publisher John Taylor:

> he says . . . that he writes for men, & that if in the former poem there was an opening for a doubt what took place, it was his fault for not writing clearly & comprehensibly—that he shd despise a man who would be such an eunuch in sentiment as to leave a maid, with that Character about her, in such a situation: & shod despise himself to write about it.   (*Letters.* II.163)

With this vindication of both Porphyro's character and his "stratagem," it becomes increasingly doubtful that the poem is simply a condemnation of dreaming. Porphyro seems much more important to the poem than Stillinger is willing to admit. Also Madeline does get what she wants, and there seems little reason to doubt Porphyro's intention when he calls her his "bride." We feel, I think, that the ending is essentially positive, not negative.

I have outlined above my own objections, especially to Stillinger, since I do not believe Sperry has succeeded in overturning this influential view of Keats's poem, which has the support of, among others, the poet's major biographer, Walter Jackson Bate,[8] as well as the advantage of exposure through reprinting, including in the widely used anthologies, *Twentieth-Century Views* and *Twentieth-Century Interpretations*. But whatever disagreements we must have with the specific details of Sperry's reading, we should not fail to acknowledge and emphasize his recognition of those elements *within* the poem which prompted Wasserman's unfortunately distorted interpretation of them, elements which Stillinger unnecessarily diminished in his effort to point out still other aspects also *within* the poem, realistic, sceptical, and anti-romantic, which his predecessor had denied.

One of the reasons for Sperry's apparent failure, it seems, is a tendency toward the kind of needless—and distorting—polarizing which he so effectively repudiates, at least with regard to the poem's position on the relative merits of the visionary imagination vis-à-vis the "real" world. Abjuring a supposed tendency in recent commentary on Keats to posit "semi-philosophical rationalizations, whether based on the letters or on schematic views of Keats's intellectual development," allegedly at the expense of "the way we are taken into the world of the poem, what happens to us there, and the way we are let out again [which is what] matters most," (41–42), Sperry would force us to choose between two approaches, neither of which is likely to prove satisfactory, though for different reasons; that is, he opposes his own awareness of the poem as methodologically preferable to interpretations which arise, not from the particular work as literary art, but from general preconceptions of Keats's thought, into which schemes the poem itself is then wrenched. Now whereas it is certainly true that Wasserman's interpretation imposes various attitudes from the letters onto the poem, it is not the case that Stillinger's argument is based too narrowly on positions outside *St. Agnes*. Despite Sperry's contention, the problems with Stillinger's reading lie not in the general scholarly method but rather in a faulty execution of an approach that is much more likely to reach Keats's intentions than Sperry's. By limiting his attention so narrowly to only the poem, Sperry greatly increases the unlikelihood of the judicious view of the complexity of *St. Agnes*, which we so badly need and which the poem itself demands.

Thus, though he is aware of the complexity of tone, texture, thought, and feeling in the poem, Sperry fails, I believe, to convince us of the precise way in which the romantic and realistic elements, as well as the mixture of affirmation and scepticism, come together to form the poem. As I have already indicated, Sperry sees in the plot "the wish-fulfilling power of the imagination." But unlike Wasserman, he quickly adds,

> If the poem continually suggests the transforming power of aroused imagination, the logic of "Adam's dream," it simultaneously exposes, through the heterogeneous devices and conventions it employs, the kinds of stratagems to which poetic magic must resort.   (41)

Nevertheless, the problems here, I believe, are several and of the utmost importance. Surely the fact of wish-fulfillment in the poem, achieved by Madeline and Porphyro but denied to the Beadsman, is principally a vehicle for larger and deeper considerations. It is simply one of the common denominators in the varied experiences of Madeline, her lover, and the ascetic Beadsman. Therefore, to insist with Sperry that "the element most central to the poem is its concern with wish-fulfillment" (30) is to distort out of all proportion this undeniable but nevertheless de-emphasized and clearly subsidiary element of the plot and so to mistake the delicate balance of the poem. What

St. Agnes calls attention to, in fact, is not the wishing and the different degrees of wish-fulfillment but rather the responses of various characters to experience.

If at this point we look outside the poem, at Keats's thought and the expression of that thought, we quickly realize the improbability of Sperry's argument that "Only in the dream—by extension the domain of romance, poetry, art—and the shelter it affords from waking consciousness is there any hope for the realization and appeasement that human longing, in all its turbulent impatience, insistently demands" (33). For throughout his all-too-brief writing career Keats was unswervingly and vehemently opposed to any belief that normal bounds can be transcended or that dreaming can be efficacious. Since Stillinger has argued this point in great detail, and been followed by Bate, I shall limit the evidence adduced to a few examples from different phases of Keats's career. *Endymion* shows how vexed and unhappy those are who forsake the real for the unreal (cf. especially IV.636–48). In *Lamia* Keats distinguishes the possibilities for men from those open to the gods: "Real are the dreams of Gods, and smoothly pass / Their pleasures in a long immortal dream" (I.127–28). In "La Belle Dame sans Merci" the Knight similarly tries to extend the impossible love of a fairy lady, only to discover as a result that the ordinary pleasures no longer carry any meaning for him. In the epistle "To J. H. Reynolds, Esq." Keats asserts that "imagination brought / Beyond its proper bound" "forces us in summer skies to mourn, / It spoils the singing of the Nightingale" (78–79, 84–85). And, to cite but one more example, in *The Fall of Hyperion* dreamers are said to vex the world because they create illusions. In this matter, then, Stillinger would seem closer to the truth than Sperry. Stillinger concludes,

It is a notable part of Keats's wisdom that he never lost touch with reality, that he reproved his hoodwinked dreamers who would shut out the world, that he recognized life as a complexity of pleasure and pain, and laid down a rule for action: achievement of the ripest, fullest experience one is capable of.   (555)

Of course, as we have seen, Sperry is too perceptive a reader to fall into the same trap that caught Wasserman. For the later writer, the romance quality of the poem, supposedly most apparent in both the general tone and the plot where the wishes of Madeline and Porphyro are realized, which itself is said to testify to the transforming power of the imagination, is qualified by a self-consciousness within the art of the poem. This self-consciousness, specifically as to convention and technique, calls attention to the story as story and thus "tests the limits and the dangers of its own devices even while employing them" (42). The result is a work which "marks the beginning of that ironical perspective on imaginative experience Keats was steadily to develop in 'La Belle Dame sans Merci,' the great odes of the spring, and *Lamia*" (42). Yet, while insisting that the self-consciousness of technique in *St. Agnes* qualifies the romance elements, Sperry is unwilling to grant the degree of scepticism regarding dreams, the imagination, and wishing that the poem seems to require and that Stillinger, Bate, and others have spent so much effort in trying to establish. Sperry's qualifications are simply insufficient to offset the forced emphasis on the power of imagination and dreaming.[9] At the same time, as I hope to show later, his account of the poem's technique is not strictly accurate in describing the ways in which it calls attention to itself as story. In any case, especially in 1819, if at all, Keats would not have relied exclusively on form or technique to balance a story line that itself expressed commitment to the imagination. But further, and most important, we can be rather sure that he would not have written a poem which in any way suggested the ability of the imagination or dreaming to create for men and women with any degree of permanence the kind of life they so much yearn for but are denied by an at best indifferent world. Can we now, proceeding on the assumption of a dual aspect to the poem but assuming as well the necessity for going outside the poem for help, provide a more satisfactory alternative than Sperry has managed?

In simplest terms *The Eve of St. Agnes* presents—and is—an intense, delightful experience. But though this fact, if not always certain implications arising from it, is widely recognized, not so thoroughly understood are elements in the poem which serve to bring this experience into sharp relief and, further, to give it significance as a sophisticated way of coping with reality. With no less care than he bestowed on the beauty of individual verses, I believe, Keats defines and emphasizes the approach to experience that lies at the heart of the poem. Probably the most important, though certainly not the only, means by which this particular response is spotlighted and defined is that of paralleling contrasts. Thus central to *St. Agnes*, it seems to me, is an intensely realized approach to experience that is carefully, and favorably, juxtaposed with other approaches presented in the poem.

The most crucial of these paralleling contrasts, it seems clear, is that of the Beadsman and his way of life with Madeline and Porphyro and their "way." Although it would appear almost impossible to ignore the Beadsman, given that we see him immediately upon entering the poem and that it is to him that we are returned in the last two lines, only in recent years have critics expressed serious interest in him and his function in the poem. In this seemingly strange mix, this "delight of the senses," where highly charged sensuous and even sensual imagery appears alongside equally prominent religious imagery, where sacred and profane come together in a precarious balance, the Beadsman represents the traditionally religious, specifically Christian approach to life. He would, then, seem to be other—and more—than Sperry claims in seeing him as creating a contrast with "the wish that creates its own fulfillment, the way of the poem" (35). Sperry fails to notice the very close parallel, and contrast, between the Beadsman's actions and those of Madeline and Porphyro. To my knowledge only James D. Boulger in a suggestive essay on "Keats' Symbolism"[10] has recognized the ways in which the Beadsman's Christian worship is unfavorably juxtaposed with both Madeline's superstitious St. Agnes' Eve ceremonies and Porphyro's "religious" adoration of his flesh-and-blood "saint" and his asceticism contrasted with their happy indulgence in the physical pleasures.

As Keats presents him in *The Eve of St. Agnes*, the Beadsman is a particular kind of Christian, an ascetic. But for Keats, because he is an ascetic, as well as a Christian, the Beadsman comes to represent *the* Christian response to life, which will soon be contrasted with a vibrant, joyous, and efficacious alternative. Although Keats is somewhat less than sympathetic to the "argent revelry" (37) in "that mansion foul" (89) on which the Beadsman turns his back, it is clear from the first that the way of this "patient, holy man" (10) is not that of the narrator or of the poem. What the old man rejects is, of course, much more than the raucous merriment of the "barbarian hordes" (85). In another work his mortification of the flesh and rejection of the earthly in favor of preparation for the eternal might stand as a positive value, but not here. In contrast to the youth, warmth, vigor, and sensuous enjoyment of both the story and the tone are the cold, age, and death associated throughout with the Beadsman. He is first glimpsed, in prayer, his "numb" fingers around the rosary, "while his frosted breath, / Like pious incense from a censer old, / Seem'd taking flight for heaven, without a death" (6–8). After prayer he moves, "meagre, barefoot, wan" (12), along the chapel aisle. What we see there strikes us, though it would not him, as emblematic of this approach to experience:

> The sculptur'd dead, on each side, seem to freeze,
> Emprison'd in black, purgatorial rails:
> Knights, ladies, praying in dumb orat'ries,
> He passeth by; and his weak spirit fails
> To think how they may ache in icy hoods and mails.
> (14–18)

For him St. Agnes' Eve is a time for such thoughts as this picture illustrates: "His was harsh penance" (24) on this promising night. In
relation to the amorous party-goers, as well as to Madeline, Porphyro,
and the narrator, his is "Another way" (25). What he chooses is to sit
"among / Rough ashes" (25–26) "for his soul's reprieve, / And all
night [he] kept awake, for sinners' sake to grieve" (26–27). Yet in the
forceful, almost brutal conclusion, Keats insists that the sacrifice, the
prayers, and the faith are all for nought: "The Beadsman, after thousand aves told, / For aye unsought for slept among his ashes cold"
(377–78).

In obvious contrast to the Beadsman's "way" is the happy fulfillment of Madeline and Porphyro. But whereas the contrasts are obvious and none too subtle, some rather close parallels are at the same
time established, parallels which will become of the utmost importance
to the poem. We might notice first of all that Madeline is engaged in a
religious ceremony, just as is the Beadsman. And like him she is a
devout adherent to her belief and fiercely obedient. Just as he successfully resists the alluring call of "Music's golden tongue" (20), so does
she exhibit her own steadfastness in rejecting the overtures of the young
men at the party. Hers, too, is a way of faith, hope, and patience; "she
heeded not at all: in vain / Came many a tiptoe, amorous cavalier"
(59–60) for "she saw not: her heart was otherwhere" (62).

What follows in the poem is rife with religious (specifically Christian) imagery. Madeline is "like a mission'd spirit" "With silver taper's
light" (193–94), and her bedchamber is said to be a "paradise" (244).
Further, Keats describes Madeline's St. Agnes' Eve ceremonies in terms
that apply to Christian ritual; according to Boulger, the poem becomes
a "sacred parody" (256). In any case, as Madeline proceeds with her
superstitious rites, the religious language becomes all the more prominent: "down she knelt for heaven's grace and boon" (219). While she
prays (as a votary of the St. Agnes legend), there appears "on her
hair a glory, like a saint: / She seem'd a splendid angel, newly drest /
Save wings, for heaven" (222–24); the description here echoes that
earlier of the Beadsman, especially 6 ff., quoted above. The intruding
Porphyro, stolen to Madeline's chambers with Angela's help, is profoundly affected by this scene: he "grew faint: / She knelt, so pure a
thing, so free from mortal taint" (224–25). Later, in bed, she is somewhat similarly described as "Clasp'd like a missal where swart Paynims
pray" (241).

By this point, however, the focus has shifted. As this last quotation
indicates, Madeline has now somehow become the object of adoration

and worship, rather than simply the faithful votary. She continues to observe the prescribed rites, but her function, now that she is in bed, at the altar in this "sacred parody," is largely passive. Porphyro replaces her as the active participant in the ritualistic observance, and his worship is directed solely to her. "Stol'n to this paradise, and so entranc'd" (244), he gazes for a while on the clothes she has just stepped out of, listening to her breathing, waiting for indication that it had wakened "into a slumberous tenderness; / Which when he heard, that minute did he bless" (247–48). Then he creeps from the closet and proceeds to heap up the food offering, which, among other things, spotlights the sensuousness which envelops the whole scene. Keats's poetry here is beautifully expressive of the sensuous ritual, especially the whole of stanza xxx.

Having performed this rite, Porphyro moves to awaken Madeline: "And now, my love, my seraph fair, awake! / Thou art my heaven, and I thine eremite" (276–77). After several more urgings, she stirs but soon begins to weep with the realization that her dream is now past. As she laments this change, Porphyro "knelt, with joined hands and piteous eye" (305). But she continues to compare the real-life Porphyro with the spiritualization in her dream. Finally, after she cries, "Oh leave me not in this eternal woe, / For if thou diest, my Love, I know not where to go" (314–15), Porphyro, "Beyond a mortal man impassion'd far" (316), acts to consummate the ritual by making physical love to her: "Into her dream he melted, as the rose / Blendeth its odour with the violet,— / Solution sweet" (320–22). Though when the love-making is finished Madeline still worries that the very mortal and physical Porphyro has simply used her, he calms and reassures her with terms that signify the nature of the experience he has just undergone. The terms remain religious, for his experience has been precisely that, though it is certainly not conventional, not one the orthodox and ascetic Beadsman would condone or even understand:

> "My Madeline! sweet dreamer! lovely bride!
> Say, may I be for aye thy vassal *blest*?
> Thy beauty's shield, heart-shap'd and vermeil dyed?
> Ah, *silver shrine*, here will I take my rest
> After so many hours of *toil and quest*,
> A *famish'd pilgrim*,—*saved by miracle*.
> Though I have found, I will not rob thy nest
> Saving of thy sweet self; if thou think'st well
> To trust, fair Madeline, to no rude *infidel*.
> (334–42; italics mine)

She does trust him, so much so that she flees "o'er the southern moors"

(351) with him. And though we can never be certain of what is there waiting for them,[11] we do know, with absolute certainty, that the poem has described an intense, satisfying, fulfilling, even if not permanent, experience, one that is counterpointed with the ineffectualness of the Beadsman's ascetic faith: "The Beadsman, after thousand aves told, / For aye unsought for slept among his ashes cold."

Clearly, by the end of the poem we are aware that we must speak of its central experience as, in some manner, religious. The precise nature of that experience, and the way in which it acquires religious significance for Porphyro at least, are yet to be determined, however. For James D. Boulger the problem is relatively simple. *The Eve of St. Agnes* is, he argues, closely patterned on, indeed is a parody of, the ritual of the Eucharist, with Love replacing the Eucharist as the sacrament in this system. He writes,

By borrowing and reworking for his own purpose the central mystery of the Christian ritual, clearly removed from its original sacred context, [Keats] was able to use the Beadsman as a foil to develop successfully, in his poem at least, the *mysterium fidei* of his own sacramental universe.   (258–59)

But despite the suggestiveness of this view, as well as its value in calling attention to the parallels between the religion of the Beadsman and the worship of both Madeline and Porphyro, a basic misunderstanding is, I believe, apparent. To pass over Boulger's highly dubious drawing of an exact parody of Christian ritual in the later events in the poem, we should note that he believes that in the religion of Love sanctified by *St. Agnes* essentially the same *kind* of thing happens as in that which it replaces, the Christian sacrament of the Eucharist; that is, though the means, end, and entire approach are completely different, a mystery, indeed a "miracle," occurs. Boulger is, in spite of obvious differences, not so far from Wasserman's general views. But the problem is that Keats uses the religious parallels and terminology not to indicate the occurrence of a "miracle" (which I doubt very much he believed in, in any literal sense), but only to suggest that for Porphyro this experience with Madeline has become religious. Keats's aim, in other words, is not to depict a miracle in the literal sense of the word but rather to indicate, through the use of religious language, that what has happened has, for Porphyro at least, become religious and, through the use of religious parallels, that this kind of religious fulfillment is the most satisfying, if not the only effective, one in these days when the old pieties are no longer believable. With Keats, I think, it is the phenomenal level (as defined so well in the "negative capability" passage in the letters) that matters.

Confirmation is readily available, both from inside and outside the poem, of the views just expressed in opposition to Boulger's assessment of the function of the religious terminology in *St. Agnes*. The poem never leaves us in any doubt as to where religious meaning lies. Here, as elsewhere in Keats, it is squarely in and through, but not beyond, the physical. If we now look at some of the further ways in which the poem defines and emphasizes its central experience, we can see that this is so.

As we have seen, complementing the romance itself is the God's plenty of both sensuous and sensual imagery, which contributes so much to making the poem a physico-sensuous delight. Since the sensuous imagery is obvious and, besides, has been emphasized above, I shall pause here only to note some aspects of the poem's sensualness, particularly the alluring richness with which Madeline's undressing is described. Her vespers completed, Madeline "frees" her hair, "Unclasps her warmed jewels one by one; / Loosens her fragrant boddice" and then "by degrees / Her rich attire creeps rustling to her knees" so that finally she is described as "Half-hidden, like a mermaid in sea-weed" (227–31). The effect of this passage is frankly titillating, and the narrator, no less than Porphyro (or the reader), enjoys the sexual prospect:[12] "Now prepare, / Young Porphyro, for gazing on that bed" (196–97). No less sensually expressive of course is Keats's beautiful and daring description of the actual intercourse. Porphyro rises, "Ethereal, flush'd, and like a throbbing star / Seen mid the sapphire heaven's deep repose" (318–19), and then "melts" into her dream "as the rose / Blendeth its odour with the violet,— / Solution sweet . . . " (320–32).

But further, while insisting on, and presenting in the most tantalizing ways, this feast of the senses, Keats works to insure that we view the physical union and its attendant delights as more than mindless indulgence and as something other than a simple alternative to the Beadsman's sacrificial asceticism. These ends he accomplishes, in part, through the implied contrast set up between both the Beadsman and the "bloated wassaillers" (346) and these "barbarian hordes" and Madeline-Porphyro. As we have seen, both Porphyro and the narrator use forceful epithets in marking their distaste for the revelers. The narrator, especially, is impatient with them; these "let us wish away" (41). In lines he ultimately deleted from the poem, Keats's intention vis-à-vis the "Hyena foemen, and hot-blooded lords" (86) is all the clearer:

> Ah what are they? the idle pulse scarce stirs.
> The Muse should never make the spirit gay;
> Away, bright dulness, laughing fools away,— . . . .[13]

Of course, in describing the Baron and his guests Keats does much more than focus on their sensuality. Indeed, that aspect of their characters is less important ultimately than their general bestiality. After first presenting the revelers as glittering and well arrayed, if also mindless, the narrator proceeds to refer to the "barbarian hordes, / Hyena foemen, and hot-blooded lords," who would be eager to set upon Porphyro with "a hundred swords" (83). Their "very dogs would execrations howl / Against his lineage; not one breast affords / Him any mercy, in that mansion foul" (87–89), except of course Angela. But clearly it is not simply that Porphyro arouses the worst in the revelers; the seeds of brutishness are already present, for, apart from that unexplained animosity, even during the festivities the "throng'd resort" (67) is said to be composed of "whisperers in anger, or in sport" (68), and Madeline in this setting is said to be " 'Mid looks of love, defiance, hate, and scorn" (69). The last reference we are given to the "bloated wassaillers" is no more sympathetic:

> That night the Baron dreamt of many a woe,
> And all his warrior-guests, with shade and form
> Of witch, and demon, and large coffin-worm,
> Were long be-nightmar'd.
>
> (372–75)

Against such a background the unconventional, even daring, Madeline-Porphyro affair appears in positive relief. Further, by juxtaposing the central love affair with the barbarian revelry, as well as with the Beadsman's asceticism, Keats suggests that not just any mode of fleshly indulgence is to be sanctioned. The presence of the Baron and his warrior-guests in the poem indicates Keats's interest in defining a *particular* approach to experience, one that is opposed to asceticism but that, while being physical, manages to avoid animalism.

We are, then, apparently to conclude that in Madeline's bedchamber, finding her "so pure a thing, so free from mortal taint," Porphyro suddenly realizes that the opportunity before him is more than simply physical or sexual, as he had earlier supposed and as it would remain for the "bloated wassaillers." Partly owing to Madeline herself and partly owing to the striking contrast within "that mansion foul" between Madeline and the "barbarian hordes," the experience now looms as extraordinary, even exalted. And significantly, in the beautiful description of Madeline at prayer in obedience to the superstition, naked, and observed by Porphyro, the two major strands of imagery, the sensuous-sensual and the religious, come together:

Full on this casement shone the wintry moon,
And threw warm gules on Madeline's fair breast,
As down she knelt for heaven's grace and boon;
Rose-bloom fell on her hands, together prest,
And on her silver cross soft amethyst,
And on her hair a glory, like a saint . . . .

(217–22)

Porphyro thus becomes "Beyond a mortal man impassion'd far" because the moment is one of supreme possibility, intensity, and beauty. It is one of those times when one no longer feels ordinary. Without in any way hinting at any spiritualization of Porphyro or of any literal or miraculous conversion of the physical, Keats suggests that this experience has acquired the significance conventionally termed religious.

That Keats would hold and express such views as I have described is highly probable. To consider first of all the nature of Keats's religious thought: as is well known, Keats was hardly a conventional believer. He was, for example, vehemently anti-clerical, so much so in fact that in 1819 he sought to avoid staying in a place with the word "bishop" in its name (Bishopsteignton, in Devon [*Letters*. II.70–71, 115]). That his unconventionality extended far beyond hatred of the clergy is abundantly clear. To Benjamin Bailey he wrote early in 1818: "You know my ideas about Religion—I do not think myself more in the right than other people and that nothing in this world is proveable" (*Letters*. I.242). In a letter to George and Georgiana Keats, April 21, 1819, he proposed his own scheme of salvation: "This point I sincerely wish to consider because I think [the vale of soul-making] a grander scheme of salvation than the chryst<e>ain religion." In the same letter he scorns conventional religion: "The common cognomen of this world among the misguided and superstitious is 'a vale of tears' from which we are to be redeemed by a certain arbitrary interposition of God and taken to Heaven—What a little circumscribe[d] straightened notion" (II.101–102). In an earlier section of the same letter, written March 19, Keats referred to "the pious frauds of religion" (II.80). Near the end of his life he said to Joseph Severn, "I think a malignant being must have power over us—over whom the Almightly has little or no influence—yet you know Severn I cannot believe in your book—the Bible."[14] To Fanny Brawne he was more temperate than at other times when he spoke of "the blood of that Christ you believe in" (II.304). More considered than some of the rash statements in the letters and written before all hope was gone, the sonnet "Written in Disgust of Vulgar Superstition" epitomizes, I believe, Keats's abhorrence of con-

ventional religious practice, as it carries a suggestion of the alternative
that Keats would develop in, among other places, *The Eve of St. Agnes*:

> The church bells toll a melancholy round,
>   Calling the people to some other prayers,
>   Some other gloominess, more dreadful cares,
> More hearkening to the sermon's horrid sound.
> Surely the mind of man is closely bound
>   In some black spell; seeing that each one tears
>   Himself from fireside joys, and Lydian airs,
> And converse high of those with glory crown'd.
> Still, still they toll, and I should feel a damp,—
>   A chill as from a tomb, did I not know
> That they are dying like an outburnt lamp;
>   That 'tis their sighing, wailing ere they go
>   Into oblivion;—that fresh flowers will grow,
> And many glories of immortal stamp.

But Keats's interests in religion were not exclusively negative, for
while he consistently expressed disapproval of conventional religion,
he was seeking a replacement for it. Although, as we have seen, Keats
once proposed what then seemed to him "a grander scheme of salvation
than the chryst<e>ain religion," we should be hesitant to accept it as
a carefully developed and consistently held solution. What seems safer
is to note the recurrent manifestations of a desire for a replacement of
conventional religion; these manifestations sometimes appear in different clothing in Keats, but it is, after all, the impulse that matters
most here. In the letter of November 3, 1817, to Benjamin Bailey we
see this persistent desire in Keats as well as the general form of his
solution: "O for a recourse somewhat independant [sic] of the great
Consolations of Religion and undepraved Sensations, of the Beautiful,
the poetical in all things" (1.179). The "Ode to Psyche" deals in part
of course with the collapse of old religion (the days of "happy pieties"
[41] are past, the old myths no longer believable) and its more effective
replacement ("O latest born and loveliest vision far" [24]). Here too the
new religion of Psyche seems to be a belief in what intensifies life and
makes it livable and is in direct contrast with the asceticism associated
with Christian myth (the "pale-mouthed prophet dreaming" [35]).

It has not been pointed out before, I believe, that the replacement
Keats proposes in *St. Agnes* is the same as that revealed in his cor-
respondence with Fanny Brawne. As we have already seen, though
Fanny was a Christian and though he respected her feelings, Keats
nevertheless made clear to her his own impatience with Christianity.
Then in October 1819 he wrote to her, "I could be martyr'd for my
Religion—Love is my religion—I could die for that. I could die for
you. My Creed is Love and you are its only tenet. You have ravish'd

me away by a Power I cannot resist . . . " (ii.223–24). The ideas here, which so closely parallel both the situation and terminology of *St. Agnes*, appear as well in poems Keats wrote around this time. In the lines "To———" beginning "What can I do to drive away . . . ," Keats speaks to Fanny of "heresy and schism" (25). In a sonnet written to her (beginning "The day is gone, and all its sweets are gone!") he concludes, "But, as I've read love's missal through to-day, / He'll let me sleep, seeing I fast and pray." And finally in the "Ode to Fanny" he writes:

> Let none profane my Holy See of love,
> Or with a rude hand break
> The sacramental cake . . . .
>
> (51–53)

The parallel terminology here and in *St. Agnes* is intriguing. It should not be lightly dismissed as either a passionate rhetorical flight or as metaphorical. Keats may well have come to feel about Fanny as Porphyro did about Madeline. In Fanny and their relationship Keats may have experienced, or at least glimpsed, the kind of human fulfillment that has conventionally been termed religious. As is widely known, their affair was well underway at the time Keats was working on *St. Agnes*, and Fanny may even have inspired it.[15]

Yet, I believe, what is important for our purposes in the above parallel between Porphyro and Keats himself is not that for both a woman becomes the source of their religious experience and the object of their worship, but that the specific love situation in each case appears as the supreme of a whole spectrum of beautiful, intense experiences. In other words, as with Keats's short-lived "grander scheme of salvation than the chryst<e>ain religion," so with his announcing to Fanny that love is his religion and she its only tenet. The point is the recurrent manifestation of a very strong and determined search for religious meaning and further the fact that, common to each of these situations as well as to others in the poetry, is the possibility of special, indeed beautiful and intense, experience. Admittedly, much of the evidence for this distinction comes from outside *St. Agnes*. Nevertheless, it does seem strong enough to be compelling.

As noted above, in the letter of November 3, 1817, to Benjamin Bailey, Keats states that the "recourse" he favors is "the Beautiful, the poetical in all things." The same answer is given and clarified in the famous opening of *Endymion*:

> A thing of beauty is a joy for ever;
> Its loveliness increases; it will never
> Pass into nothingness; but will keep

> A bower quiet for us, and a sleep
> Full of sweet dreams, and health, and quiet breathing.
> Therefore, on every morrow, are we wreathing
> A flowery band to bind us to the earth,
> Spite of despondence, of the inhuman dearth
> Of noble natures, of the gloomy days,
> Of all the unhealthy and o'er darkened ways
> Made for our searching: yes, in spite of all,
> Some shape of beauty moves away the pall
> From our dark spirits.

This "faith" is at least implicit in "Sleep and Poetry" (245–47, 255–93, for example) and in the epistle "To J. H. Reynolds, Esq." (67–85). In 1819 Keats advises the victim of "the melancholy fit" to "glut thy sorrow on a morning rose, / Or on the rainbow of the salt sand-wave, / Or on the wealth of globèd peonies," or, finally, to "feed deep, deep upon [thy mistress's] peerless eyes" ("Ode to Melancholy," 15–17, 21), And finally, to cite but one other example here, that this consolation is at once prominent, consistent from his earliest major work to his last, and seriously proposed is apparent from *The Fall of Hyperion*. There the speaker learns the frequently heard Keatsian message: the true poet "is a sage; / A humanist, physician to all men" (II.189–90) and he "pours out a balm upon the World" (I.201), creating additional beauty and intensity.

But alongside this sustaining belief in experience that will make life livable is an equally prominent scepticism as to the likelihood of any settled solution to life's problems. Nowhere is this scepticism better illustrated than in *St. Agnes*. The insistence on cold and even death in the frame that surrounds the romance proper puts the story of Madeline and Porphyro squarely in a harsh, cruel, "real" world (even if one containing "sleeping dragons" [353]) and thus suggests that the beautiful, exalted moments, which in this case have acquired the aspect of religious fulfillment, are temporary and fleeting. (*Lamia*, similar to *St. Agnes* in several important ways, presents these intense moments in collapse.) As the lovers are deep in enjoyment, a storm rages outside, symbolizing the "real" that is forever present to break in upon the fulfilling experience. They soon run headlong into the storm, even in fleeing from the "mansion foul." Of course, the cold, cruel, brutish, even deathly, is never far away in the poem, appearing prominently in the revelers. But it is perhaps clearest in the presentation of the Beadsman. For despite his piety and his faith, there is no reward, for there is no benevolent ruler to make right in another world the wrongs incurred in this one—"What a little circumscribe[d] straightened notion" to think that "we are to be redeemed by a certain arbitrary interposition of God

and taken to Heaven." To Keats the possibilities for human meaning
and fulfillment seemed severely limited. In *The Eve of St. Agnes*,
though one of the three approaches to experience treated is shown as
effectual, its limitations are never denied, forgotten, or diminished.

My necessarily schematic analysis of *The Eve of St. Agnes* has so
far emphasized its intellectual content, disproportionately perhaps and
no doubt at the expense of its poetic beauty. That imbalance must now
be corrected, for if Keats believed so strongly in the consolatory and
restorative powers of certain kinds of experience, it is likely that poetry
would count importantly among these possibilities. We should, then,
expect *St. Agnes* to participate in the beauty and intensity it pinpoints
and advocates. That it does so, and is therefore much more than a
simple statement, "message," or thesis-poem, can easily be shown.

The place to begin, I suggest, is with the poem's realistic frame, since
there is no point here in simply citing its many and obvious beauties.
The presence of the realistic frame about the romance can mean more
than one thing: the romance quality inside the different frame can indicate that in such a brutish world some kind of momentary paradise is
still attainable; the frame can also emphasize the ephemeral quality of
the spotlighted experience. Both of these effects are, I think, evident in
St. Agnes, but without negating any affirmation, as Bate, Stillinger, and
others would have us believe. Rather, the constant awareness of the
brutish and mortal tugging at us helps prevent any illusion that paradise could be found and maintained. (This the Knight in "La Belle
Dame," as well as Lycius, does not understand.[17]) By heightening the
romance terminology at the end (Porphyro refers to the "elfin-storm
from faery land" [343], and the narrator speaks of "dragons" [353],
"phantoms" [361], and witches [374]), the poem calls attention to itself as story. The frame is thus functional within the complete story
that is the poem and also designed as a reminder, for the reader's benefit, of the totally fictive nature of the enchantment he has just witnessed
and enjoyed. What Keats works hard to prevent is the illusion that the
momentary can be made permanent, that the consciously contrived
world of art and dreams can exist in the "real" world apart from recognition of what they, and thus their limitations, are.

There is, then, as Sperry has argued, a notable self-consciousness
within *St. Agnes* about its own art. The significance of that self-
consciousness has not, however, been adequately explained. To begin
to do so we must look outside the poem. Consistently Keats affirmed
what he understood as early as "I Stood Tip-toe" (that the poet
"Charms us at once away from all our troubles: / So that we feel up-

lifted from the world" [138–39]) and "Sleep and Poetry" ("the great end / Of Poesy [is] that it should be a friend / To sooth the cares and lift the thoughts of man" [245–47]). In *The Fall of Hyperion*, at the opposite end of Keats's writing career, appears the same view:

> The poet and the dreamer are distinct,
> Diverse, sheer opposite, antipodes.
> The one pours out a balm upon the World,
> The other vexes it.
>
> (I.199–202)

A dreamer, we are told, is "A fever of [one]self" (169) and "venoms all his days" (175), whereas the poet is "A humanist, physician to all men" (189). In the words of *Endymion*, the poet heals by wreathing for us "A flowery band to bind us to the earth" by creating "Some shape of beauty [to move] away the pall / From our dark spirits." Thus, to refer again to "Sleep and Poetry," "they shall be accounted poet kings / Who simply tell the most heart-easing things" (267–68). But the most heart-easing things come not from dreamers, or simple escapists, for they vex the world by creating illusions, by taking us away from the viable possibilities before us. Apparently, then, the most heart-easing things are those which take into account the brutishness of life and still find something in the midst of the horror to bind us to the earth. As early as "Sleep and Poetry" Keats knew that he must leave behind the realms of Pan and Flora in order to deal, realistically yet restoratively, with the problems of the world: I must pass up these joys "for a nobler life," Keats writes, "Where I may find the agonies, the strife / Of human hearts . . . " (123–25).

In more than one sense, we may say, *The Eve of St. Agnes* performs the Keatsian function of poetry, that is, a balm for the world. The poem graphically illustrates that some human fulfillment is possible, and in thus showing this possibility for consolation it acts as balm. Of course, as art the poem is itself one of the experiences of beauty capable of replacing the no longer effectual consolations. That Keats intended the poem as, at least in part, an object of beauty is clear. Stanzas become tableaux, richly decorated; scenes, stanzas, lines, phrases, with their luscious descriptions and imagery, sonorous language, and enchanting rhythm, are meant to be relished and enjoyed. The poem is, then, "a thing of beauty" and "a joy for ever." There is no hint, though, that art is thereby superior to life. Art is consolatory and restorative—and limited: it is a conscious, fictional creation. Poetry memorializes exalted moments and crystalizes them, but such moments, after all, are best actively and directly, not vicariously, experienced. In Keats's own words,

"Nothing ever becomes real till it is experienced—Even a proverb is no proverb till your Life has illustrated it" (*Letters*. II.81). For Madeline in *The Eve of St. Agnes* the real experience proves even more intense than her dream, and thus preferable, for in reality she has Porphyro in the flesh.[18]

NOTES

[1] William Michael Rossetti, *Life of John Keats* (London, 1887), 183. The first quotation is from Hugh Miller, *Essays* (London, 1856–62), I, 452.

[2] In *The Finer Tone: Keats' Major Poems* (Baltimore: Johns Hopkins Univ. Press, 1953). After the first citation, for all editions and studies throughout, references by page number and, where appropriate, volume will be included within the text.

[3] *The Letters of John Keats*, ed. Hyder E. Rollins (Cambridge, Mass.: Harvard Univ. Press, 1958), I, 184; hereafter cited as *Letters* with specific references as to volume and page given in the text.

[4] "The Hoodwinking of Madeline: Scepticism in 'The Eve of St. Agnes'," *SP* 58 (1961), 533–55, rpt. in Stillinger's collection *"The Hoodwinking of Madeline" and Other Essays on Keats's Poems* (Urbana: Univ. of Illinois Press, 1971). Reprinted as well in W. J. Bate, ed., *Keats: A Collection of Critical Essays* (Englewood Cliffs, N.J.: Prentice-Hall, 1964), 71–90 (abridged), and in Allan Danzig, ed., *Twentieth Century Interpretations of "The Eve of St. Agnes": A Collection of Critical Essays* (Englewood Cliffs, N.J.: Prentice-Hall, 1971), 49–71. Page references in the text are to the original article.

[5] *Studies in Romanticism* 10 (1971), 27–42.

[6] The text used for the poems throughout is *Keats: Poetical Works*, ed. H. W. Garrod (1956; rpt. London and New York: Oxford Univ. Press, 1966). For the sake of convenience I have included line numbers to references in the text.

[7] Though Stillinger notes the passage quoted and grants the narrator's delight in Porphyro's prospect, he still feels that the poem shows Porphyro's actions to be wrong. I do not see this. What follows in the present essay will, I think, show Stillinger to be mistaken. For now, as further proof of Keats's delight in matters sexual, and thus as added doubt that delight and condemnation would occur together, we might note, as just one example, Keats's reaction to the Paolo-Francesca episode in *The Divine Comedy*. Rather than chasten, a dream destroyed any moral significance in the story and became a sexual fantasy: "The dream was one of the most delightful enjoyments I ever had in my life—I floated about the whirling atmosphere as it is described with a beautiful figure to whose lips mine were joined at [sic] it seem'd for an age—and in the midst of all this cold and darkness I was warm—even flowery tree tops sprung up and we rested on them sometimes with the lightness of a cloud till the wind blew us away again—I tried a Sonnet upon it . . . " (*Letters*. II.91). See also below, n. 12.

[8] *John Keats* (Cambridge, Mass.: Harvard Univ. Press, 1963), 438–51. For a recent essay showing the influence of Stillinger, see Rosemarie Maier, "The Bitch and the Hound: Generic Similarity in 'Christabel' and 'The Eve of St. Agnes,' " *JEGP* 70 (1971), 62–75. See also the recent essay by Leon Waldoff, "From Abandonment to Scepticism in Keats," *Essays in Criticism* 21 (1971), 152–58.

[9] Admittedly, Sperry qualifies his argument regarding Keats's belief in the power and place of the imagination, but it is not enough: "Yet the particular kind of 'intensity' *St. Agnes* achieves is less the result of any pure or final com-

mitment to imagination than a complex awareness of the strains and tensions that are bound to develop within any romantic attempt to satisfy the sum of human expectations once aroused" (42). In rejecting Sperry as unsatisfactory on the degree of distrust of the imagination in Keats, I do not want to suggest that we should therefore join with Stillinger *et al.* in viewing *St. Agnes* as merely a condemnation of dreaming. Though the issues are complex, I hope to sort at least some of them out and so work toward a more probable position on the degree and nature of Keats's scepticism.

[10] "Keats' Symbolism," *JELH* 28 (1961), 244–59. My ideas here were developed independently of Boulger, who nevertheless has proven quite helpful in details, sometimes for disagreement, sometimes for confirmation. Later in this essay I shall treat Boulger's argument at some length. Strangely, that essay seems to be ignored by commentators on *St. Agnes*. For somewhat similar views applied largely to another poem, see the suggestive essay by David Ormerod, cited below (n. 12).

[11] Contrasting views of the ending (the first, positive and happy) are offered by Arthur Carr, "John Keats' Other 'Urn'," *University of Kansas City Review* 20 (1954), 237–42, and Herbert G. Wright, "Has Keats's 'Eve of St. Agnes' a Tragic Ending?", *MLR* 40 (1945), 90–94.

[12] According to David Ormerod, in the "Bright Star" sonnet, apparently composed in April 1819, while he was still working on *St. Agnes*, Keats opposes "his own pagan and sensual approach, where body and soul are mingled and harmonized," to Christian ascetic spiritualism. He writes further that the last line "envisages nothing less than an eternity of coitus—an embrace lasting forever, or, what comes to the same thing, recurrent swooning to death in the sexual climax" ("Nature's Eremite: Keats and the Liturgy of Passion," *Keats–Shelley Journal* 16 [1967], 74–75.

[13] For an informative discussion of Keats's revisions, and of the care expended on *St. Agnes*, see M. R. Ridley, *Keats' Craftsmanship* (London: Oxford Univ. Press, 1933), 96–190. See also Jack Stillinger, "The Text of 'The Eve of St. Agnes'," *Studies in Bibliography* 16 (1963), 207–12, rpt. in *"The Hoodwinking of Madeline" and Other Essays on Keats's Poems*.

[14] Quoted in Robert Gittings, *John Keats* (London: Heinemann, 1968), 425. As Gittings notes, Keats eliminated from the poem certain potentially offensive oaths, spoken by both Porphyro and Madeline. He kept the oath in 145, however (" 'I will not harm her, by all saints I swear' "), as well as the following two lines where Porphyro says, apparently none too carefully, " 'O may I ne'er find grace / When my weak voice shall whisper its last prayer . . . . ' "

[15] Gittings, 273–74, though, thinks the poem reflects an affair with Isabella Jones.

[16] By Book IV Endymion has learned the folly of forsaking the concrete for a dream: "I have clung / To nothing, lov'd a nothing, nothing seen / Or felt but a great dream" (636–38). His conclusion: "There never liv'd a mortal man, who bent / His appetite beyond his natural sphere / But starv'd and died" (646–48).

[17] About the Lycius-Lamia love affair Keats writes, " 'Twould humor many a heart to leave them thus, / Shut from the busy world of more incredulous" (I.396–97), but he does not fail to note the truth, concluding at the beginning of II that "That is a doubtful tale from faery land, / Hard for the non-elect to understand" (5–6).

[18] Lamia is aware of this truth and puts that awareness to good use: "Of all the sweets of Faeries, Peris, Goddesses, / There is not such a treat among them all, / Haunters of caverns, lake, and waterfall, / As a real woman . . ." (I.329–32).

The University of Kansas

ROBERT D. ARNER

PASTORAL PATTERNS IN
WILLIAM BARTRAM'S *TRAVELS*

Like many of the classic works of American literature, William Bartram's *Travels* is structured around a three-part pastoral pattern that
begins with the naturalist's withdrawal from society, focuses upon an
encounter with nature, usually intensely personal and fraught with am-
biguities, and ends either with the explorer's return to civilization or
with some ironic qualification of pastoral idyllicism. In its broadest
sense, the book is enclosed by this thematic and narrative pattern,
starting with Bartram's departure from Philadelphia in April of 1773
and concluding in the final sentence of Part III with his return to that
city and to his father's house on the banks of the Schuylkill River in
January 1778; the fourth part is totally devoted to the Indians Bartram
encountered on his journeys, and while it is thus loosely related to the
main body of the *Travels*, its separate title page suggests that he thought
of it as a separate composition. At the heart of the book, of course, are
the explorations of Georgia, the Carolinas, and East and West Florida
which supplied so much raw material for the imaginations of Coleridge
and Wordsworth, among others.[1] Bartram's emotionally and philo-
sophically complex experiences with nature are registered by the disparity of styles employed in the book, now mundanely scientific and
purely factual, now soaringly poetic and highly figurative. The tension
between the styles enforces the tension in Bartram's mind between
cultivated and untrammeled nature, productive and merely picturesque
or sublime landscapes, garden and wilderness.[2] The style, in other
words, dramatizes a rhythm of consciousness[3] which underlies the

133

whole of the *Travels* and which in various ways provides the work with unity and meaning.

In the first two sections of the *Travels*, Bartram's ambivalent feelings toward the wilderness are most strikingly evident in a number of brief, largely self-contained episodes which can be isolated from the body of the text for convenience in discussion. The two landscapes, garden and wilderness, are juxtaposed in his lament for a "venerable grove"[4] on the shores of Lake George which he had visited fifteen years earlier in the company of his father. At that time, he says, "in that uncultivated state it possessed an almost inexpressible air of grandeur" (99). Now, however,

all has been cleared away and planted with indigo, corn, and cotton, but since deserted: there was now scarcely five acres of ground under fence. It appeared like a desart to a great extent, and terminated, on the land side, by frightful thickets, and open pine forests.   (100)

There appears to be a contradiction here, for Bartram alternately praises one "uncultivated state" and characterizes another as a "desart" bounded by "frightful thickets." A closer look at the "uncultivated" countryside reveals, however, that Bartram's appreciation of the earlier scene had depended upon his perception of unity and order in the landscape. As he describes it,

what greatly contributed towards completing the magnificence of the scene, was a noble Indian highway, which led from the great mount, on a straight line, three quarters of a mile, first through a point or wing of the orange grove, and continuing thence through an awful forest of live oaks, it was terminated by palms and laurel magnolias, on the verge of an oblong artificial lake, which was on the edge of an extensive green level savanna. This grand highway was about fifty yards wide, sunk a little below the common level, and the earth thrown up on each side, making a bank about two feet high. Neither nature nor art could any where present a more striking contrast, as you approached this savanna.
    (99)

Bartram's style in this passage becomes almost a metaphor for the idea of order which he sees underlying "untamed" nature. The elements of his sentences, particularly of the first sentence, are neatly parceled into separate clauses and phrases, their relationship to each other defined by grammatical rules of modification and their boundaries firmly established by commas. In the same way, Bartram's eye perceives each feature of the landscape separately, then in juxtaposition one to the other, and finally as part of a vista into which all elements are integrated by means of the implicitly metaphoric "striking contrast," a phrase that suggests the rules of formal landscape painting.[5] Providing linear visual unity for the entire composition are the Indian highway and the geographical and mathematical lines of demarcation associated with it. The eye travels along the *straight* road, which is *three quarters of a mile long*, about *fifty yards wide*, and *lined* with embankments about *two feet high*; the road passes a *point* of the orange grove and ends at a stand of palms and laurel magnolias, which is on the *verge* of an *artificial* lake, which is on the *edge* of the *level* savanna (my emphasis). Demonstrably, Bartram's aesthetic appreciation of the uncultivated depends upon man-made refinements, the remnants of an ancient civilization which create geometrical designs on the landscape, not upon wilderness. The artificially defined spatial relationships, which imply chronological sequences as well, are precisely what he misses in the "desarts" and "frightful thickets."[6]

In the animal kingdom, Bartram seeks (and most often is able to convince himself that he has found) a moral order corresponding to the physical order which he values in the landscape. Thus he argues the basic benevolence of the rattlesnake (267–73) and the wolf (158–59). So, too, when his life is threatened and then spared by a Seminole renegade, he offers the reader this profitable speculation:

Can it be denied, but that the moral principle, which directs the savages to virtuous and praiseworthy actions, is natural or innate? It is certain they have not the assistance of letters, or those means of education in the schools of philosophy, where the virtuous sentiments and actions of the most illustrious characters are recorded, and carefully laid before the youth of civilized nations: therefore this moral principle must be innate, or they must be under the immediate influence and guidance of a more divine and powerful preceptor, who, on these occasions, instantly inspires them, and as with a ray of divine light, points out to them at once the dignity, propriety, and beauty of virtue. (22–23)

When Bartram cannot detect evidence of this underlying moral principle and cannot ground his pastoral idyllicism firmly in the ideas of order and benevolence, the result is often a version of the pastoral which admits reality and thus brings subtle irony to bear against the idea of retreat into nature. At times, Bartram seems to be aware of the pastoral design he is creating, though not of all its implications, as when he extols the rural hospitality he received on the island of St. Simon. "Our rural table," he writes, "was spread under the shadow of Oaks, Palms, and Sweet Bays, fanned by the lively salubrious breezes wafted from the spicy groves" (61). For music, he and his host, who seems a character fitted for residence in Oliver Goldsmith's Auburn in its happier days, enjoy the

responsive love-lays of the painted nonpareil, and the alert gay mock-bird; whilst the brilliant humming-bird darted through the flowery groves, suspended in air, and drank nectar from the flowers of yellow Jasmine, Lonicera, Andromeda, and sweet Azalea. (61)

Altogether, he paints a scene of beauty, innocence, and ease to rival Eden before the Fall.

In the very next paragraph, however, he apparently wishes to remind us that there is another side to nature, a destructive and anarchic one, and so he contrasts the birds' singing with the roar of the ocean to the east: "the solemn sound of the beating surf strikes our ears; the dashing of yon liquid mountains, like mighty giants, in vain assail the skies; they are beaten back, and fall prostrate upon the shores of the trembling island" (61).[7] The defeat of the assaulting waves signals a victory for order and for the ideal pastoral environment, but the threatening power of the ocean functions to contain Bartram's rhetorical flight within a vision of reality that is markedly different from the one represented by his insistence upon underlying order and harmony.

A similar tension between ideal and actual is generated in the following episode, which makes use of the tripartite pastoral pattern of withdrawal, encounter, and return identified at the outset of this paper:

> Whilst my fellow travellers were employing themselves in collecting fire-wood, and fixing our camp, I improved the opportunity in reconnoitring our ground; and taking my fusee with me, I penetrated the grove, and afterwards entered some almost unlimited savannas and plains, which were absolutely enchanting . . . .
>
> How happily situated is this retired spot of earth! What an elysium it is! where the wandering Siminole, the naked red warrior, roams at large, and after the vigorous chase retires from the scorching heat of the meridian sun. Here he reclines, and reposes under the odoriferous shades of Zanthoxylon, his verdant couch guarded by the Deity; Liberty, and the Muses, inspiring him with wisdom and valour, whilst the balmy zephyrs fan him to sleep.
>
> Seduced by these sublime enchanting scenes of primitive nature, and these visions of terrestrial happiness, I had roved far away from Cedar Point, but awakening to my cares, I turned about, and in the evening regained our camp.
>
> (107–108)

The key words in this passage are to be found in the last paragraph: "seduced," "enchanting," and "visions." The "visions" are explicitly contrasted to the geographical reality represented by Cedar Point, mention of which ties Bartram firmly to the actual physical universe. Both "seduced" and "enchanting" suggest unreality and an excess of fantasy, as if Bartram were always conscious that the imagined life of his "naked red warrior" is more fairy tale than fact, a poetic rather than a possible existence. The very luxuriance and richness of nature seem to indicate danger, and the traveler awakens to his cares with something of the sense of relief experienced by the speaker of Frost's "Stopping by Woods on a Snowy Evening," turning his back on the dark and deep forests to return to the routine of work in the world of the village. On the one hand, the woods offer an aesthetic experience that provides a necessary psychological release from the spiritually deadening duties of normal daily life; on the other hand, it is precisely this routine which keeps man from going out too far and in too deep, from becoming totally a creature of natural instincts who does nothing but sleep while balmy zephyrs fan him. Bartram here appears to reject his own vision of terrestrial happiness in favor of the organized white man's world of work.

Nor is this the only paradise which Bartram discovers to be an illusion. Observing the "innumerable bands of fish" (166) in the "Elysian springs" (168) near Lake George, one of the scenes that helped to inspire the crystal fountains and subterranean rivers of Coleridge's "Kubla Khan," he calls attention to the peaceful behavior of the inhabitants of the deep. Here alligators, gar, trout, bream, catfish, spotted bass, and other fish swim around each other "with free and unsuspicious intercourse . . . ." There are "no signs of enmity, no attempt to devour each other . . . " (167). But this, Bartram warns us, is no peaceful kingdom, no piscatorial Garden of Eden. Although this "paradise of fish" seems to exhibit the "happy state of nature which existed before the fall," it is all deception.

For the nature of the fish is the same as if they were in Lake George or the river; but here the water or element in which they live and move, is so perfectly clear and transparent, it places them all on an equality with regard to their ability to injure or escape from one another . . . .   (168)

The central tension in this passage is generated between pre- and post-lapsarian states of nature, between innocence and corrupt aggressiveness. It is significant that Bartram identifies post-lapsarian nature as reality, for this identification implicitly suggests that hostility and violence lie at the heart of the natural world, not benevolence and moral order as he had earlier asserted in his account of the generous Indian who spared his life. His view of nature in the "paradise of fish" episode reminds us of Ishmael's perception that the beautiful undulating surface of the ocean is also a mask for voracious sharks. The more thoroughly one becomes acquainted with nature, the more he learns of her subtleties and deceits.

Thus it is that in the third part of the *Travels* Bartram pays increased attention to the unpleasant and sinister sides of nature. The general conformity of the book to the pastoral pattern of withdrawal, encounter, and return is, of course, largely accidental, since any narrative of exploration necessarily follows the same development. But it is a fortunate accident nevertheless, for it underlines a change in attitudes which the text reveals from Parts I and II to Part III, the excursions into the land of the Cherokees and thence into West Florida. If the first two sections are characterized by many encomiums to wilderness, or at least to Bartram's personal version of uncultivated nature, the third section reverses the emphasis. Bartram now experiences more depressing and frightening moments than exhilarating ones. He begins with a zest for discovery, and on several occasions, driven by the "restless spirit of curiosity" (73), he braves the wrath of Indians and the elements to venture into undiscovered country. His sense of mission is explicitly stated:

My chief happiness consisted in tracing and admiring the infinite power, majesty, and perfection of the great Almighty Creator, and in the contemplation, that through divine aid and permission, I might be instrumental in discovering, and introducing into my native country, some original productions of nature, which might become useful to society.   (73–74)

There is never any serious doubt about his fulfilling the second part of his goal, and his conviction that God operates benevolently through nature can survive even the challenge of the rattlesnake. But as his travels continue, evidence begins to accumulate that the wilderness is not, in fact, under the guidance of moral law, but that it is hostile or at best indifferent to man. Like Thoreau climbing "Ktaadn," Bartram becomes aware of the threatening and chaotic attributes of nature.

At first, the sinister side of the natural world shows itself in the broad sweep of a landscape which is inhospitable to travelers. Journeying from Fort James in the Carolinas, Bartram gazes upon

chains of hills whose gravelly, dry, barren summits present detached piles of rocks, which delude and flatter the hopes and expectations of the solitary traveller, full sure of hospitable habitations; heaps of white, gnawed bones of ancient buffalo, elk and deer, indiscriminately mixed with those of men, half grown over with moss, [which] altogether, exhibit scenes of uncultivated nature, on reflection, perhaps, rather disagreeable to a mind of delicate feelings and sensibility, since some of these objects recognize past transactions and events, perhaps not altogether reconcileable to justice and humanity.   (322)

In a book characterized by eighteenth-century circumlocution and indirection, this passage is remarkable for its equivocation, as if Bartram sensed that the implications of this scene of "uncultivated nature" would eventually lead him to a point where to continue exploration would be to challenge and perhaps to disprove the idea of natural benevolence. The barren summits testify to nature's deceitfulness, her power to thwart the hopes and expectations of man. Then, says Bartram, *perhaps* the sight of human bones scattered in this wasteland is *rather disagreeable* to some people because *perhaps* the bones are evidence of actions *not altogether reconcileable* to justice and humanity (my emphasis). So many qualifications and evasive negatives indicate, I think, a mind seriously engaged in debate with itself and genuinely uncertain as to the outcome.

Emerging from this valley of dry bones, Bartram continues his journey to the Cherokee town of Sinica and travels the next day to Fort Prince George Keowe in the Vale of Keowe. The valley is surrounded by "lofty, superb, misty and blue mountains" and is "at this season enamelled with the incarnate fragrant strawberries and blooming plants, through which the beautiful river meanders" (330). Bartram greets the prospect as ample recompense for the hardships of his journey, yet his passage in praise of the vista curiously devotes more attention to his remote situation and to his difficulties than it does to a description of the valley itself.

Abandoned as my situation now was, yet thank heaven many objects met together at this time, and conspired to conciliate, and in some degree compose my mind, heretofore somewhat dejected and unharmonized: all alone in a wild Indian country, a thousand miles from my native land, and a vast distance from any settlements of white people. It is true, here were some of my own colour, but they were strangers; and though friendly and hospitable, their manners and customs of living so different from what I had been accustomed to, administered but little to my consolation: some hundred miles yet to travel; the savage vindictive inhabitants lately ill-treated by the frontier Virginians; blood being spilt between them, and the injury not yet wiped away by formal treaty: the Cherokees extremely jealous of white people travelling about their mountains, especially if they should be seen peeping in amongst the rocks, or digging up their earth.   (331)

From dark thoughts such as these, the Vale of Keowe offers a temporary sanctuary, and Bartram becomes a sojourner in Elysium. He compares the valley to the "Fields of Pharsalia or the Vale of Tempe" (354). It is, in short, a terrestrial paradise, and about it hangs the rich odor of ripe strawberries. Here he and his companion, a young trader, come upon a band of Cherokee virgins "collecting strawberries, or wantonly chasing their companions, tantalizing them, staining their lips and cheeks with the rich fruit." The "sylvan scene of primitive innocence" proves too great a temptation and, "nature prevailing over reason," the two men approach the "joyous scene of action." There follows a passage charged with sexual innuendo which ends with the maidens whom Bartram and his friend have cornered in a grove "half unveiling their blooming faces, incarnated with the modest maiden blush, and with native innocence and cheerfulness, . . . [presenting] their little baskets, merrily telling us their fruit was ripe and sound." Had it not been for the watchfulness of the Indian matrons, Bartram confesses, there is no telling "to what lengths our passions might have hurried us, thus warmed and excited . . ." (357). Even in this apparently idyllic interlude, then, two concepts of nature are juxtaposed and contend for supremacy: natural innocence, as represented by the young Indian virgins, and instinctual nature, particularly sexual aggressiveness, on the part of the two white men. The contextual ambiguity of the maidens' offering their "ripe and sound" fruit suggests that Bartram may again be bringing a gentle irony to bear against the ideal of innocence in a garden setting.[8]

Two days after this event, Bartram sets out from the Vale of Keowe for the territory of the Overhill Indians, who are presently "in an ill humour with the whites, in consequence of some late skirmishes between them and the frontier Virginians . . ." (359). His determination to explore their country in spite of their hostility reminds the reader of his earlier decision to go to St. John's Island in East Florida in spite of the Indian trouble that had recently developed. Then he had persevered, but now the outcome is far different. When the old trader, Mr. Galahan, parts company with him, he feels the depressing weight of the solitude and oppressiveness of the wilderness descend:

I was left again wandering alone in the dreary mountains, not indeed totally pathless, nor in my present situation entirely agreeable, although such scenes of primitive unmodified nature always pleased me.

May we suppose that mankind feel in their hearts a predilection for the society of each other; or are we delighted with scenes of human arts and cultivation, where the passions are flattered and entertained with variety of objects for gratification?

I found myself unable, notwithstanding the attentive admonitions and persuasive arguments of reason, entirely to erase from my mind those impressions which I had received from the society of the amiable and polite inhabitants of Charleston; and I could not help comparing my present situation in some degree to Nebuchadnezzar's, when expelled from the society of men, and constrained to roam in the mountains and wildernesses, there to herd and feed with the wild beasts of the forests.   (360)

So far as any single moment in so rich and diverse a book can be identified as crucial without exaggerating its importance, this dark moment when Bartram discovers God's curse on Nebuchadnezzar rather than the evidence of benevolence he had anticipated finding marks the psychological turning point of his travels. In his Introduction, he had advised the traveler to search out God's endless abundance in nature and had, in fact, made natural variety the underlying theme of his prefatory remarks. When he employs the term nature, he includes, of course, men and manners, but the bulk of his Introduction he devotes to a celebration of the variety of wild nature. Now, however, he thinks only of the "variety of objects for gratification" that may be found in "scenes of human arts and cultivation." The awesome solitude of the wilderness appears at last to have overcome his psychological resources and left him defenseless to despair.

In this context, the allusion to Nebuchadnezzar is especially enlightening, since it associates madness with the wilderness. Perhaps unwittingly and certainly without full awareness of all he was implying, Bartram casts himself in the role of one who has been stricken by God, an outcast from humanity by divine decree, and thus the passage stands in stark contrast to his earlier proclamation of his sense of mission. The rational mind proves ineffectual in combating the despair engendered by the wilderness and by the loneliness of Bartram's surroundings, for the wilderness inspires emotions far more powerful than rational thought. In terms of the biblical allusion and of Bartram's primitive psychological analysis of his state of mind, the wilderness is both the cause and the symbolic setting of man's degeneration into a bestial or semi-bestial condition in which the irrational dominates the rational. At this moment in his travels, Bartram has arrived at a point as close to the divine and natural heart of darkness as he will ever go. Two days later, still pushing on slowly towards the Overhill Indians' territory, he abruptly decides that the "slow progress of the vegetation in this mountainous, high country" (366) makes the journey scarcely worth the effort. "I suddenly came to a resolution to defer these researches at this time" (366), he tells us, though we have seen this resolution forming for some time. In a few days he has returned to the Indian town and the company of Mr. Galahan. Thus his "lonesome pilgrimage," as he aptly termed his trip through Cherokee country, comes to an unsuccessful conclusion.

We might pause here to speculate why the Carolina wildernesses should have proved so frightening and depressing to Bartram when even his battles with the alligators in East Florida did not seem to dampen his enthusiasm for exploration. Three reasons can be advanced. The first is that he had by this time been three years absent from Philadelphia, most of which he spent in wilderness environments. Long exposure may have helped to intensify whatever negative reactions earlier experiences might have begun. Second, Bartram spends much of his time alone in this aborted expedition, and, as some of the passages already quoted show, the loneliness he felt greatly affected his response to his surroundings. The third reason, and probably the decisive one, is that the wilderness of the Carolinas is a very different country from East Florida. As the abundant references to mountains, cascades, and waterfalls establish, it is a mountainous area where forests are tall and dense, emphasizing the darkness and the gloom, and where hills slope down to narrow valleys which do not provide the visual relief of the savannas. For the most part, it is a wilderness which surrounds and contains the human figure. That Bartram responded to this difference and that sweeping vistas were necessary parts of his psychological landscape are revealed in his account of his passage through a forest in which he saw "vast heaps of . . . stones, Indian graves undoubtedly."

> After I left the graves, the ample vale soon offered on my right hand, through the tall forest trees, charming views, which exhibited a pleasing contrast, immediately out of the gloomy shades and scenes of death, into expansive, lucid, green, flowery fields, expanding between retiring hills, and tufty eminences . . . .[9]
>
> (348)

After Bartram returns from the wilderness area of the Carolinas, he immediately begins preparations for the journey into West Florida. In this expedition, he never ventures into the wilderness alone, but always has human company, even if, as he says, it is only three slaves. He spends almost as much time describing the plants that flourish in cultivated gardens on plantation estates as in discussing the wild vegetation (429, 436, and 469, for example). This is not accidental, since he does not stray far from settlements of some sort, Indian or white, and consequently this section of the book is the least interesting to read. Admittedly, the region was more inhabited than other areas he had explored, excluding his early excursions into Georgia, and possibly there were simply fewer natural wonders to relate. But even his first glimpse of the storied Mississippi River does not seem able to inspire the old enthusiasm or stimulate his imagination. When we recall his poetic flights in praise of the Altamaha and compare them with his attempt to portray the Father of Waters as "a prospect of the grand sublime" (428), chiefly in terms of depths and distances, who does not feel that Bartram's ardor for the wilderness and for scenes of wild magnificence, even if only for the carefully controlled wilderness of his mind, has cooled considerably?

Moreover, the few encounters with wild nature that Bartram does experience in West Florida carry forward the established theme of nature's hostility to man, to human enterprise, and to rational modes of consciousness. Bartram devotes more space to an account of the extreme heat and tormenting flies of Florida than he gives to the Mississippi, and when he describes the insects as "evil spirits," "persecuting spirits," and "demons" (385–86), he employs a metaphor that, perhaps unintentionally but nevertheless significantly, links the Florida wildernesses to the demon-haunted woodlands of medieval legend and fable. Nor does he attempt to argue the benevolence of these insects as he might have done earlier. The heat and flies combine to sap the energy of the entire company with which he is traveling. "The animal spirits sink under the conflict," he writes, "and we fall into a kind of mortal torpor rather than refreshing repose; and startled or terrified at each others [sic] plaintive murmurs and groans" (386). Almost literally, the wilderness seems to have extinguished all human faculties and to have reduced the travelers to the level of beasts, communicating with each other in inarticulate groans.

One misery succeeds another, as Bartram and his companions are drenched by a heavy thunderstorm which, however, temporarily revives them. For a brief moment, they contemplate the familiar smiling face of nature: "The birds sung merrily in the groves, and the alert roe-buck whistled and bounded over the ample meads and green turfy hills" (387). Yet even now the implicitly metaphoric "meads" suggests that Bartram is describing more a landscape of the mind than of actuality. The sinister side of nature reappears when he develops the symptoms of a fever, which quickly grows worse and threatens his sight and his life. Though he recovers, vision in his left eye is seriously impaired (418, 436). Mosquitoes plague the travelers, swollen rivers confront them with nearly impassable barriers, and Indians once again pose a problem that necessitates a change in the proposed route of travel. In the end, his ill health causes Bartram to cut short his trip into West Florida, but the reader is left with the distinct impression from the brief four chapters recounting these final experiences with the wilderness that the traveler was not disappointed to be forced to end his explorations.

This reading of the last part of the *Travels* depends, of course, upon emphasis, not upon any absolute shift in attitude. Ambivalence characterizes Bartram's responses to nature throughout the book, but in Part III his reactions seem to be more negative than positive, a reversal of Parts I and II. There is one important piece of biographical evidence in support of this interpretation, which is that Bartram did not undertake another expedition, even though he was later offered the chance to head a group of naturalists who were to explore the identical territory of the Overhill Indians which he had wished to visit in his travels. His attendant spirit, curiosity, seems to have deserted him in this instance, and perhaps we need look no further than the last hundred pages of the *Travels* to discover sufficient explanation.

Although it is not an attempt at fiction, Bartram's account of his travels, in its concentration upon man's confrontation with nature and in its use of the central device of the journey of withdrawal, can be recognized as an important piece of American literature related to such works as Poe's *Narrative of Arthur Gordon Pym*, Cooper's *Prairie*, Melville's *Moby-Dick*, Faulkner's *The Bear*, Dickey's *Deliverance*, and to the non-fiction essays *Nature* and *Walden*. Like these later writers, Bartram can reconcile garden to wilderness, order to chaos, benevolence to hostility, and beauty to terror only through the force of imaginative metaphors or transcendent vision, and for him, as for them, the psychological tension is reflected in the style and form of his narrative. If the line of descent from the *Travels* to these and other works of later American literature is not direct, there is nevertheless sufficient family resemblance to establish the authenticity of the lineage beyond dispute.

NOTES

[1] The indebtedness of English romantics, and of certain American romantics as well, is discussed in John Livingston Lowes' *The Road to Xanadu* (Boston: Houghton, 1927), Ernest Earnest's *John and William Bartram: Botanists and Explorers* (Philadelphia: Univ. of Pennsylvania Press, 1940), Nathan Fagin's *William Bartram: Interpreter of the American Landscape* (Baltimore: Johns Hopkins Univ. Press, 1933), and Josephine Herbst's *New Green World* (New York: Hastings House, 1954). Of these, Fagin's offers the most comprehensive treatment of Bartram's influence on later literature.

[2] Roderick Nash, *Wilderness and the American Mind* (New Haven: Yale Univ. Press, 1967), 54–55, briefly notes Bartram's negative responses to the wilderness.

[3] The phrase is Leo Marx's in "Pastoral Ideals and City Troubles," *JGE* 20 (1969), 251–71. See also his *The Machine in the Garden* (New York: Oxford Univ. Press, 1967) for a discussion of some of the tensions of the American pastoral.

[4] William Bartram, *Travels Through North & South Carolina, Georgia, East & West Florida...* (Philadelphia: James & Johnson, 1791), 100. Further references to the *Travels* are to this edition and will be noted in the text by page number only.

[5] Elsewhere in the *Travels*, Bartram shows the artist's sensitivity to tones of color, especially to shades of green (335–36, for example), and to perspective and line (esp. 102, 179–80, and 187–88).

[6] This reading of Bartram's passage differs widely from that of Josephine Herbst, who is inclined to accept his "uncultivated nature" at face value. See *New Green World*, 256.

[7] Note Bartram's use of alliteration, particularly of sibilant *s*'s as counterpoints to the weightier consonants, to convey the sound of the sea.

[8] Bartram most often romanticized the noble savage he encountered in the American wilderness, but, as his tale of the unfortunate trader with the conniving Seminole wife (111–12) demonstrates, he was not totally blinded by the appearance of virtue and innocence; he could also see to moral realities lying under the appearances.

[9] Additionally, we might note that mountainous scenery was not much appreciated by any traveler during the first half of the eighteenth century and for a good while thereafter. See Ola Elizabeth Winslow, "Seventeenth-Century Prologue," *Essays on American Literature in Honor of Jay B. Hubbell*, ed. Clarence Gohdes (Durham, N. C.: Duke Univ. Press, 1967), 27, and Samuel Holt Monk, "The Sublime in Natural Scenery," *The Sublime* (Ann Arbor: Univ. of Michigan Press, 1960), 203–32.

The University of Cincinnati

JOAN R. SHERMAN

TENNESSEE'S BLACK POET:
GEORGE MARION McCLELLAN

Although over one hundred black men and women published poetry in America during the nineteenth century, only a handful have been recognized in anthologies of black literature. Among the neglected poets, George McClellan of Tennessee, a contemporary of Paul Laurence Dunbar, is outstanding not only for his accomplishments as a scholar, teacher, and minister, but also for his talents as a poet of nature and love. Moreover, McClellan emerges as the archetypal black artist described by W. E. B. Dubois in *The Souls of Black Folk*, a man whose "double consciousness" of himself as an American and a Negro inspired and crippled his endeavors.

In a sketch, "The Goddess of Penitentials," appended to McClellan's *Poems* (1895), a Goddess bestows on a poet at birth acute sensitivity to beauty and capacity to love, and she takes him into "the service of human sorrows." She forecasts that the child shall have "learning and the cultivation of aesthetic tastes" but will win no recognition for his talents, that he will feel brotherhood with all who are oppressed but will stand helpless to alleviate their misery. Finally the Goddess promises: "Of all the disgrace and degradation of thy race thou must be a part" and learn wisdom through bitterness. This sketch is McClellan's self-portrait at age thirty-five and an uncanny presentiment of the frustrations and tragedy that darken his later years.

The poet was born in Belfast, twenty-five miles southeast of Columbia, Tennessee, on September 29, 1860, the son of George Fielding and Eliza (Leonard) McClellan. His life history until age twenty-one is still unknown. About 1881 McClellan enrolled at Fisk University in

147

Nashville where he earned the Bachelor of Arts degree in 1885. From 1885–1887, he studied at Hartford (Connecticut) Theological Seminary and in 1887–1890 served as a Congregational minister in Louisville, Kentucky.[1] During this ministry, on October 3, 1888, McClellan married Mariah Augusta Rabb of Columbus, Mississippi, in that city.[2] From about 1890, however, the couple was frequently separated. Mrs. McClellan graduated from Fisk's Normal Department in 1891, served on the Fisk faculty (1891–1892), and earned her B.A. in 1895.[3] Meanwhile, McClellan continued his studies at Fisk to earn the M.A. in 1890, and simultaneously he commuted to Hartford which granted him the Bachelor of Divinity degree in 1891. The following year, McClellan was a minister in Nashville, and from 1892–1894 he traveled extensively through New England as financial agent for Fisk University. The Fisk *Catalogues* record his next position as chaplain of the State Normal School in Normal, Alabama, from 1894–1896.

In 1895, McClellan published *Poems*, a collection of fifty-seven verses and five sketches, and a year later he reprinted twelve of the verses as *Songs of a Southerner*. McClellan had composed these poems at odd places and times: when he was a student teacher on vacation in the swamps of Mississippi during college days; at train stations while traveling for Fisk; and about his native hills of the Highland Rim of Middle Tennessee. The scenes and activities of his youth and young manhood became the substance of his art. McClellan's poems describe the beauties of spring and summer in the Cumberland Mountains, in Mississippi, Massachusetts, or Alabama; they dwell on innocent joys of a Southern boyhood, the pain of separation from the South and loved ones, and hostility encountered in white society. Likewise, McClellan's stories, "A Creole from Louisiana" and "Essie Dortch" (1906) and "Gabe Yowl" (1916), are set on Fisk University's campus or in the city of Nashville; and his tales, "Old Greenbottom Inn" and "For Annison's Sake" (1906), take place on the campus of an "Industrial and Normal School of 400 Negro students" in Northern Alabama where the narrator is chaplain.

Literature was necessarily only McClellan's avocation. He confesses in *Poems* that his work lacks "special merit" because he never had "leisure and freedom from the constant struggle for daily bread" to devote continued effort to poetry (p. 7). McClellan's poverty is painfully evident in an application for scholarship aid he submitted to Hartford Seminary in his senior year, 1890. He had received $72 in 1889, but now has on hand "$.0000," and is $35 in debt. He requests funds for Seminary expenses to supplement what he may earn from "chance preaching" which must go to support two sisters in school and his wife.[4] Within a few years, McClellan gained two more dependents, his sons Lochiel (born about 1892) and Theodore (1895).

From the turn of the century, fulfilling the prophecies of his Goddess, McClellan enjoyed a successful teaching career in Louisville, Kentucky, but was beset by financial and personal woes. From 1899–1911 he taught geography and Latin at Central Colored High School, and from 1911–1919 he succeeded his friend, the poet Joseph Seamon Cotter, Sr., as principal of the Paul Dunbar School.[5] During the first decade, in 1906, McClellan paid $500 to publish and advertise *Old Greenbottom Inn*, a novella and four stories. The publisher held back all but 250 of the 1,000 copies because McClellan owed him $100. To raise this sum and get his books for a Christmas sale, he resorted to a "prize offer," sending out 100 circulars; he received only $8 in reply.[6]

Such publication problems seemed minor beside the greater misfortune which befell the poet ten years later. His younger son, Theodore, was stricken with tuberculosis, and for money to save Theodore's life, McClellan privately published *Path of Dreams* (1916). Among the ten new poems in this collection, one is a tender tribute, "To Theodore" (dated February 22, 1916):

> No more are echoes of your flying feet.
> Hard by, where Pike's Peak rears its head in state,
> The erstwhile rushing feet, with halting steps,
> For health's return in Denver watch and wait.
> But love and memories of noiseless tread,
> Where angels hovered once, all shining fair,
> To tuck you in your little trundle bed,
> Kneel nightly now in agony of prayer.

A recipient of McClellan's prospectus for *Path of Dreams* with his letter of appeal mentions the "heroic struggle of an intelligent and loving father, on behalf of his sick and despised son, despised because of his race."[7] McClellan took Theodore to Los Angeles for treatment, probably in July of 1916. Although details of the boy's battle for life are vague, it is clear that he was refused admission to a sanitarium on account of his race. Theodore's death certificate, written in McClellan's own hand, records that his son died of tuberculosis in Los Angeles on January 5, 1917, at the age of twenty-one.[8] Offering a second edition of *Path of Dreams* twelve years later, McClellan wrote: "When I lost the fight, I was so utterly broken in soul and body over the death of the boy, all further effort to sell the book was dropped." McClellan's suffering was compounded by estrangement from his wife, perhaps as early as 1895, and almost surely in the 1920's when he resided in

California. He had returned to Louisville for a few years after his son's death, but from 1921 through 1925 he lived in Los Angeles. He attended the University of California Extension Division (Los Angeles) as a "special student" in 1921 and worked as a probation officer for the county and as a teacher.[9] His whereabouts in 1926–1928 are unknown. In 1929, from his "home" in the YMCA of Nashville (Fourth Avenue and Cedar Street), McClellan wrote to Hartford Seminary, requesting a list of alumni to whom he mailed his "Especial Book Announcements." This twelve-page prospectus offered a package of three books for $1.50: a second edition of *Path of Dreams*; *Gabe Yowl*, a murder story, included in the 1916 *Path*; and a new work, *The History of American Literature*.[10] During his long experience as "a teacher of secondary and college English and of English and American Literature," McClellan found that students and teachers were ignorant of work by Negro authors. Therefore he planned a text book of black and white literature, an integrated text because "all forms of segregation carry with them in some measure disrespect and lowered estimation of the segregated." He hoped to publish the *History* in the spring of 1930, but either the Great Depression or personal problems intervened, and none of the volumes appeared.

In the four years from his "Announcements" until his death, McClellan may have taught school in Nashville or in Louisville where he was living in 1933. In April of that year, he again requested an alumni list from Hartford and the date of the Seminary's May commencement. He planned to leave Louisville shortly, he wrote, travel East, and arrive in Hartford for commencement, the first since his own in 1891. There was no further word from George Marion McClellan. The Seminary records his death date as May 17, 1934, place unknown.[11]

McClellan's life spanned four decades of the nineteenth century and three of the twentieth. He was a transitional figure in many ways. His art reflects the plight of Afro-Americans who, in their leap from slavery to citizenship, felt compelled to forswear their heritage, abandon their culture, and bleach their souls. Moreover, for McClellan and many other black writers, especially Southerners, the passage from servitude to seemingly unbounded freedom of the post-War era, then back to legislated "enslavement" in post-Reconstruction years proved as traumatic as the passage from freedom to slavery had been for their ancestors. McClellan continually struggled to adjust to the demands of the unstable new world. He felt duty-bound to raise himself to a position of respect and influence in order to bring credit to the race and promote its advancement. To this end, McClellan overcame poverty, misfortune, and prejudice to earn three college degrees in ten years while working as a minister, and he taught school for thirty years.

McClellan also wrote and published in the interest of race-elevation. He privately printed *Poems* in 1895 to counteract charges that the Negro was incapable of high development since he "had contributed essentially nothing to literature." This absurd charge, he writes, overlooks the facts that "superior excellence in literary instinct and capacity is a plant of slow growth, the cultivated gift of many generations," and that a race's literature must express "its national and social life." The black writer, only thirty years away from slavery, suffers the great disadvantages of lack of education, time, security, and an "inspiring history" necessary to produce "song-materials as well as singers." McClellan's contributions to race literature, he says, are not "Negro songs purely, but songs of beautiful landscapes, wherever I have seen them, ... or of touches of human loves and feelings, as I have felt them."[12] His sixty-seven lyrics treat traditional "white" subjects—nature, love, and religion—in graceful classical meters, with restrained diction, sober thought, and refined sensibilities. The landscapes, broad summery vistas, evoke reveries of childhood; they confirm God's benevolent presence and illustrate by analogy frailties of human nature. The poet's enthusiasm for Nature and faith in God's Providence create a serene, optimistic mood; however, strains of melancholy disillusionment and despair darken his nostalgic visions.

Thus, in all areas—theme, style, and tone—McClellan's poetry manifests his devotion to Whittier, Longfellow, and hundreds of lesser traditionalist poets of his age. Such orthodoxy exemplifies the work of most black poets from 1880 until the Harlem Renaissance of the 1920's as they turned away from the militantly race-conscious polemics of ante-bellum writers.[13] Afro-Americans discovered that accommodation to white standards was the most politic way to respectability both in life and literature.

The black artist, compelled to write "white," became a man torn between two cultures and a stranger to them both. His impossible task was to create a dual-purpose literature: one that would be meaningful to his own people by being faithful to their deepest feelings and race experience, and, at the same time, one that would convince a white audience of the race's capabilities and the poet's worthiness to be published. In 1903, W. E. B. DuBois described this feeling of dual allegiance as "double consciousness": the sense of "measuring one's soul by the tape of a world that looks on in amused contempt and pity" while longing to express the "soul-beauty" of the race.

One ever feels his twoness,—An American, a Negro; two souls, two thoughts, two unreconciled strivings; two warring ideals in one dark body, whose dogged strength alone keeps it from being torn asunder.[14]

George McClellan suffered keenly from "double consciousness" because he was so gifted a man, highly intelligent, sensitive, ambitious, and race-proud. His sense of "twoness" and of estrangement from both the black and white worlds is the major theme of his poems, whatever their ostensible subject.

McClellan's poems are spiritual autobiographies, and the speaker is the poet (as he admits in the introduction to *Poems*). He usually lies "in indolent repose," daydreaming. The dreamer longs to recapture the innocence, peace, freedom, and ecstatic harmony with Nature his soul enjoyed before it was corrupted and splintered by experience in the white world; or he envisions a transcendental integration of all souls with the Spirit of his landscapes that will lead mankind to full Christian fellowship. "Lines to Mount Glen" (a poem of eighty-two lines) expresses all elements of McClellan's separation-estrangement-regeneration theme. The poet lies at the base of Mount Glen, his "early childhood friend" which he has come home to worship:

> And so
> It was Old Glen we came at first to love
> In this soft scented air now long ago,
> When first I brought my youthful heart to thee,
> All pure with pulsing blood still hot
> In its descent of years in tropic suns
> And sands of Africa, to be caressed
> By thee. And to your lofty heights you bore
> Me up to see the boundless world beyond,
> Which nothing then to my young innocence
> Had aught of evil or deceptive paths.
> With maddening haste I quit thy friendly side
> To mix with men. And then as some young bison
> Of the plain, which breathes the morning air
> And restless snorts with mad excess of life,
> And rushes heedless on in hot pursuit
> Of what it does not know: So I, Old Glen,
> As heedlessly went out from thee to meet
> With buffeting, with hates, and selfishness,
> And scorn. . . . And in the fret
> And fever of the endless strife for gain
> I often sigh for thee, my native peaks,
> And for that early life for me now past
> Forevermore.

The "stranger" luxuriates in the "gentle grace so indefinable" flowing from the mountain's heart to his, but such bliss, he knows, is temporary. He cannot regain childhood's "all-believing innocence" and must

return to the fretful life of men. The poem concludes with his vision
of a new Eden:

> And here in this perfume of May, and bloom
> Luxuriant, and friendly rioting
> Of green in all this blooming waste, is seen
> A glimpse of that which He, the Lord of all,
> Intended there should be with things and men
> In all this earth, a thing which yet will be,
> A universal brotherhood.

Contemplation of a beloved landscape gives rise to similar sentiments
in many poems, including "To Hollyhocks," "In Summer," "The Path
of Dreams," "Heart Yearnings," "The Harvest Moon," and "May."
The poet has lost a part of himself, the African part, or, as DuBois
put it, the Negro soul. This lost soul is invariably exemplified by the
Southland with its lush foliage and pulsating life in hazy moonlight or
shimmering sunshine, and by childhood.

"A September Night" describes a bayou surrounded by great cotton
plantations; it links the sensual odors and rhythmic sounds of nature
to the black man's exuberance, all of which the poet can observe but
not share:

> Aromas wild and sweet
> From muscadine, late blooming jessamine,
> And roses, all the heavy air suffuse.
> Faint bellows from the alligators come
> From swamps afar, where sluggish lagoons give
> To them a peaceful home. The katydids
> Make ceaseless cries. Ten thousand insects' wings
> Stir in the moonlight haze and joyous shouts
> Of Negro song and mirth awake hard by
> The cabin dance. O, glorious is this night!
> The Summer sweetness fills my heart with songs
> I can not sing, with loves I can not speak.

In "The June" (106 lines), the Southern countryside vibrates with
sound and blazes with light and heat. It is described as brilliant, gleam-
ing, golden, shimmering, "teeming everywhere with life and hope." A
dreamer, "stretched full length upon the ground," recalls his idyllic
childhood in these hills:

> The June has come with summer skies and glow,
> Reflecting bliss and Junes of long ago—
> Bare feet, and careless roving bands of boys
> That haunted lake and stream in halcyon joys,
> The bow and arrow, hunting ground and snares,
> The sudden flight of quails and skulking hares,
> The wild and joyous shouts along the glen
> Come back in all the month of June again.

> Then other days and solitary dreams
> Are come again with flash of flaming gleams,
> . . . .
> Unseen but felt, the spirit of the wood
> Without a dogma teaches of the good
> In God sublime. An all-pervading sense
> Is everywhere of his resource immense,
> His love ineffable—infinite power,
> In storm resisting oaks, and purple flower . . . .

The poet summons all to drink deep of June's true love and joys, to wear once more the "boyish spirit"; and he contrasts the lost world with present reality:

> In these no hot contentions, endless strife,
> Nor aching hearts, consuming greed of life,
> No soul-corrupting lusts, debasing sin,
> Nor blighted lives where innocence has been
> Are ever brought by June. But to assuage
> The sorrows of mankind from age to age
> A subtle charm, a bliss, a merry tune
> Abideth in the country lap of June.

McClellan's tributes to his native state, such as "The Hills of Sewanee," "A Song of Nashville," "May Along the Cumberland," and "After Commencement at Fisk University," also express nostalgia for familiar haunts, unfulfilled dreams, and the self now lost.

McClellan's nature poems, viewed in the context of nineteenth-century verse, appear to offer little originality of subject, sentiment, or detail. Idealization of the past, backward-looking reverie, contemplation of the oneness of God, Nature, and man's spirit—these are staple ingredients of the century's poetry. McClellan, however, employs these themes not to escape from realities of life, as most of his contemporaries did, but to magnify the reality of his struggle to merge two selves into one, to be an American poet without abandoning his Negro soul. McClellan's scenes of the South and boyhood with their typical image clusters,—light, heat, luxuriant vegetation, heights, dreams—symbolize the original self, the black soul, spontaneous, vibrant, warm, singing in harmony with the land and its guiding Spirit. The poet has repressed this self, but he cannot (and would not) extirpate it; nor does he want to embrace a new self proffered by society, the white soul, selfish and calculating, rushing in heartless pursuit of materialistic gods.

The black man who pursues whiteness repudiates the law of Nature which, to McClellan, is the law of God. He points up the hazards of forsaking the old for a new self in another group of poems in which the natural qualities of rivers, insects, birds, and flowers lend themselves to direct analogy with man. These poems illustrate the dangers of leaving one's native place, the foolishness of pride, trustful naiveté, and reckless ambition. In "The Sun Went Down in Beauty," the poet watches the Mississippi River rush to the sea: "Its swelling current resembling / The longing, restless soul, / Surging, swelling, and pursuing / Its ever receding goal." The "restless tide" carries "phantoms of loved ones" away from him. A young man in "Youthful Delusions" is reproached for yearning to roam abroad too soon; he will encounter the "lurking woe" of the world and be poisoned for his ambition. Flowers blighted by winter are like this young man. In "The Bridal Wreath's Lament," the haughty flower opens its tender leaves and buds to the "soft, deceitful, sighing winds" of spring, only to be frozen by a stealthy storm. Likewise in "A January Dandelion," the thoughtless weed is misled by premature warm days to leave its natural bed:

> And yet, thou blasted, yellow-coated gem!
> Full many hearts have but a common boon
> With thee, now freezing on thy slender stem.
> When once the heart-blooms by love's fervid breath
> Is left, and chilling snow is sifted in,
> It still may beat, but there is blast and death
> To all that blooming life that might have been.

In "A Belated Oriole" the poet recognizes his kinship with the shivering bird caught in a December storm up North:

> Why hast thou lingered here so late
>   To face the storms that rise
> When all thy kind, and yellow mate,
>   Have sought for southern skies?
>
> Hast thou, like me, some fortune ill
>   To bind thee to this spot?
> Made to endure against thy will,
>   A melancholy lot?

The poem concludes with the hope that God will lend "his great love and care" to keep both bird and man from harm.

The North, dull winter skies, treacherous icy winds and snow, and adulthood (in contrast to the South, brilliant hot summers, and childhood) symbolize the alien world where the all-white soul dwells. Although he longed to be part of it, McClellan found this world uncongenial and often hostile and destructive.

The two thoughts expressed in "A Belated Oriole" are expanded in his poems on love and religion: youthful love is inevitably lost through death of passion or lovers' separation; and the God of mercy and justice will, in the long run, heal, comfort, and save. A tone of bittersweet pain and yearning sighs through McClellan's love poems: "Resent-ment," "The Message of a Dead Rose," "To Kitty Wysong," "Love is a Flame," "Estrangement," "An Autumn Day," "An Octaroon's [sic] Farewell," and "A Faithless Love." As in the nature poems, happiness belongs to the past, linked to images of spring and summer in the South "when love's wild glow / Made fervid youth a tenement of dreams / Back in the long ago." Typical is "A Faithless Love" (in seven stanzas):

> But O, my heart, my heart of hearts!
>   What hope is there for me?
> For what was hope and what was joy
>   For me have ceased to be.
>
> The woodlark's tender, warbling lay,
>   Which flows with melting art,
> Is but a trembling song of love
>   That serves to break my heart.
> .   .   .   .
> O May! my heart had found a rose
>   As lovely as the morn,
> Which charmed awhile, then faithless went,
>   But left with me its thorn.

McClellan's poignant love poems join other expressions of loneliness and homesickness, such as in "My Madonna," in response to a photo-graph of his wife and infant son sent "From my own sunny south . . . north to me," and in "Thanksgiving Day in New England": "My home-sick heart gives useless sighs / For love beneath my southern skies."

No humor and little joy brighten the verses of *Poems* and *Path of Dreams*. McClellan's most hopeful mood combines selfless stoicism and devotion to God, as in "Hydromel and Rue," "Service," "Prayer," "The New Jerusalem," and "As Sifted Wheat." His faith in God's heal-ing power finds strongest expression in his best-known poem, "The Feet of Judas," originally published in the *Fisk Herald* (1885). Trav-eling to Fisk in August of 1884, McClellan was forcibly evicted from a train in Alabama. The humiliation left him with "a burning hatred which was consuming" him; "I prayed to have the hatred taken out of my soul," he writes, and "followed the prayer by writing 'The Feet of Judas,' and all feeling of hatred for any human being left me forever."[15] Repetition of the theme line through five stanzas and the simple diction give strength to his earnest testament:

> Christ washed the feet of Judas!
>   The dark and evil passions of his soul,

His secret plot, and sordidness complete
　His hate, his purposing, Christ knew the whole,
And yet in love, He stooped and washed his feet.
· · · · · · · · · · · · · ·

Christ washed the feet of Judas!
　And thus a girded servant, self abased,
Taught that no wrong this side the gate of Heaven
　Was ever too great to wholly be effaced,
And though unasked, in spirit be forgiven.

And so, if we have ever felt the wrong
　Of trampled rights, of caste, it matters not,
What ere the soul has felt or suffered long,
　Oh, heart! this one thing should not be forgot;
Christ washed the feet of Judas!

McClellan's devotion to Gospel idealism prompts him to compose "The Legend of Tannhauser and Elizabeth," a Christian version of the myth in some 460 lines of blank verse. Handling the meter with ease and in unadorned language, without moralistic digressions, McClellan swiftly narrates Tannhauser's enchantment by Venus and year-long stay in Venusberg, his singing in praise of Venus before the Thuringian court, and his fruitless pilgrimage to Rome where the Pope denies his plea for mercy: " 'you may hope / For God's forgiveness when my staff puts forth green leaves.' " When Tannhauser fails to return with the pilgrims from Rome, fair Elizabeth dies of a broken heart. Later, Tannhauser dies of grief just as messengers from the Pope come singing

Of a great marvel wrought by God, for now
The staff put forth green leaves in token of
Tannhauser's full redemption from his sins.

This "Legend," and, even more, McClellan's nature and love poems are distinctly his, readily distinguishable from other black poetry on similar subjects. No other black poet offers his metrical and stanzaic variety and faultless rhyming so smoothly executed as to appear effortless; nor does anyone achieve his complexity of structure and texture, for McClellan combines description of generic panoramas, overt analogical statements, and restrained, graceful diction to generate a cool, detached tone when, in fact, beneath the surface his poems seethe with deeply personal emotions and the strife of double consciousness. It is as if McClellan's poems were white outside and black inside; like the poet, they lack organic unity (which is indeed their "message"). The reader feels these unresolved tensions and is puzzled, disturbed, and haunted by McClellan's poetry far more than by the work of any other black poet of his time.

Although the poems are not "Negro songs purely," they affirm McClellan's love of Negro "soul-beauty" and commitment to his black identity. He makes explicit his feelings on black-white relations in only a few poems and in his fiction. A twelve-stanza poem, "Daybreak," calls for race activism but more emphatically counsels patience and piety:

> Awake! arise! Oh, men of my race,
>   I see our morning star,
> And feel the dawn-breeze on my face
>   Creep inward from afar.
>
> I feel the dawn, with soft-like tread,
>   Steal through our lingering night,
> Aglow with flame our sky to spread
>   In floods of morning light.
> . . . .
> Though wrongs there are and wrongs have been
>   And wrongs we still must face,
> We have more friends than foes within
>   The Anglo-Saxon race.
>
> In spite of all the babel cries,
>   Of those who rage and shout,
> God's silent forces daily rise
>   To bring his will about.

The race is urged to endure "Ignoble, arrant prejudice" with Christian fortitude, trusting that "Endurance, love, will yet prevail."

This conciliatory posture is clarified by McClellan's account of the genesis of "The Feet of Judas." Most black men, he says, quietly accepted Jim Crow segregation on trains;

But there were a few Negroes who would fight and I was one of them from boyhood up. I made it a rule never to carry a pistol. I had many "rows" and I knew if the whites ever put hand on me as they did many Negroes I would use a pistol if I had it on me.

Twice McClellan was told to leave the train; twice he refused. At a station "noted for its mob spirit," a group of white men approached the car: "I could have gone out of the car in time to save myself from being dragged out but I had never run in my life. I think that will be true when I die."

Not conciliation, but violence was the law of McClellan's nature which he suppressed with great anguish. As a black man in the hands of an Alabama mob in 1884, he courageously chose passive resistance, the technique that opened doors to his race throughout the South seventy-five years later.

McClellan's contempt for the abuses of slavery and for contemporary racial discrimination breaks forth undisguised in his fiction. His melodramatic and sentimental tales involve miscegenation, concealed identity, murder, seduction, and suicide. Plots are burdened with unintegrated historical and descriptive materials and didactic moral and social commentary. Although these stories of retributive justice and the saving power of love and faith have little aesthetic merit, they reinforce our presumption of race-consciousness and race pride as the theme of McClellan's poetry. The stories parallel the poems in their Southern settings and, very often, in their structure utilizing flashbacks and dream visions.

In "Old Greenbottom Inn," on a lovely day in May, a "Professor" reclines on a grassy slope overlooking "Greenbottom Inn, with all its jovial history, its poetry, its romance, its comedy and tragedy of slavery days." Giving himself up "wholly to sensations of mingled joy and sadness," he gazes at the old slave track passing the Inn door "over which many chain-gangs of slaves with broken hearts have passed to the Southern cotton plantations of Alabama and Mississippi." This view triggers a vision of the Inn "in all its glory of ante-bellum days," and the tale unfolds. It concerns a fateful octoroon, Daphne, whose black lover, John Henry, is lynched for accidentally killing her white lover. John Henry is an outspoken, educated black gentleman; this is the crime for which "cruel and merciless hands dragged him from his cell and from the jail steps he saw a sea of faces."

And there were devils incarnate there. See once a mob lynching a Negro with all the hate and cruelty of the heart let loose, and there can be no doubt of a personal devil. . . . He [John Henry] said: "I thank you for this last chance to address you. I was born here and all who know me know that my conduct from childhood has been blameless. . . . I am no murderer. I did speak against lynching last May, and I do so again to-night. I said then no brave and true man ever helped to lynch a man; only cowards and cut-throats did. I say the same to-night. That is what you are, every one of you."

The enraged mob drags John Henry (the mythical steel-driver) off to die: "torture and death common to savages was to be outrivaled by the high civilization of the white South." The lynching is accomplished (in gory detail) "by five hundred of Alabama's best citizens." McClellan's bitter reproaches fade as he rejoices at the ironic transformation of Old Greenbottom Inn from a bastion of slavery into an industrial school for blacks, and he finds in the birth of Daphne's child (by her white lover) on Easter Sunday "new life and new hope in the new order of things."

"Gabe Yowl" is a tale of miscegenation, murder, and detection which, we are told, actually occurred twenty-five years previously in Nashville. Again, it is May: "I was lying on my back on the soft grass in the campus of Livingstone Hall." The narrator sees Fisk's Jubilee Hall "glimmering in the sun on Fort Gillum":

> The former earth works of Fort Gillum, raised for the throwing shot and shells to sustain a system of slavery then struggling even unto death to bind forever into the most abject servitude and degradation, every Negro boy and girl then living in the South and those of generations yet unborn, now served to elevate towards the sky for Negro girls one of the most costly and most beautiful college dormitories of the South.

From this vision of past and present the narrator travels back to his student days at Fisk University when Gabe Yowl, a militant mulatto, was indicted for murder. Everyone knew that indictment in the South "was tantamount to a death sentence, either by a lynching or a court of law for any one of the Negro race." Gabe is saved by the last-minute confession of his white socialite mother (whose identity and guilt Gabe had concealed); but the long trial scenes ably expose the hypocritical, crooked politicians who, without a shred of evidence, planned to play up race prejudice for the jury and hang the "bigoted and murderous educated nigger."

The poet from Tennessee was also an "educated nigger." The contradiction between these terms, "educated" and "nigger," in his heart and in the minds of white society, formed McClellan's double consciousness and made his life and poetry battlefields of warring white and black ideals. Yet, his objective seems a simple one, to be both an American and a Negro: "to be a co-worker in the kingdom of culture, to escape both death and isolation, to husband and use his best powers and his latent genius."[16] McClellan could not achieve this synthesis. He bore the blows inflicted on him by man and God with deep faith and great personal courage, wasting no time or words on self-pity. There is something heroic, in the ancient sense, about George Marion McClellan and, perhaps more than any black poet of his age, he epitomizes the sacrifice of superior talent, intelligence, and energy to race prejudice.

NOTES

[1] Chronology of 1885–96 in *Catalogues of Fisk University*, 11 vols. Brief biographical data on McClellan is found in Newman I. White and W. C. Jackson, eds., *An Anthology of Verse by American Negroes* (Durham, N. C.: Trinity College Press, 1924), 92; *Who's Who of the Colored Race*, ed. Frank L. Mather (Chicago, 1915), I, 187. A selection of McClellan's poetry is in *Early Black American Poets*, ed. William H. Robinson (Dubuque, Iowa: W. C. Brown, 1969),

122–37, but biography and bibliography are inaccurate, as they are for all poets in this anthology.

² Marriage certificate, Lowndes County, Miss., copy in my possession.

³ Sylvester Dunn, registrar, Fisk University, in a letter to me.

⁴ Photocopy courtesy of Mr. Nafi Donat, archivist, Case Memorial Library, Hartford Seminary Foundation. I am greatly indebted to Mr. Donat for his helpful letters to me and for photocopies of McClellan's correspondence, "Especial Book Announcements," and other papers held by the Seminary.

⁵ Charles E. Patterson, administrative assistant, Louisville Public Schools, in a letter to me.

⁶ McClellan, letter to an anonymous recipient of his "prize offer" from Hartford, Nov. 24, 1906. Reviews of *Old Greenbottom Inn* appear in *Alexander's Magazine* 3 (Feb. 15, 1902), 210, and 6 (June 15, 1908), 87–88. The date of the first review suggests that an edition earlier than 1906 was published, but I have not located it.

⁷ James H. Roberts, letter to Professor Jacobus, Hartford Seminary, March 30, 1916.

⁸ Theodore's death certificate, copy in my possession, states he had been a California resident for six months; he was buried in Rosedale Cemetery, Los Angeles, on Jan. 8, 1917.

⁹ Los Angeles *City Directory* (1922–30), references courtesy of Miss Marian Marquardt. McClellan's address in 1922–25 was 1669 East 50 Place. His "special student" status is noted in "Especial Book Announcements," p. 1, and enrollment is confirmed by Helen H. Gibbs, recorder, University Extension, University of California, in a letter to me.

¹⁰ The first edition of *Path* was 500 copies of which 360 were sold ("Announcements," p. 3). "Announcements" includes commendations of *Path* from Reuben Post Halleck, Bliss Carman, Joseph S. Cotter, Alice Hegan Rice (author of *Mrs. Wiggs of the Cabbage Patch*), J. E. Spingarn, and others.

¹¹ McClellan's death is not on record at the Bureaus of Vital Statistics in Nashville, Louisville, or Los Angeles.

¹² "Race Literature," *Poems*, 8–10.

¹³ See, for example, the poetry of Josephine Heard, Mary W. Fordham, T. Thomas Fortune, Albery Whitman, H. Cordelia Ray, Mrs. Frances Ellen Harper (after 1877), John W. Menard, Joseph Seamon Cotter, Sr., Daniel W. Davis, James E. McGirt, and Charles Clem. The poets were strongly influenced by Booker T. Washington at the turn of the century.

¹⁴ *The Souls of Black Folk* (Chicago: A. C. McClurg, 1903), 3.

¹⁵ "Especial Book Announcements," 11–12.

¹⁶ DuBois, 4.

GEORGE MARION McCLELLAN'S WORKS

Library locations of McClellan's books and manuscripts: DHU—Moorland and Spingarn Collections, Howard University; DLC—Library of Congress; HaSem—Case Memorial Library, Hartford Seminary Foundation; NNSch—Schomburg Collection, New York Public Library.

POETRY

POEMS. / By / George Marion M'Clellan. / Printed for the Author. / Nashville, Tenn.: / Publishing House A. M. E. Church Sunday School Union. / 1895. 145 pp., 5½" x 7½". Dark red cloth. 57 poems. "Contents," pp. 3–5; "Race Literature" (Author's essay), pp. 7–10; "Passing Songs," pp. 11–95; Prose (five sketches), pp. 95–145. COPIES: DHU; DLC. (A facsimile edition of this work has been published recently [Freeport, N. Y.: Books for Libraries Press, 1970].)

SONGS OF A SOUTHERNER / By George Marion McClellan / Boston: Press of Rockwell and Churchill / 1896.
16 pp., 6″ x 8½″. Blue paper. Portrait facing title page. 12 poems. "Songs of a Southerner," pp. [5]–16 (all reprinted from *Poems*, 1895). COPY: DHU.

THE PATH OF DREAMS / By / George Marion McClellan / John P. Morton & Company / Incorporated. / Louisville, Kentucky / [n.d]
© 1916.
76 pp., 5½″ x 8″. Green cloth. 43 poems. "Contents," pp. [i–ii]; Poems, pp. 1–76 (10 new poems; 33 from *Poems* [1895]). COPIES: DHU; DLC; NNSch. NNSch copy, gift of Joseph S. Cotter to A. A. Schomburg, inscribed August 18, 1925.
SAME: A. M. E. Sunday School Union / Nashville, Tenn. / [n.d.]
© 1916.
206 pp., 5″ x 7″. Green cloth. 43 poems. "Contents," pp. [1–2]; Poems, pp. [3]–57 (same as Louisville ed.); "Gabe Yowl" (murder tale), pp. [58]–86; "Old Greenbottom Inn" and three other stories (from 1906), pp. [87]–206. COPIES: DHU; NNSch. NNSch copy inscribed facing title page: "George Marion McClellan—author / Jan. 3rd, 1934/"

PROSE

Fiction

OLD GREENBOTTOM INN / AND OTHER STORIES / BY/ George Marion McClellan [n.p., n.d]
[Publ. 1906].
210 pp., 5″ x 7½″, rebound.
Dedication, "To Professor W. H. Councill," dated Louisville, Ky., 1906, p. [iv]; "Proem" (on tragedy), p. [v]; "Contents. Old Greenbottom Inn. For Annison's Sake. A Creole from Louisiana. Essie Dortch. The Death of Hanover," p. [vi]; Stories, pp. [7]–210. COPIES: DHU; NNSch.

Essays

"Especial Book Announcements." 1929. 12 pp. Includes portrait, testimonials, poems, and essay. COPY: HaSem. "The Negro as Writer." In *Twentieth Century Negro Literature*. Ed. D. W. Culp. Naperville, Ill., 1902; rpt. New York: Arno, 1969. Pp. 275–86.

Letters

Correspondence with Hartford Seminary, 1906–1933. COPY: HaSem.

Rutgers University

CONTRIBUTORS

ROBERT D. ARNER, Assistant Professor of English at the University of Cincinnati, has written articles on colonial American literature, Nathaniel Hawthorne, Kate Chopin, and Ernest Hemingway for such journals as *Early American Literature, Southern Literary Journal, New England Quarterly*, and *Mississippi Quarterly*.

G. DOUGLAS ATKINS, Assistant Professor of English at the University of Kansas, has as his field the Restoration and eighteenth century and has contributed articles on Dryden and Pope to *Texas Studies in Literature and Language* and to *The Huntington Library Quarterly*.

JOHN SCOTT COLLEY, Assistant Professor of English at Vanderbilt University, teaches Shakespeare and Renaissance drama. His publications include the Blackfriars Edition of *Troilus and Cressida* and articles for *Shakespeare Studies* and *English Literary Renaissance*. He is currently preparing a study of the drama of the children's theaters, 1599–1609.

CARL DENNIS, Associate Professor of English at the State University of New York at Buffalo, has published several essays on American and English literature, including an introduction for a facsimile edition of Sidney's *Arcadia* and a Shakespeare article for *Philological Quarterly*.

RENÉ E. FORTIN, Professor of English at Providence College in Rhode Island, has taught primarily Shakespeare and Milton courses and recently served as department chairman. He has written articles on Shakespeare for *Shakespeare Quarterly, Studies in English Literature*, and other journals.

JEFFREY A. HELTERMAN, Assistant Professor of English at the University of South Carolina, is the author of articles on *Beowulf*, Chaucer, and Shakespeare, which have appeared in *ELH* and other journals.

JAMES QUIVEY, Assistant Professor of English at Eastern Illinois University, has published *The Sinclair Lewis Newsletter*, *Ball State University Forum*, and *Discourse*.

JACK E. REESE, Associate Vice-Chancellor for Academic Affairs and Associate Professor of English at the University of Tennessee, Knoxville, has contributed articles to such journals as *Studies in English Literature*, *College English*, *Shakespeare Quarterly*, and *Review of English Studies*.

HUGO M. REICHARD, Professor of English at Purdue University, has previously published two articles on *Gulliver's Travels*, four on Pope's poetry, and single articles on Johnson, Gray, Hardy, and Conrad.

CHARLES SCRUGGS, Associate Professor of English at the University of Arizona, has published on Swift in *Texas Studies in Literature and Language* and on Jean Toomer in *American Literature*.

JOAN R. SHERMAN, Assistant Professor of English at Rutgers University, has a forthcoming book on nineteenth-century Afro-American poets and has written for *Negro History Bulletin*, *CLA Journal*, *Journal of Negro History*, *Connecticut Review*, and *The Virginia Magazine of History and Biography*.

FRANK H. WHITMAN, Associate Professor of English at the University of British Columbia, specializes in Old English and has recently completed a book on the Old English riddles. In addition he has been a contributor to such journals as *Chaucer Review*, *Studia Neophilologica*, *Notes and Queries*, *Neuphilologische Mitteilungen*, *English Language Notes*, and *Philological Quarterly*.

ACKNOWLEDGMENT

The editors would like to express their appreciation to Professors Lorraine Burghardt and Barry Gaines for the editorial assistance rendered in the preparation of this volume.

FORTHCOMING SPECIAL ISSUES

The next three issues of *Tennessee Studies in Literature* will be devoted to the following topics: 1974, the eighteenth century; 1975, nineteenth-century British literature; 1976, American literature. The deadline for submissions to the first of these has now passed, but contributions for the other two are solicited.